GHOSTS

A HISTORY OF PHANTOMS, GHOULS
& OTHER SPIRITS OF THE DEAD

GHOSTS

A HISTORY OF PHANTOMS, GHOULS
& OTHER SPIRITS OF THE DEAD

P. G. MAXWELL-STUART

TEMPUS

Sunt geminae somni portae; quarum altera fertur
cornea, qua veris facilis datur exitus umbris,
altera candenti perfecta nitens elephanto,
sed falsa ad caelum mittunt insomnia manes.

Vergil: *Aeneid* 6.893-6.

First published 2006

Tempus Publishing Limited
The Mill, Brimscombe Port,
Stroud, Gloucestershire, GL5 2QG
www.tempus-publishing.com

© P. G. Maxwell-Stuart, 2006

British Library Cataloguing in Publication Data.
A catalogue record for this book is available from the British Library.

ISBN 0 7524 3935 9

Typesetting and origination by Tempus Publishing Limited
Printed in Great Britain

CONTENTS

I

THE ANCIENT WORLD:
MAPPING THE AFTERLIFE, CALLING UP
THE DEAD

INTRODUCTION

An eleventh-century German monk, Otloh of St
Emmeram, tells the story of two brothers who were
travelling on horseback when they suddenly saw a large
crowd of people in the air, one of whom (to all appearances
a knight richly accoutred in full armour), stepped forward
and identified himself as their dead father. He explained that
while he was alive he had misappropriated some lands from
a monastery, and that if his sons did not right the wrong by
returning these estates to the monks, both he and his whole
progeny would end up in Hell fire. At first, the young men
argued with their father's spirit, urging that they should
not be asked to impoverish themselves and observing that,
judging by the quality of the armour he was wearing, he
did not seem to be in any need himself. To this their father
retorted that he was in constant pain because his armour and
clothing burned him with intolerable heat; and then, with a
final injunction to them to fulfil his wishes, he disappeared.
The brothers discussed his request and decided to do as they

were bid. Immediately, their father reappeared, wearing different clothes, and thanked them for their decision. 'Already
by the grace of God I have been assigned to cross over to
rest', he said and vanished once more from their eyes.

About two hundred years later, Boccaccio related the tale
of a young nobleman from Ravenna, Nastagio degli Onesti,
desperately in love with a young girl who did not return
his love. Indeed, she held herself aloof from him and scorn-
fully spurned his advances. Nastagio was persuaded to leave
Ravenna to help him forget his despair; but he continued
to brood on the girl's cruelty and suddenly one morning,
near a wood not far from Ravenna, he saw a beautiful naked
maiden running out of the wood towards him, pursued by a
knight on horseback and a pack of ravening dogs. It was clear
her life was in danger, so Nastagio stepped forward with the
intention of trying to intervene and save her, but the knight
explained that interference was pointless as both he and the
girl were dead. Apparently the knight had killed himself when
the girl refused to love him, and not long after the girl, too,
had died exulting in her lover's suicide. The sins of both being
so great, they had both been condemned to re-enact each
succeeding Friday a bloody chase which would end with the
knight's ripping out the girl's unfeeling heart and feeding it to
his dogs. This done, she would resurrect and the chase would
begin once more; and sure enough, these same bloody events
then took place before Nastagio's horrified eyes. Appalled by
what he had seen and heard, Nastagio arranged for his own
beloved and her family to come to the place the following
Friday and see it for themselves. This they duly, if reluctantly,
did and the young girl was so moved by the sight that her
dislike for the knight turned to love at once and the two of
them were married very soon after.[1]

These two medieval stories are typical of their period and
genre. They interweave the wonderful with the everyday

and the supernatural with the natural. They convey a moral lesson to the living in the story and to the story's external audience. They remind the listener that there is an existence after death and that there is a Power which governs it. Their effect as anecdotes is therefore greater than the transitory pleasure afforded by their entertainment. Medieval stories diverted, but only for a more serious purpose. We may note, too, that in these tales the supernatural and preternatural elements merge seamlessly with the natural. The appearance of ghosts may be startling, but principally because of what they do or say, not because their very existence and intrusion upon the living is a source of amazement in itself. But is this ready acceptance of the reality of another mode of existence peculiar to the Middle Ages, or can we see therein both an inheritance from an earlier period and a tradition handed down into modern times?

Of all those manifestations which are said to illustrate the parochialism of the modern essentially materialistic conception of existence, ghosts may surely stand foremost as that with the longest uninterrupted history of acceptance by a majority of people. For it is remarkable how many in the past have averred, and how many in the present continue to claim, that they have had some kind of experience either of a ghost itself or of phenomena associated with the tangible presence of the dead, even though modern sensibilities tend to express themselves with a degree of reluctance to admit the possibility of a non-natural explanation. 'I believe in ghosts: that is, I know that there are times, given the place which is capable of suggesting a phantasy, when those who are sufficiently impressionable may perceive a dream projected as if external to the dreamy mind: a waking dream due both to the dreamer and the spot.'[2] Modern empiricists are, by the very nature of their world-view, impelled to relocate spirits, transferring them from the external world where they were seen and heard by our ancestors, to the inner world of the imagination because, as Castle points out, 'as long as the external world is populated by spirits – whether benign or maleficent – the mind remains unconscious of itself, focused elsewhere, and unable to assert either its autonomy or its creative claim on the world'.[3] Modern self-consciousness, however, demands above everything else that it be in control, 'control' principally manifesting itself as the claimed ability to explain any and every phenomenon in accordance with the requirements of scientific materialism; and it is worth noticing, for example, that popular television programmes in particular invariably try to account for phenomena such as ghosts, werewolves, witches, and demonic possession, in terms of magnetic fields, physiological disturbance triggered by unusual diet, mass neurosis, or hallucination, ergot poisoning, etc. There is never any attempt to step beyond the physical, even as a theoretical possibility.

But ghosts, it seems, will not leave us alone. Like the poor, they are always with us: and no matter what religious system may direct a society's spiritual needs, the ability of the dead to return in some form to contact the living, whether by transient vision or sound, mysterious or purposeful conversation, offers apparent proof that the gulf between two worlds, the material and the unearthly, is not unbridgeable. Indeed, it seems to offer proof that such worlds exist, and if this be so, that humans are not alone in a purely physical universe. Even when a society's political régime is hostile to religion, as it was in the former Soviet Union, official attitudes may not make any deep inroad into people's private beliefs. 'For all that Soviet citizens have claimed for decades, in questionnaires and surveys, that they do not believe in an afterlife, their children still go along to the graves to talk. People from every kind of social background pack into trams with their evergreen branches and bags of fruit at Easter and Trinity. They half-believe, or choose to hope, that someone listens. There are some favoured cemeteries where they even write their messages for the dead on the monuments, combining, as their grandparents once did, an ill-assorted selection of religious fantasies – belief in ghosts, belief in ancestral spirits, belief in the efficacy of graves, in consecrated ground.'[4]

Societies from very ancient times to modern have also had in common the notion that in some sense their dead form a community which is an extension of the living. They inhabit, as it were, a separate but connected country which the living may glimpse from time to time through the medium of individual and often familiar visitants: a mirror existence whose laws, customs, and modes of behaviour are disturbingly like ours. Hence, 'death is not the opposite of life but rather a weak form of it, and the dead, in however attenuated a form, retain many of their own distinctive features and characteristics which they had in life. No doubt they are shadows of their former selves, but still it is of their former selves that they are shadows'.[5] Thus, the father of Otloh's two brothers is recognisable once he has identified himself, presumably by raising his visor so that the youths can see his face, although it is always possible he was altered in death in such a way that identification was necessary, but that once such identification had been made, recognition was instantaneous. Mary Magdalene, for example, was unable to recognise Jesus after His resurrection until he spoke to her and thus stimulated identification and recognition [*John* 20.14–16]. Appearances of the dead to the living also illustrate the bond which exists between the two worlds. Otloh's father speaks to his sons because he wants them to right a wrong which he committed during life, and the moment the youths decide to accede to his request his state is altered. The armour and clothes which burned him are replaced. He is reclassified; assigned to another place, like a soldier seconded from his unit to service somewhere else; the pruning to which hitherto he has been subjected is now complete and he is prepared for a fresh season's growth. The verb he uses [*deputatus sum*] is capable of all these meanings. This reassignment made, he has been enabled to cross over [*transire*] from a burning state to a peaceful or restful one [*ad requiem*]; the geography of the otherworld implies that there is more than one bourn or condition in which the dead may dwell, and that they can cross from one to another like travellers in the physical world. Time in the otherworld, too, is like, but not *quite* like ours. Events can be repeated again and again in dramas apparently complete in themselves – Boccaccio's knight would pursue and kill the girl whether there were spectators of his chase or not: they do not need an audience – but which may also serve as warnings or messages to the living.[6]

But does the presence of the living cause the drama to become visible? Who makes the rules governing the appearance of the dead to the living? By what mechanism can the dead be seen and heard by the inhabitants of a world not their own? The questions are answered indirectly during the course of the two stories above. By what authority were the knight and the girl condemned to act out their private nightmare? 'By the just decrees of almighty God'. By whose decision was Otloh's knight released from his pains? 'By the grace of God'. The otherworld and its territories, therefore, do not exist *in vacuo*. They, like the world of the living, are subject to God: and so God enters the relationship between the living and the dead and provides the authority not only for what happens in each, but also for the breach of the veil which parts the two. The wrongs of the dead can be righted after their death, or the living may be startled or frightened into righting a wrong of their own before they die, and it is God who makes these possibilities available.

One further consequence of this notion is that the living feel some continued responsibility for their dead, some obligation to fulfil their possible needs. Hence graves are tended, prayers said, anniversaries observed. Western twenty-first-century urban dwellers, however, have become accustomed to hand over their dead to commercial organisations which deal with the physical details of preparing the corpse for its funeral. Grieving friends and relatives are thus denied that intimate contact with the body which washing, dressing, and laying out afford, and children are frequently shielded even from the sight of it. Even the funeral ceremonies themselves are frequently turned from a burial of the dead into a 'celebration' of his or her life, as if to deny that the death has actually happened – a kind of refusal to soil the present with the actuality of someone's passing. Fear of death, then, along with fear of the dead has become predominant in such communities who have thus deprived themselves of a dramatic opportunity to acknowledge the possible existence of another world and the transit of one of their number to its shadow community. In previous times, of course, fear of the dead was also predominant; but it could be tempered by careful observation of apotropaic rituals – carrying the body feet first out of the house, placing a metal instrument on the bier or in the coffin, untying all knots in the clothing of the deceased, watching over the dead with prayers and lamentation – all of which resisted the impulse to which the modern West too frequently yields itself, to reduce the lives of the living to a mere sequence of experiences which leave no trace when they are dead.[7]

For Westerners tend to be dominated by a linear rationality derived from and dependent upon the physical sciences for its justification, and in consequence too much reminder of or care for the dead is liable either to be dismissed as morbid superstition or patronised as 'folk observance'. Science, as the West has developed it, is a highly aggressive 'ism' which sees other systems of knowledge or ways of knowing as rivals which need to be eliminated. Moreover, as Graves puts it, 'the pursuit of science (to borrow its own jargon) produces no abnormal psychosomatic effect in its devotees. At its best, it furnishes fascinating intellectual problems for a few bright research fellows to solve, and makes possible the manufacture of numerous labour-saving amenities. But it also destroys numerous ancient amenities; dulls the minds of its countless mechanical servitors; separates man more and more from his natural context in wild nature; and so far enthrones the intellect as the greatest of all human attributes as to remove all checks on its irresponsible functioning'.[8] It is difficult for Westerners to break free of this intellectual constraint and allow themselves to see the living and the dead through differently focussed eyes. Nevertheless, the effort can and should be made; for the ghost, as we are reminded by Gordon, 'is not simply a dead or a missing person, but a social figure, and investigating it can lead us to that dense site where history and subjectivity make social life… Being haunted draws us affectively… into the structure of feeling of a reality we come to experience, not as cold knowledge, but as a transformative recognition… In haunting, organised forces and systematic structures that appear removed from us make their impact felt in everyday life in a way that confounds our analytic separations and confounds the social separations themselves'.[9]

The effort to dislocate one's cultural conditioning, then, is more or less a prerequisite for a meaningful encounter between the present and the past; and as ghosts have loomed large in human consciousness since earliest recorded times up to and including our own, they may be able, if caught in that desirable disjunction of our intellectual preconceptions, to afford a fruitful introduction to the concept of otherness.

ANCIENT GHOSTS

From the very start, the sleeping and the dead have been regarded as alike. The soul, the personality, whatever it was that made someone an individual, had left its fleshly encasement and gone somewhere else, that 'somewhere else' often being imagined as a dark, silent place where the dead existed as melancholy entities, sometimes in human shape, sometimes in other. Thus, the Babylonians thought of the otherworld as an underground citadel in which the dead were locked, like prisoners:

> the house whose entrants are bereft of light,
> where dust is their sustenance and clay their food.
> They see no light but dwell in darkness.
> They are clothed like birds in wings for garments,
> and dust has gathered on the door and bolt.

In Greek religious mythology, death sent souls squeaking like bats to the house of Hades, not so much a house as an extensive underground territory with its individual districts, rivers, woods, and sacred groves, peopled by non-human inhabitants, causes of little but fear. Hesiod, however, had a somewhat different perspective. In his eyes, the underworld, Tartaros, might be a walled enclosure from which there would be no escape, a house which could be entered or left, a great deep gorge, and all of these at once, for, as Johnson points out, '[this] representation of Tartaros is multiple because the underworld has multiple tasks to perform', although in the end, to be sure, whatever its various aspects, it still amounted to the same thing – a prison for the dead.[10]

Plato turned Tartaros into a vast chasm in the earth, through which all rivers flowed downwards and then out again to the surface. There are many such streams, he said, but four in particular: Okeanos which flows round the earth; Akheron which flows through various desert places until it goes below ground and comes to the Akherusian lake. 'The souls of most of the dead come here, stay for their appointed times (longer for some, shorter for others), and are then sent off to be born to living creatures.' Pyriphlegethon flows between Okeanos and Akheron and falls into a huge, boiling, muddy lake; and opposite this flows the Kokytos which begins as the River Styx, the colour of lapis lazuli. When people die, their souls undergo judgement. Those who have not been irredeemably wicked travel in boats upon Akheron until they reach the Akherusian lake where they are purified. The thoroughly wicked, however, are thrown into Tartaros and never come out again. The ancient Israelites, too, envisioned their dead as having a shadowy existence underneath the earth in a place of darkness and silence sometimes known as Sheol in 'the land of gloom and deep darkness', as *Job* 10.21-22 puts it, 'the land of gloom and chaos, where light is as darkness'. The Psalms paint an equally grim picture. Death is a city with gates, or a raging torrent which sweeps people away, or a pit which closes its mouth upon them, or a place equipped with ropes and snares intended to catch people and hold them helpless.[11]

But concomitant with this overwhelmingly sad and frightening view of the afterlife is one which either mitigates its gloom or posits a happy location for some of the dead, at least. Thus, a funerary epigram by Kallimakhos (*Anthologia Palatina* 7.524), is cast in the form of a conversation between someone passing by a tomb and the occupant of the grave.

A. Does Kharidas rest beneath you?
B. If you mean the son of Arimmas of Kyrene, yes.

A. What is it like down there, Kharidas?

B. Very dark.

A. What about coming back?

B. It's a lie.

A. And Pluto?

B. He's a myth.

A. We're completely destroyed!

B. What I'm telling you is true, but if you want [to hear] something pleasant – a large ox in Hades comes cheap.

The Blessed Isles and the Elysian Field offer the dead a kind of golden age similar to the one enjoyed by mortals in the distant past. No one has to work for a living; the dead are free to enjoy themselves in horse-riding, or playing board-games or music; and they also have an opportunity to recline on couches and talk and drink wine, spending their eternity, in fact, in a state of intoxication, a view of the afterlife frequently expressed in funeral iconography.[12] The fifth-century BC Athenian playwright Pherekrates took this notion and exaggerated it for comic effect in his play, *The Miners*:

Everything in the world yonder was mixed with wealth and fashioned with every blessing in every way. Rivers full of porridge and black broth flowed babbling through the channels, spoons and all, and lumps of cheese-cake, too. Hence the morsel could slip easily and oilily of its own accord down the throats of the dead. There were blood-puddings, and hot slices of sausage lay scattered by the river banks, just like shells. Yes, and there were roasted fillets nicely dressed with all sorts of spiced sauces. Close at hand, too, on platters, were whole hams with shin and all, most tender... Roast thrushes... flew round our mouths, entreating us to swallow them as we lay stretched among the myrtles and anemones... Girls in silk shawls, just reaching the flower of youth, and shorn of the hair on their bodies, drew through a funnel full cups of red wine with a fine bouquet for all who wished to drink. And whenever anyone had eaten or drunk of these things, straightaway there came forth once more twice as much again.[13]

These are examples of the way in which the horrors of the afterlife could be mitigated, at least for those who had lived exemplary lives or died exemplary deaths according to the requirements of their culture, or had not committed any great wrongs during life. It is a modification found elsewhere, too. Hence, the pre-Columbian Mexica believed that men who had died in battle or perished as human sacrifices, and women who had died while giving birth to their first child, went skywards, while the wicked and the unworthy went below to an underworld which was dark and dank. Likewise, the Nahuatl envisaged a region of the dead below the earth where they stayed for four years before their separate existence came to an end, as well as other places, such as Tlalocan where 'there is never a lack of green corn, squash, sprigs of amaranth, green chillies, tomatoes, string beans in pods, and flowers'. Ancient Japan, too, had its version of Hades with regions full of terror and others offering peace and earth-like delights for the dead.[14]

Before they could enjoy or endure the delights or pangs of the afterlife, however, the dead might have to pass through some kind of judgement or test. In Egypt, the soul came before Osiris, the god of the dead, who listened to him or her reciting a declaration of innocence: 'I have not committed iniquity, I have not ill-treated animals, I have not done wrong in the Place of Truth, I have not sought to know the future, I have not tolerated evil', and so forth. Thereafter, the soul made a second similar declaration in front of a panel of forty-two divine judges before his or her heart was weighed in a balance against Truth, hieroglyphically represented as a feather. For those who failed the judgement, there seems to have awaited some kind of second death as they were devoured by the monster Ammut or were burned in pits of fire, although according to the *Book of Caverns* from the tomb of Ramses VI, souls and the shades of sinners were punished by being boiled in a cauldron. To assist the newly-dead through these ordeals, the so-called *Book of the Dead* was compiled as a kind of manual whose spells would provide keys to safe passage into a happy shadow-existence. The *Tibetan Book of the Dead* does something similar, and contains an extraordinary episode of judgement in which the Lord of Death looks into a mirror and sees the dead person's good or evil acts reflected in it; whereupon the body of the deceased is subjected to a multiplicity of torments. 'Then [one of the Executive Furies of] the Lord of Death will place round thy neck a rope and drag thee along; he will cut off thy head, extract thy heart, pull out thy intestines, lick up thy brain, drink thy blood, eat thy flesh, and gnaw thy bones; but thou wilt be incapable of dying [a second death]. Although thy body be hacked to pieces, it will revive again. The repeated hacking will cause intense pain and torture. Even at the time that the pebbles are being counted out, be not frightened, or terrified; tell no lies; and fear not the Lord of Death' – an exhortation, one cannot help thinking, more easily said than done. So, too, the Hindu *Bhagavata Purana* describes tit-for-tat punishments meted out to those whose karma is bad; and the Aztec dead were obliged to meet a series of obstacles on their four-year journey to the oblivion of Mictlan.[15]

Likewise, judgement awaited both angels and human beings according to the second-century BC *Book of Enoch* (1.22). Therein, the eponymous figure makes a series of visionary journeys, one of which brings him to a place of dreadful fire stretching, it seems, for ever into an abyss. The archangel Uriel explains that this is a prison for rebellious angels, a place in which they will be kept for eternity. From there, Enoch is transported to a mountain which has in it four huge hollows. These, the archangel Raphael tells him, are where the souls of dead humans are incarcerated until the final day of judgement. Three of the hollows are dark: one is for those who have died before their misdeeds could be punished in life, and so here they await a perpetual retribution; a second is for those who suffered violent deaths and have complaints to bring against their murderers; and a third is for those who weakly co-operated with sinful people even though they themselves were not particularly sinful. A kind of prefiguring of Hell and of Purgatory seems to be visible here. The fourth hollow is light, with a spring of water in its midst. This is reserved for the righteous dead.

The afterlife, then, tended to be envisaged as dark, cheerless, and frightening, with exceptions for certain groups or kinds of people. In some cases, it implied a close relationship between the dead person's spirit and his or her corpse, most notably, of course, in Egypt. But this was also true of Mexican belief – a belief, incidentally, which continues into the present – for according to this all live human beings produce emanations originating in their actions and emotions, and these vaporous residues are released after death to be seen as shadowy doubles of the once-living, or as animals; and in these forms they enter the body of a still-living person where they assume some other form and induce a chill which, in turn, causes illness and bad dreams.[16] The implication of such a belief, and others like it, was that the dead could both contact and be contacted. This brought in its wake a number of implications: (1) since the dead could well be unhappy in their new existence, they might in some fashion ask the living to help them; (2) if the living failed to respond, the dead might either continue in their suffering or even die a second, permanent death, or they might harass the living and cause them unhappiness in return until their needs were met; (Thus Otloh's knight threatened his own sons and the rest of his posterity with Hell fire unless they agreed to put right a wrong which he himself had committed); and (3) the dead could be consulted by the living, for as they were now spirit forms and existed in a world wherein the usual human limitation of time did not appear to operate, they were in a position to know the future as well as the past and present, and could thus assist the living by accurate prediction.

In Mesopotamia ghosts appeared because their funerary rites had not been correctly celebrated, or because death had happened as a result of execution or accident. Anyone who had ceased to receive the customary offerings to the dead was thus angered and distressed, and by way of punishment might inflict diseases upon the living or persecute them in some fashion; and there survives a series of one hundred magical incantations, called *Maqlû*, which were intended to ward off the attentions of hostile ghosts. Such beliefs continued to flourish centuries after the antique period. A Corsican folk-tale, for example, says that on the Day of the Dead a dreadful storm arose because someone had failed to leave out the traditional drink of water for the dead; and in Ariège and Roussillon, chestnuts were placed on the stairs on All Souls' Day not only to gratify the dead but also to distract them from coming to disturb the living while they lay asleep.[17] Similarly, when the Romans neglected to make offerings to the dead, large numbers of the living suddenly died and ghosts issued from their tombs and howled round the city and its environs; and in Apuleius's novel, *Metamorphoses*, the heroine warns her lover that if they were to marry prematurely, her former husband's ghost would

rise and kill him (8.9). Belief in ghosts' potential hostility
is not confined to Europe, of course. The first Emperor of
China had hundreds of sets of stone armour buried with
him. They were destined for the spirits of his own soldiers
who had been killed in battle, and were intended to placate
them so that they would not turn against him in death and
so become vengeful ghosts. In India, *bhuta* are ghosts of those
who have died untimely or violent deaths, or have been
insane or deformed, and are invariably hostile to the living;
while the *brahm* is the vengeful spirit of a Brahman who has
died a bad death, and the most ferocious is that of a Brahman
who has fasted to death in revenge for some offence against
him, for this spirit will kill members of one generation after
another of the family which has angered him, and cannot be
laid to rest until its vengeance is complete. Similarly, the *irã*
(ancestral spirits) of Guinea-Bissau may be persuaded by a
magician to leave the realm of the dead and do harm to the
living, not for any wrong done to themselves, but to avenge
a perceived wrong done to the magician's client.[18]

A further mark of the dead as powerful spirits with access
to preternatural powers can be found in the *defixiones*, the
curse tablets. They have various purposes and call upon a
variety of divine and semi-divine entities, but their general
intention was to bind the free will or free action of the
person against whom they were aimed – hence their Greek
name *katadesmoi*, 'tying down'. The Latin term is more violent –'nailing down'. These tablets, usually made of lead,
although the ancients also used papyrus, wax, and several
other materials capable of being inscribed, were buried in
places most appropriate to the powers they were meant to
invoke, and in consequence many have been discovered
in graves and tombs. Sometimes written by the aggrieved
individual, sometimes by a professional magician on his or
her behalf, they are found all over the Classical world and

assume that the dead person is now able to exert powers well beyond these accessible to humans. 'I invoke you, spirit of someone who died before his time', says one, 'bind the horses whose names and pictures I entrust to you on this [magical] instrument ..... so that tomorrow morning in the hippodrome they will not be able to run or walk or win' – a fearful way to try to ensure the success of a bet. But the dead themselves could curse from the grave, as did Arsinoe 'who died before her time'. According to her *defixio*, she now raises her hands in supplication and begs that if anyone poisoned her, or killed her by venomous magic, or rejoiced at her death, or even if anyone will do so, God and the Sun and the goddesses of vengeance will persecute them.[19] Rituals directed towards ghosts were therefore attempts to assuage their anger and dispel their unwelcome attentions, although there is also evidence that offerings were made to them with a view to enlisting their help in the fight against disease. The English word 'ghost' reminds us of the irritable and dangerous aspect of the dead, for it seems to be derived from a pre-Teutonic *ghoizdo-z*, meaning 'fury', and there is an obsolete verb *gast*, meaning 'to terrify', which lingers in the still current participial adjective *aghast*.

But the dead were not always vengeful. Indeed, they could not afford to be, because in most ancient cultures they depended on the living for continued sustenance. In Egypt, for example, it was thought that each person had two spirit-forms, the *ka* and the *ba*. The *ka* was an individual's life-force, created with him or her at birth and surviving after death in a statue or replica of the living person set up in his or her tomb. It required regular offerings of food and drink. The *ba*, often translated as 'soul' (misleading, however, if it is conceived in Christian terms), was represented as a human-headed bird free to leave the tomb at night. There was also an entity known as the *'akh* which appears to have been either some kind of supernatural force which helped the dead person in his or her new condition, or the dead person as a sort of glorified being, having successfully negotiated, with the help of magical recitations, all the perils which awaited the dead at the start of their second existence. But, unlike other Near Eastern dead, the Egyptian was not necessarily confined to a new world underground. For him or her there might be two locales: the mummified corpse and its decorated tomb where the *ka* was able to enjoy a kind of shadowy substitute of a living existence through the decorations, furniture, and artefacts provided in the tomb; or a dark world in the west ruled over by Osiris, which was illuminated every night when the sun-god traversed it on his way back to the east. The ancient Israelites also believed that the dead needed sustenance (a belief which may have been theirs or one which they borrowed from the Egyptians), and provided them with grave goods for their comfort and enjoyment. The Athenians, too, fed their dead, especially at the festival of the Anthesteria which took place in February. On one of its days, the dead came back from the otherworld to visit their houses and feed upon a gruel made from all the crops of the year, the *panspermia*. The Romans had a somewhat similar festival, the Parentalia, also held in February, when food and drink were left for the dead near their tombs; and they sometimes built pipes into their tombs, down which both food and drink could be passed to the spirit of the corpse. Funerary gardens, too, were common, often extensive pieces of land planted with vegetables, trees, and other plants gathered around a tomb with space sufficient for the family to convene at specific intervals to take part in a banquet which included the dead, a custom which continued well into the Christian era.[20]

Pliny the Younger tells what is perhaps the most famous of all Classical ghost stories, about a haunted house in Athens, whose ghost frightened successive inhabitants by appearing as an old man clanking chains round his wrists and legs. The ghost never spoke, but indicated to a philosopher who had decided to investigate the phenomenon that he should follow him. Upon reaching a certain spot in the garden, the ghost vanished, and when people dug up the place next day they found some bones entwined with chains. The bones were given proper burial and thereafter the haunting ceased (*Letters* 7.27.5-11). This haunting, then, was a cry for help. Cicero provides another:

> Two close friends from Arcadia were making a journey and came to Megara. One of them put up at an inn, the other at a friend's house. Once they had had a meal they went to sleep, and in the dead of night, while he was dreaming, it seemed to the former that the man who was staying in the inn appeared to him and begged him to come to his aid, because the innkeeper was preparing to kill him. At first, terrified by the dream, he got up, but then pulled himself together and decided that what he had seen was nothing in particular, and went back to bed. Then while he was sleeping, the same man seemed to be asking him [a favour], saying that since he had not come to help him while he was alive, he should not allow his death to go unpunished. The innkeeper had killed him, thrown him into a cart, and covered him with dung. [The dead man] asked his friend to be at the city gate in the morning before the cart went out of the town. Deeply moved by this dream, he met the plough-man [who was driving the cart] in the morning and asked him what was in the cart. The driver was terrified and fled. The dead man was rescued, the situation made clear [to the authorities], and the innkeeper paid the penalty.[21]

Now, all this raises the question, what did ghosts look like? The various English synonyms suggest above all that these emanations of the dead can be *seen*. Thus, *phantom* comes via French from Greek *phantazo* = 'I make visible'; *spectre*, from Latin *spectrum* = 'something emanating from a physical object, which gives rise to a visual or mental image' (as though the ghost were a reflection of a person rather than the person him or herself); and *apparition* from Latin *appareo* = 'I am visible, I materialise'. The word *ghoul*, however, is derived from an Arabic verb 'to seize', while *spook* is a nineteenth-century usage, derived from German *spuch*, 'goblin'. Pliny the Younger tells an anecdote about the historian Gaius Fannius who foresaw his own death in a dream or dream-like state. 'During the quietness of the night, it appeared to him that he was lying quite calmly on his couch, the way he usually did while he was applying himself to his books, and that (as was his custom) he had his writing-case in front of him. Shortly afterwards he had the impression that [the dead Emperor] Nero came, sat down beside him on the bolster, and picked up the first volume Fannius had published about his [Nero's] crimes. He read it through to the end, did the same thing with the second and third volumes, and then went away. Fannius was terrified and interpreted it as follows: that he would finish writing just as much as Nero had read – and so it turned out.'[22]

Now, when Pliny tries to tell us what was going on in Fannius's mind, he uses two verbs which mean that Fannius 'saw' the whole scene, although whether he saw it happening before his waking eyes, like a spectator watching a scene in a theatre, or whether he saw it in his head while he was still aware of his actual surroundings is not quite clear. In the sentence preceding the story, Pliny says that Fannius *praesensit*, 'perceived [his fate] beforehand with his senses', and then goes on to say that when Nero appeared, Fannius *imaginatus est*, 'had a picture of him'. To a Roman, the word *imago* carried certain emotive meanings. Every patrician house had its wax portrait images of the family's ancestors. Under the Republic, these tended to be masks which were worn by relatives and friends of the deceased during his or her funeral procession; so the dead were conceived as taking part, expressionless but recognisable, in a ritual of the living, both communities combining, as it were, to assist the newly dead in his or her passage to a new existence. These masks were *imagines*, a word connected with the verb *imitari*, 'to copy, to resemble'. Masks were replaced, to some extent, by busts under the Empire. These were carried during the funeral procession, and the basic meaning of their presence had not altered; but inevitably the sense of theatre conveyed by masked figures must have changed. Actors in plays wore masks, and with the active co-operation of their audience's imaginations were taken to 'be' the person represented by their mask. Republican funerals drew upon this dramatic convention for religious purposes. The practice of having the living wear masks to represent the dead had a long subsequent history. During the Middle Ages and later, for example, in both France and Italy young men used to wear masks at times of Charivari and were taken to signify the spirits of the dead.[23] Several of the Greek and Latin words commonly translated as 'ghost' imply recognisability: *eidolon*, 'something which is seen, a form, a representation'; *simulacrum*, 'a likeness, a statue, a picture'; *effigies*, 'a copy, a reproduction'. Hence, when the dead King Darius appears to his wife in Aeschylus's play *The Persians* (680 sq.), everyone who sees him knows at once who he is, just as Fannius recognised Nero. The dead, then, were recognisable because, in spite of their changed condition, they still looked like themselves, and this has an important consequence for the meaning of the word 'imagination'. For by this is meant the faculty of perceiving likenesses, and both it and its adjectives 'imaginary' and 'imaginative' have positive connotations, not the negative associations which are frequently present in modern English usage.

But what were the sources of all this information? Did knowledge of the dead spring from dreams alone, and was death, as Hamlet says, really that bourn from which no traveller returns – as Euripides lamented, 'Do you think your child will come back from under the earth? Which of the dead has ever returned from Hades'? (*Hercules Furens*, 296-7) – or could the living and the dead communicate directly, with the living visiting the dead in their own realms and then coming back unscathed? Visits there were indeed, partly recorded by myth, partly by accounts derived from some form of trance or ecstasy. Hercules, for example, performed his last and most difficult labour by descending into the underworld and fetching the guardian three-headed dog Kerberos to the surface of the earth, an act whose dreadful impiety Seneca makes the goddess Juno express in awe-struck terms. 'Look, he has broken open the doorway of the underworld and brought back to the upper regions the spoils of the King he defeated... The treaty [governing] ghosts has been destroyed. A way back from the deepest underworld has been laid open, and the sacred things of grim Death lie in open view... I have seen the daylight tottering at the sight of Kerberos, and the Sun stricken with terror.' It was a legend, however, which the fifth-century BC comic playwright Aristophanes seized on as material for one of his best-known plays, *The Frogs*, in which the god Dionysos and his slave Xanthias go down into the underworld. Dionysos pretends, at one point, to be Hercules and is threatened with physical violence by Aiakos from whom the real Hercules stole Kerberos (462–78). Orpheus, too, famously braved the horrors of death in an attempt to bring back his wife to the upper world. 'He even went through the jaws of Taenarum, the high entrance of [King] Dis, and the grove which is misty with black terror. He went to the dead and their frightening king and to hearts which do not know how to become soft at human prayers. Moved by his chanting, there started to come from the lowest regions of Erebus the thin shades and likenesses (*umbrae tenues simulacraque*) of those who lack the light... mothers and men and the lifeless bodies of great-hearted heroes, boys and unmarried girls, and young people placed on the pyre in front of their parents' faces.'[24]

But unlike dreams and myths, necromancy, the art of consulting the dead to gain foreknowledge of the future or to learn the secrets of the created universe, demanded a contact between the two worlds which was deliberately engineered by the living and open to their control. We have many examples of such engineering, such as an extraordinary late Greek love-spell which consists of an incantation to be placed beside the grave of someone who had died an untimely or violent death. The operator is to sing a hymn to the Sun, while holding a part of the corpse, and then its ghost will be compelled to rise and go about the magician's bidding. The Roman poet Lucan gives a famous and highly exaggerated picture of a necromancer at work. She is called Erictho and Lucan describes her wandering over a battlefield, looking for the body of someone who has not yet been buried, so that she may resurrect it and ask it questions anent the future. When she finds a suitable corpse, she stabs it several times in the chest, fills the new wounds with fresh blood, washes out the old, clotted gore, and then pours in *virus*, poisonous secretions or acrid plant juices with medicinal or magical properties. This done, she embarks on a lengthy incantation to summon the spirit of the dead man back to earth and knows she has succeeded when she sees his *umbra*, his shade or ghost, standing beside her. Erictho wants the spirit to re-enter the body, but the ghost 'is afraid to go into the opened chest cavity, the entrails, and the bowels which were burst apart by the fatal blow'. Erictho's magic, however, forces the spirit to do so:

> and immediately the clotted blood grew warm, heated the black wounds, and ran into the veins and extremities of the arms and legs... Every limb quivered, the sinews stretched themselves, and the corpse lifted himself from the earth, not little by little, one limb at a time, but thrusting himself upright and standing erect at once. His mouth gaped and his eyes were wide open. His appearance was not yet that of someone who was alive, but of someone who was in the process of dying. His pallor and stiffness remained.

The corpse is unable to speak, for he is permitted only to reply to questions. Erictho promises that if he answers truthfully, she will make sure he is free from the threat of necromancy in future; and with this, the revivified corpse utters a number of prophecies. Satisfied with these, Erictho then applies herbs to him and chants spells, before building him a pyre upon which he stretches himself and dies a second time amid the flames.[25]

Uplifting an actual corpse to answer questions, however, was not the only way to conduct a necromantic operation. The dead could be summoned as spirits and, as spirits, converse with the living, although in these cases, as the sixteenth and seventeenth centuries were to point out, it was a moot point whether the spirit was actually that of the dead person or a demon mimicking the voice and possibly the appearance of the dead. This last, indeed, was openly acknowledged by the first-century AD magician, Simon

Magus, who, we are told, 'separated the soul of a child from its body by dreadful incantations', and later explained, 'You know I separated a soul from a human body. But I know you *don't* know that it is not the soul of the dead person who acts as a servant to me, because [the soul] does not exist. It's a demon who does the work, pretending to be the soul'. Simon may have been sincere in his beliefs and claims, but the possibility of fraud always existed, of course, and one such forms a distinctive episode in a late Byzantine verse novel, *Rhodanthe and Dosikles*, in which a magical wonder-worker, Satyrion, seeking to astonish an important politician at a banquet, strips off down to a multicoloured garment round his waist and reveals a shaven head and a scrawny body covered with ash and soot. He then stabs himself in the throat and falls down, gushing blood and apparently lifeless. At the command of another man present, however – presumably an accomplice – Satyrion gets up from the floor and begins to sing and accompany himself on the lyre. Clearly his weird appearance was intended to imitate that of a ghost – he is described as 'someone who scares others' [*mormolytton*] and 'an unsmiling Hades' – an impersonation of the dead by no means uncommon during both this and earlier periods.[26]

But the best-known example of necromantic rite involved the raising of Samuel by the so-called 'witch' of Endor. King Saul, about to fight a huge army of Philistines, wants to know what will be the outcome of the battle. He instructs servants to find a woman who can predict the future with the help of a ghost. Saul is taken to such a woman, but when he says, 'Make divination for me by means of a ghost. Raise up [*suscita*] the person I shall tell you to resuscitate', the woman becomes frightened because she will be breaking an edict against such practices, which Saul himself had issued. But Saul reassures her she will suffer no punishment if she does as she is told. 'Then the woman said, Whom shall I raise up [*suscitabo*] for you? and Saul replied, Resuscitate [*suscita*] Samuel.' The Latin verb used here refers to raising from a recumbent position, or restoring to health, or waking up from sleep. Clearly this context implies that a dead person is to be woken, and thus the passage is reminiscent (without the histrionic accompaniments), of the revivification performed by Erictho. Readers of the Latin Bible, then – and these will have been a majority of scholars throughout the Middle Ages and early modern period – will have had no doubt that a rite of necromancy was about to be performed.

Samuel appears and the woman cries out at the sight of him. She reproaches Saul, whom she now seems to recognise for the first time, for coming to her in disguise; but the King reassures her and asks her what she has seen. 'Supernatural beings rising up from the earth', is her reply. Saul answers in the singular. 'What kind of shape does it have?' to which the woman replies, 'An old man has risen up, and he is draped in a large cloak'. At this, Saul realises that the ghost is that of Samuel and throws himself to the ground in veneration.[27] Could Saul see Samuel? It is difficult to tell. He seems to be dependent on the woman for at least the initial description of the spirit, and the information that it is wearing a large cloak is hardly enough to allow Saul to realise it is Samuel. (There are variations in the text which offer 'erect man' or even 'startling man' instead of 'old man', so the age of the spirit cannot here be taken into account as a guide). The Septuagint (Greek) version of the text, however, offers us a possible explanation. It calls the diviner a *gynaika engastrimython*, 'a woman who speaks from the stomach'. These ventriloquists were common in the ancient world and were credited with the ability to act as a vessel for the spirit who then spoke through them. Plutarch, referring to oracles rather than necromancers, disapprovingly observed that it was extremely silly to believe that 'the god himself, after the fashion of ventriloquists... who are now called *pythones*, enters the bodies of his prophets and speaks in a low voice, using their mouths and voices as his instruments'. But one is reminded of modern mediums, many of whom also claim to have the power to provide just such a vessel: as, for example, the twentieth-century medium, Helen Duncan, who on occasion 'began speaking in the deep voice of a "Dr Williams", a spirit guide whose name was spelled in smoke from an extinguished candle'. Helen's later control, Albert Stewart, was 'given to making cryptic comments... His voice was a peculiar hybrid: not merely Scots inflected with Australian, but what sitters most commonly described as an "Oxford" accent'.[28]

The ghosts we have met so far, then, were usually thought of as recognisable in some way, and several Greek and Latin terms for them emphasised this. Other terms, however, drew attention to a more uncertain appearance of the dead. Thus, Erictho's spirit is called an *umbra*, 'shadow', the Latin word implying a dark distorted outline rather than a clear, immediately identifiable individual, a scarcely noticeable attachment to the person who invited him. It has been suggested that this umbrageous (or sometimes smoke-like) appearance of ghosts springs from the practice of cremating the dead, since the last glimpse mourners had of the body was that of a charred, blackened, and distorted shape. The custom of pouring wine on the embers of a pyre before collecting the corpse's bones for burial is likely to have produced steam mixed with the final smoke, and this too may have helped to suggest that a ghost might look vaporous. If, on the other hand, the ghost was very pallid, this may reflect the mourners' view of the corpse's face just after death, because when circulation ceases, the blood is drawn downwards by gravity;

so if the body is lying supine, the blood will sink to the back and the buttocks, leaving the face pale and colourless. The Roman poet Lucretius associates the outline shapes [*figurae*], and images [*simulacra*], and the shades of the dead [*umbrae*], in a passage which seeks to explain that such images are like the pale film over an animal's eye or the sloughed skin of a snake [*membrana*]. The implication of all these notions is thus that the ghost is recognisable as the person it used to be, but pale and insubstantial.[29]

But the dead did not always return in the form of ghosts. The second-century AD author, Phlegethon of Tralles, tells a story of whose incidents he claims to have been an eyewitness (a favourite device to suggest authenticity), anent a girl, Philinnion, who came back secretly to her old home six months after she had died and been buried. What drew her thither was a young male house-guest called Machates, and when Philinnion's parents challenged him to prove his story that he had been sleeping with their daughter, he produced a gold ring and a breast-band, both of which Philinnion's mother recognised. The following night, at Machates's suggestion, the parents suddenly entered his room and found Philinnion sitting beside him. They embraced her, but she was furious and immediately after reproaching them became a corpse once more. An inspection of the family vault next day revealed that Philinnion's body was missing, but that a ring and a cup which Machates had given her on their first meeting were lying on the shelf her body should have occupied. On the advice of a local diviner, Philinnion's body was taken beyond the town boundaries and then burned. Machates committed suicide. Throughout the narrative, most of the words used to describe Philinnion refer to a being of flesh and blood: *nekros*, 'corpse', and *soma*, 'body'. We should therefore regard Philinnion not as a ghost but as a revivified body, a *revenant*. Philinnion claimed divine permission for her return and, to judge by Machates's reactions to her, does not seem to have given any indication that she was both dead and buried. Two other obvious examples of revivified corpses which did not shock or disgust those who saw them are, of course, Lazarus and Jesus. Not that people did not expect to be disgusted. When Jesus came to Lazarus's tomb, the dead man's sister, Martha, said, 'Lord, he is stinking, for he has been dead for four days'. But Lazarus was able to answer Jesus's summons, shuffle out of his tomb, and be unwrapped from his grave cloths and bandages without exciting any further comment about decay. Both the Greek and Latin texts of the Gospel of St John describe him as 'the man who had died', thereby emphasising that this was a revivification. Similarly, after His resurrection Jesus makes it clear to doubting Thomas that He is a body of flesh and not simply an apparition: 'Bring your finger over here and look at my hands, and bring your hand and push it into my side'.[30]

Now, revenants in particular illustrate the belief that if the dead are not buried and honoured properly in the world of the living, they will either fail to find entry into the other-world or will actually be forbidden to enter it, thus being condemned to a perpetually restless existence betwixt and between the two worlds, intruding upon this one because they are not yet fully convinced that they are dead. Their frustration and attendant distress must inevitably turn to or be allied with hostility towards those who have failed to ensure them proper passage between the worlds. Hence their disconcerting intrusions upon the living. The same may be said of those who have died before their allotted time and those who have died violent deaths. Apuleius (admittedly a late Latin author) distinguishes some restless ghosts as *larvae* who 'because of their misdeeds during life are condemned to have no fixed abode, to wander about all over the place as in a kind of exile. 'This type', he says, 'is a hollow bogeyman to all good people, but on the other hand a harmful bogeyman to the wicked.' Likewise, *lemures* were later interpreted as being the souls of evil people who had been excluded from any hierarchy of good spirits. They roamed around the earth, seeking to molest those who were living a wicked life; and similarly, the spirits of the dead called *manes* could be vengeful, as in the case of a young girl, Verginia. In order to save her from rape and slavery, her father knifed her to death. After a long struggle, justice was finally obtained against her would-be oppressors, 'and so Verginia's *manes*.... after wandering through so many houses in search of satisfaction for the wrong done to her... finally found rest'.[31] Apuleius's description of the *larva* is clearly intended to make a moral point. To good people, the larva is a *terriculamentum*, a source of terror, small in size, which is *inane*, 'empty, hollow, deserted, dead, insubstantial, illusory'. The adjective conveys both the sense of non-corporeality and of ineffective fright. *Larva* itself can also mean 'mask' or 'model skeleton'. To the wicked, however, this miniature source of terror is *noxium*, 'capable of doing wrong or harm or injury'. But Apuleius's explanation of these terms was roundly denounced by St Augustine who, in any case, had no time for the notion that the souls of the dead could impinge on the world of the living.[32]

The term 'ghost', then, has a wider application than simply the insubstantial spirit of a dead person. Felton summarises the ancient concept. 'In antiquity both the terminology used to describe such beings and the concept of "spirits of the dead" itself were much more generalised. Some ghosts were indeed considered to be the insubstantial spirits of the deceased; but the general title of "ghost" was also applied to all sorts of impersonal semi-divine apparitions, *daimones*, and other kinds of supernatural being, none of which were considered to be the spirits of people who had died.' *Daemon* (plural *daemones*), originally Greek, is a word of complex meanings ranging from supernatural entities who acted as intermediaries between human beings and the gods, to Christian usage which equated them with specifically evil spirits and therefore servants of Satan. According to their behaviour, the dead might display the characteristics of the former or the latter. The Hebrew word for the dead, *rephaim*, may indicate weakness and insubstantiality, but it has also been suggested that it is actually derived from a verb meaning 'to heal' or 'to mend', and this, if accurate, would stress the role of the dead as beneficent assisters of the living. But one should also note that the dead could appear in non-human guise as well. Both snake and butterfly are recorded, for example, and with these one may compare the observation of the sixteenth-century Protestant minister, Ludwig Lavater, that '[ghosts] appear also in the form of brute beasts sometimes four-footed, as of a dog, a swine, a horse, a goat, a cat, or a hare: and sometimes of fowls, and creeping worms, as of a crow, a night owl, a screech owl, a snake, or dragon'. This view of their protean capabilities has lasted into modern times. In nineteenth-century Sweden, a farmer recorded that one of his crofters' wives and another woman had seen the ghosts of two brothers – one a suicide, the other an accidental death – hopping in the form of crows along a couple of cart-tracks; and in Madagascar, ghosts merge with various nature spirits and can be seen in the form of butterflies and moths. So the dead may show themselves to us in almost any shape, and exhibit a near-comprehensive array of powers to help or frighten, beg for help or threaten. It was an extraordinary legacy to be inherited by the Christian world.[33]

II

THE MIDDLE AGES:
PITEOUS REVENANTS, NECROMANTIC SPIRITS, AND VAMPIRES

If ghosts were considered to be a category of non-human entity which included beings other than spirits of the dead, it is easy to see that the dead, by process of association, inhabited a curious hinterland of consciousness in the living, at once remembered as they were in life and yet now permanently alien. Expelled by death from the world in which they were accustomed to exist, the dead became the children of death, born into a different life in which they were both dead and not-dead, since they were deprived of a material existence and yet still continued in memory and, sometimes, in more tangible form such as painting and sculpture. A later age, indeed, would emphasise this disturbing double life with the invention of photography and voice-recording, both of which preserved the dead even more distinctly as they had been in their material shape. Even in ancient times, however, the link with their erstwhile humanity was maintained in a variety of ways. If they were buried in ancestral lands, for example, their bones constituted a continuing guarantee of ownership of that territory by the living, a guarantee reinforced by the preternatural powers to which the dead now had access. Among the Sámi of northern Norway, a pregnant woman or shaman might see a dead relative in a dream and decide to name the new child after the deceased, thus reintegrating the dead into the living family. Fifteenth-century Florence saw the same custom, but carried it out more in fear of than respect for the dead, but among the Abruzzi, godparents and godchildren had a special relationship, for whoever died first waited to guide the other across 'the River Jordan' or 'the Valley of Jehosaphat' to bring him or her safely into the realm of the dead. Giving a child a name was very important, of course, because this implied that she or he had been baptised. Without baptism, the child might become a ghost, as a Scottish Gaelic story illustrates:

> In Bohaldy Forest a young child which had not been baptised died. It was buried and after that people in the locality thought there was a ghost in the place. They used to hear splashing sounds in the pool close to the place and they made out it was the child's ghost that was there. One night a bold man came past. He heard the sound and said, 'So you are busy, Puddlefoot!' 'Now I've got a name', said the child-ghost, 'and I will never again cause any trouble'.

The Nuer of southern Sudan, too, perpetuate the dead by not allowing widows to remarry or to be inherited by other members of the family. The women continue to be married to their dead husbands and any children they may bear after the death are considered to be those of the dead man, not of the living impregnator. The woman is then known as *ciek joka*, 'the ghost's wife', and her male child as *gat joka*, 'the ghost's son'. 'In honouring and reincarnating the dead', says Klaphisch-Zuber, 'the living avoid alienating them; they neutralise them, "buy them off", and prevent them from floating free in the indefinite and threatening space reserved for shades.' The relationship between living and dead is well-described in relation to Kongo belief but, *mutatis mutandis*, applicable to earlier periods in European society. 'Beginning with the individual, the total community, like a series of concentric waves, spreads first into the members of the living community; then outward to the recent dead, who are in process of becoming revered ancestors; and finally to those who have achieved the status of ancestors or little gods, who watch over, guide, and protect the community of the living.'[1]

This, however, still leaves the question of where the dead went and existed, for notions regarding this question underwent changes after the ancient and the Classical periods. The ancient concept of the afterlife and the underworld was, as we have seen, principally gloomy, although there were notions, frequently expressed, that places of light and enjoyment also existed for those entitled to inhabit them. One common idea throughout the Near East was that 'Heaven' was the residence of the gods and that human dead went elsewhere. *Psalm* 113.16–17 (Vulgate) for example, is explicit for Israelite belief. 'The heaven [and] the heavens [belong to] the Lord: but He has given the earth to the sons of human beings. The dead will not praise you, O Lord: neither will all those who go down to the underworld'. This realm of the dead may reflect, in one way or another, the structure of the world with which the dead had been familiar in physical life, the heavenly Jerusalem thus beginning as a city reminiscent of its terrestrial counterpart until it developed in such a way that all such connection finally disappeared.[2] But *Psalm* 113 also expresses another notion common to most of the ancient texts: that there are multiple heavens above or near the earth, and that these can actually be penetrated by living humans in dream or in ecstasy. *The Greek Testament of Levi*, one of the so-called *Testaments of the Twelve Patriarchs*, dating from the second century AD, gives a description of several:

> Then there fell upon me a sleep, and I beheld a high mountain, and I was upon it. And behold the heavens were opened, and the angel of God said to me, Levi, enter. And I entered from the first heaven, and I saw there a great sea hanging. And further, I saw a second heaven far brighter and more brilliant, for there was a boundless height also therein. And I said to the angel, Why is this so? And the angel said to me, Marvel not at this, for thou shalt see another heaven more brilliant and incomparable... Hear, therefore, regarding the heavens which have been shown to thee. The lowest is for this cause gloomy unto thee, in that it beholds all the unrighteous deeds of men. And it has fire, snow, and ice made ready for the day of judgement, in the righteous judgement of God; for in it are all the spirits of retributions for vengeance on men. And in the second are the hosts of the armies which are ordained for the day of judgement, to work vengeance on the spirits of deceit and of Beliar. And above them are the holy ones. And in the highest of all dwelleth the Great Glory, far above all holiness. In [the heaven next to] it are the archangels, who minister and make propitiation to the Lord for all the sins of ignorance of the righteous... And [in the heaven below this] are the angels who bear answers to the angels of the presence of the Lord. And in the heaven next to this are thrones and dominions, in which always they offer praise to God.[3]

Other, apocalyptic writings describe even more. *Baruch* sees five, *Enoch* ten, and others seven, and one can discern a

gradual evolution in the early Judaeo-Christian concept of
the cosmos to produce parallel pictures of a simple tripartite
structure of Heaven, Earth, and Underworld – a structure
derived from those Biblical texts regarded as authoritative
(one which actually mirrored the three-tiered universe of
Mesopotamian belief), and a series of interconnected but
separate worlds – supernal, planetary, terrestrial – whose
purpose is to house equally complex hierarchies of beings,
from God Himself to angels to various kinds of spirits to
humans to the dead, and to provide places where the human
dead may receive reward or punishment in accordance with
their ethical or non-ethical behaviour in life.[4] The general
notion is clearly set out in the first-century AD Jewish historian Josephus's description of Essene belief:

> They have a fixed belief that the body is corruptible, that
> the matter of which it is composed is not permanent, and
> that the soul is immortal and cannot perish. These souls,
> which emanate from the thinnest air, become entangled,
> so to speak, in the gaol which is the body, to which
> they are dragged down by a kind of natural incantation.
> Once they have been set free from the chains of the flesh,
> however, then, as though liberated from a long servitude,
> they are happy and are carried upwards. They share the
> belief of the children of Greece and maintain that virtu-
> ous souls have a dwelling-place reserved for them beyond
> Ocean, a place not oppressed by rain or snow or heat, but
> refreshed by the perpetual gentle breath of the west wind
> which comes in from the sea. Worthless, wicked souls
> they assign to a dark, storm-ridden dungeon which is
> big with everlasting punishments... Such are the religious
> beliefs of the Essenes anent the soul, which prove irresist-
> ibly attractive to all those who have once had a taste of
> their philosophy (*Bellum Judaicum* 2.154-58).

The vision of the afterlife delineated in the *Book of Enoch*, which we noted earlier, described several hollows in a mountain, one for the irredeemably wicked, one for the righteous, one for those whose sins were not unforgivable, and one for those who died violent deaths and had complaints to bring against their murderers. It is possible here to detect a faint prefiguring of Hell, Heaven, and Purgatory, and a state of being from which it might be possible for the dead to return in some fashion to the world of the living in order to seek retribution for wrongs they had suffered. Final judgement in orthodox Christian doctrine is, of course, postponed until the end of creation when Christ will come a second time and make a final division between the souls of both dead and living according to whether they are innocent or guilty, thus rendering them justified or unjustified, saved or damned. Meanwhile, a kind of provisional judgement is made whereby the souls of the dead are directed into that state or place appropriate to their moral condition. Caesarius of Heisterbach tells the story of a lay brother who comes back from the dead and describes Heaven as a place full of trees and flowers; and the French King, Charles the Fat, had a vision of evil bishops burning in valleys of pitch, sulphur, lead, wax, and soot. He was suddenly attacked by demons who tried to seize hold of him with hooks made of fire, but he managed to escape and found himself, first on a mountain where all kinds of metals were melting into each other, and then in a valley with two springs, one of boiling water, the other of cold. Here he saw his father who was condemned to be plunged first into one stream, then into the other, on alternate days. At last, however, King Louis reached Heaven where he was greeted by a dazzling light which surrounded the Blessed who were sitting on an enormous topaz of extraordinary beauty.

As late as the nineteenth century, people were still speaking of the afterlife in remarkably physical terms. An old army man, for example, told Lady Gregory:

I have seen Hell myself. I had a sight of it one time in a vision. It had a very high wall around it, all of metal, and an archway in the wall, and a straight walk into it, just like what would be leading into a gentleman's orchard, but the edges were not trimmed with box but with red-hot metal. And inside the wall there were cross walks, and I'm not sure what there was to the right, but to the left there was five great furnaces and they full of souls kept there with great chains. So I turned short and went away; and in turning I looked again at the wall and I could see no end to it. And another time I saw Purgatory. It seemed to be in a level place and no walls around it, but it all one bright blaze, and the souls standing in it. And they suffer near as much as in Hell, only there are no devils with them there, and they have the hope of Heaven. And I heard a call to me from there, 'Help me to come out of this!' And when I looked it was a man I used to know in the army, an Irishman and from this country, and I believe him to be a descendant of King O'Connor of Athenry. So I stretched out my hand first but then I called out, 'I'd be burned in the flames before I could get within three yards of you'. So then he said, 'Well, help me with your prayers', and so I do.

Christianity, therefore, has developed over time a very distinctive geography of the afterlife. There is Heaven for the just, Hell for the irredeemably unjust, Purgatory for those who are not irredeemable but require to be punished for, and thus cleansed of, their sins before warranting admission to the Beatific Vision of God, and Limbo to accommodate

those just people who died before knowing Christ, a category which includes virtuous pagans as well as infants who
have died before receiving baptism.[5]

Of these states, Purgatory was to be the most significant in relation to ghosts, and it is therefore useful to ask
where people believed Purgatory was located. One popular
assumption said that it was not far from Eden, that it lay
in the east, and that it was cut off from everywhere else by
inaccessible seas or mountains or desert regions. Another
maintained that it could be found on an extraordinarily
high mountain, so high that its summit touched the sphere
of the moon, a notion which clearly had an effect on Dante's
conception which described Purgatory as a high mountain
with seven concentric circles gouged from its sides, in which
the seven capital sins are purged. On its summit lay Eden
and at its base, two further circles wherein were received
the souls of those who had made a late repentance of their
sins, and those who were excommunicate. Purgatory, then,
was conceived as a very particular geographical location, if
not on earth itself, at least within the bounds of the created
universe. For those who believed the former, it was possible
to see for themselves the entrance to Purgatory by going to
Lough Derg in Ireland, where a cave enclosed by the walls
of the abbey there drew pilgrims from all over Europe until
it was destroyed by Protestants in October 1632.[6] So since
Purgatory was often thought of in physical terms as a place
with a real existence which could not only be imagined but
also approached by those yet living, it is hardly surprising
that people also accepted that the dead could venture forth
from their realm into this, since the two were contiguous.

Indeed, the souls in Purgatory had every incentive to
return to the living and demand or implore assistance, or even
perform penance for sins they had committed while still alive,
for the length of their existence in that place was not eternal

and time spent there could be varied not only by their own continuing conduct but by that of the living, too. Caesarius of Heisterbach, for example, tells the following story:

> Three years or so ago, at about the time of Advent, a little girl aged nine years died in Mount St Saviour, a house belonging to our order [*Cistercian*]. Not long afterwards, the sisters had assembled in the choir when she entered in clear daylight and, bowing low before the altar, went to the place where she used to stand while she was alive. Another girl of almost the same age saw the dead girl take her place beside her, and was struck with such fear that the lady abbess (who told me this story) noticed it. The abbess asked the girl why she was so frightened, and she replied, 'I have just seen Sister Gertrude come into the choir and at Vespers, when they mentioned Our Lady, she prostrated herself''. The abbess was afraid the girl was being deceived by the Devil and said to her, 'If Sister Gertrude comes back, say "Benedicite" to her, and if she answers "Dominus", ask her where is it she comes from and what is it she is looking for'. Next day [the ghost] came again. She was greeted, gave the answer 'Dominus', and asked why she had come. 'I have come here', she answered, 'to do penance. I used to whisper with you in choir, and I have been ordered to make atonement for this in the same place where I used to sin in this way. Unless you take care, you will suffer the same punishment when you die'. After she had done penance like this on four separate occasions, she said, 'Now my atonement is complete. Henceforth you will see me no more'. The next thing that happened was that, as her living friend watched, she made her way towards the cemetery and passed through the wall by supernatural power (*Dialogus miraculorum* Book 12, chapter 36).

If we compare this with the stories told by Otloh and Boccaccio, we can see several common themes. There is a Power which can give instruction to the dead and shape their existence in the otherworld; sin is punished, but punishment comes to an end and the dead may be released from the torment or burden which has been imposed on them; the living may be threatened unless they pay heed to or co-operate with the dead; the very existence of the otherworld is confirmed by the account of it given by eye-witnesses; and the existence of that otherworld reinforces a sense of community – the dead and the living are not entirely separate and the actions of each can affect the lives of the other.[7]

Medieval ghost stories, however, are not uniform accounts and Schmitt has divided them into three different categories: (a) *exempla*, which are told for a number of moral and doctrinal purposes; (b) *mirabilia*, which combine elements of lay culture with clerical in their composition, and (c) *miracula*, which are intended principally to enhance the reputation of specific ecclesiastical establishments, with (b) emerging particularly during the twelfth century and (c) during the thirteenth. Pope Gregory I (*c.*540–604) had been responsible in part for giving encouragement to *exempla* and *miracula* since, in the last book of his *Dialogues* in particular, he chose to ignore St Augustine's well-known dismissal of the belief that ghosts were in any sense real and, in an effort to undermine remnant pagan notions of the afterlife, provided his readers with uplifting Christian stories about dead people who returned to tell the living about the otherworld and warn them to reform their present mode of behaviour.[8]

Ghost stories, therefore, are capable of development and diversity. After AD 1000, for example, autobiographical stories of ghosts began to appear, that is, stories which recounted the immediate and personal experiences of the narrator, and even the Church's liturgy was susceptible to change. For at the end of the eleventh century and the beginning of the twelfth there emerged a new ritual, commemorating the dead on a Monday morning. It consisted of a Requiem Mass followed by a procession to the cemetery, the blessing of the tombs, and a sounding of the church bells. Ringing the bells was intended to frighten away ghosts and evil spirits, a belief about which the Protestant Godfredus Spinaeus waxed sarcastic in an essay deprecating the practice. There is also evidence that during the twelfth and thirteenth centuries some people began to regard the dead as particularly alien and dangerous, and in consequence more changes were made to the liturgy, barring the presence of any actual body of a deceased from any Masses said for the living. But the Middle Ages themselves did not form a unitary, unchanging period. From the Christian centres of Europe missionaries were constantly streaming out to convert or reconvert whole communities, according to whether those communities were pagan or, having once been orthodoxly Christian, had lapsed into heresy; while between the early seventh century and the middle of the eighth the new religion of Islam spread westwards as far as France and eastwards as far as modern Pakistan, with the result that Pope Honorius I (625–38) and the twenty-one Popes who followed were faced by the spectacle of this new religion seeming to sweep all before it, with whole areas such as North Africa, Syria, and Spain lost to Rome either permanently or for a considerable time. Representatives of the Church were thus constantly coming across and having to assimilate large numbers of unorthodox ideas about almost every aspect of life, but perhaps especially the non-Christian religious or spiritual beliefs of the communities to which they had come or been sent; and naturally, these included attitudes to the dead.[9]

Among the Scandinavian peoples, for example, we find a pre-Christian belief in the dead as immensely powerful guardians of the family to which they belonged in life, so powerful, indeed, that they might almost be said to rival the sky-god. This has its parallel in the Greek concept of the dead as *daemones*, transmuted by their passing across the river of death into near-divine beings with preternatural, if not supernatural powers. But those dead who had not died worthily became restless ghosts, cast out from the ancestral part of the clan, and condemned to wander in the world in a kind of exile. After Christianity had reached the various Nordic countries, however, we find, in the words of Thomas Dubois, that 'a strong and pervasive interest in ghosts, paralleled throughout Europe, had acquired a particular ethnographic bent, as the customs of non-Christians became the source and sometimes the cure of malevolent returns from the dead'. Thus we are told that stakes should be driven through the breasts of the dead, and then later (perhaps much later), a Christian cleric would come along, uproot the stakes, pour holy water into the cavities, and sing Mass over the corpses. The *Eyrbyggja Saga*, written about the mid-thirteenth century, tells us about Thorgunna, a woman from the Western Isles of Scotland, who had settled down in Iceland and accumulated enough possessions to rouse the envy of the local land-holder. Eventually she became very sick and on her deathbed gave explicit instructions about her funeral, including her desire to be buried in a place some distance away. After she died, it looked as though some of her last wishes were going to be ignored or subverted; but her ghost returned and made sure that everything was done properly. The lesson is clear. To guard against unwanted hauntings, observe all the details of a Christian burial and do not thwart the dead. In Greenland, by contrast, a Christian burial was not considered sufficient to lay a ghost, so the body needed to be burned on a pyre and its ashes scattered to effect the required dismissal of the dead who had been the cause of all the hauntings throughout the winter months. With the advent of the Church's teaching on Purgatory, of course, there was bound to be tension between what the Church required of her adherents by way of belief and practice and the tug of older entrenched pagan norms, and this tension can be seen not only in relation to mortuary and post-mortem customs, but also anent the great range of magical operations common among all ranks, not just in Scandinavian society, but in European society as a whole.[10]

A brush with non-Christian themes can also be seen in the incorporation into Christian ghost tales of the army or procession or hunt of the dead, a motif with a very much older history than the tales in which it often appears. Orderic Vitalis, for example, gives a lengthy account of a French priest called Walchelin who was called out to attend a sick person on 1 January 1091. There was a bright moon to light his return through deserted countryside. Suddenly he heard the noise of soldiery. Fearful for his safety, he tried to hide but a huge figure shouted at him not to move, and then came and stood beside him. There passed by a long, motley procession which included people Walchelin recognised as fellow-villagers who had died not long before. Dwarfs, women, clerics, monks, and well-known local knights followed, all dead, all apparently suffering in some fashion. Dead they may have been, but when Walchelin refused to carry back a message from one of the knights to his living wife and son, the dead man seized him by the throat and Walchelin felt a physical pain and carried the marks for some time thereafter. Finally he had a conversation with another of the knights who identified himself as Walchelin's brother. (We may recall that the brothers of Otloh's story did not recognise their own father, either, until he told them who he was). The knight-brother asked for Walchelin's prayers and alms-giving to help release him from his present condition, and warned the priest to reform his own sinful life; and with this the incident comes to an end. A non-Christian confrontation has been absorbed into a Christian story and made to serve a purely Christian purpose. Yet it is easy to envisage a version of the tale which would remain entirely pagan. A man walks alone in the countryside, sees the ghostly procession, and is warned by his dead father not to neglect the rites proper to the dead, otherwise retribution will follow. A pagan view of the afterlife and what was appropriate to it thus merges so easily with Christian attitudes and belief that one is tempted to say the differences between them are doctrinal rather than essential.[11]

But what of those beliefs and attitudes which were Christian but unorthodox? There might be two types: popular or heretical. By 'popular', I do not mean to imply an absolute distinction between the beliefs and practices of the common people and those of the educated or aristocratic élites. It is well known that this is an artificial dichotomy, since the beliefs and attendant practices of the community as a whole overlapped and shaded into each other, thus forming a complexity which could easily embrace contradictory as well as variant notions and attitudes. As Schmitt warns, 'We must be careful not to reify belief, to turn it into something established once and for all, something which individuals and societies need only express and pass on to each other... A belief is a never-completed activity, one which is precarious, always questioned, and inseparable from recurrences of doubt'.[12] Indeed, 'popular' and 'heretical' should not be taken as representative of a genuine distinction of belief in this instance either; for popular beliefs might well be regarded as heretical according to strict interpretation of Church doctrine, and heretical beliefs might owe more to popular convictions than to deliberate deviance from the Church's teaching. The Waldenses, for example, did not seem certain about their position. On the one hand, a popular Vaudois proverb said, 'In the other world there are only two ways, that is Heaven and Hell, and there is no such thing as Purgatory'. On the other hand, many of them continued to pray for the dead and to leave money for such prayers to be said. The Cathars of Montaillou, however, seem to have expressed convictions which appear to owe little or nothing to regular Christian teaching. Thus Guillaume Fort, a farmer, maintained he did not believe in the resurrection of the body, and yet claimed that the souls of the dead were real enough and existed as flesh and blood, a notion he based on the visions of local people who said they had seen evil spirits leading these physical ghosts across rocks and slopes before hurling them down some cliffs, at the bottom of which they suffered but did not die. Demonic dangers apart, though, the dead were accustomed to meet in churches where oil-lamps were left burning at night to welcome them. Because they had bodies, like ours but more beautiful, they could feel the cold and would therefore enter people's houses and relight fires from the banked-up embers, and drink wine in great quantities. Ghosts rushed about restlessly, went on pilgrimage, and met socially after Mass. Purgatory, however, is mentioned very little in records from Montaillou. The rushing about, the sociability, the visits to churches were done while the ghosts prepared to undergo a kind of second death. This could be hastened by the prayers and Masses of the living, but once the ghosts had reached their place of rest (however it was envisaged), that seemed to put an end to their wandering. Purgatory for Cathar ghosts, therefore, was located within those living communities of which they had once been a part.[13]

Two themes in particular can thus be found, the restlessness and the physicality of the dead, neither of which could quite be approved by official teaching, although the Church was by no means averse from accommodating these views to her own purposes and using them to forward instruction among the people. On the one hand, the Church regarded the dead as occupying one of several places which together formed a hierarchy of locations both within and outwith the created universe. On the other, there was a general notion permeating society that the dead were neighbours to the living in a kind of extended community, part of which, while usually invisible, might manifest itself at command or in accordance with its own wishes. In this view, the dead occupy (in some sense of the word) not only an occult place such as Heaven, Hell, or Purgatory, but also the grave itself and the surface of the earth local to their erstwhile relations and neighbours. Hence, bearing in mind also those notions which placed Purgatory somewhere upon or near Earth, we may not find it difficult to see why the dead should have been frequently conceived as taking physical form. Their immediate universe was both natural and localised, a concept underlined by the usual European practice at this time of burying, not cremating, the dead. Place them in earth: from earth they will return, made of earthly substance.[14]

Experience by the living of such a return tends to fall into two broad categories. The dead are seen, and sometimes heard, as visions or apparitions: or they are seen, and sometimes felt, as physical entities, frequently manifesting in a state of decomposition. We have already come across a number of examples of the former, but let us look in detail at another for the sake of the specific points it illustrates. Here is an anecdote related to Peter the Venerable, ninth abbot of Cluny (1092–1156), and retold by him to his readers:

At the time Alfonso, King of Aragon, inherited the kingdom at the death of Alfonso the elder, King of the Spaniards, it

happened that he moved his army against certain men who
were fighting him in that region called Castile, and that he
issued an edict that individual infantrymen and cavalrymen
from the separate parts of his kingdom be sent to him.
Compelled by this edict, I earmarked for the army one of
my servants, whose name was Sancho. After a few days had
gone by and all those who had taken part in that expedition were coming back home, Sancho also came back, but
then, after a short time (in human terms) had elapsed, he
was overcome by illness. He did not struggle long with it,
and died. Then about four months after he had departed
this life, while I was lying in my house at Estella in winter,
next to the fire, suddenly Sancho appeared to me, about the
middle of the night, while I was still awake. He sat down
by the fire and turned over the coals here and there as if
to produce warmth or light; then he turned round and
began to show himself to me as a much more recognisable
[figure]. He was naked and wore not a stitch of clothing
except for a small cheap piece of cloth with which he
concealed his more shameful parts (so to speak).

When I saw him, I said, 'Who are you?'

He said in a low voice, 'I am Sancho, your servant'.

'What are you doing here?' I asked.

'I am coming to Castile', he said, 'and a large army is
keeping me company on the way so that we may pay
the due penalties for our misdeeds in the place where
we did the wrong'.

'Why have you turned off here?' I asked.

'I have hope of pardon', he said, 'and if you are willing
to show pity, you will be able to obtain for me a quicker
rest [requiem]'.

'How?' I asked.

'When I took part in the recent expedition which you
know about', he replied, 'egged on by the enemy's disor-

derly behaviour, I plunged into a church with a number
of companions and stole things I found inside. I even
carried away the priest's vestments with me For this I
have been subjected to dreadful punishments and am in
torment. So I implore a remedy from you, as my [former]
master with as many prayers as I can. For you will be
able to help me if you make the effort to assist me with
spiritual acts of kindness. Moreover, I ask you to do something for me and beg my lady, your wife, on my behalf
not to delay paying eight shillings which she owed me
as proper payment for my service, and distributing them
to the poor, and so paying for my soul (which requires
these things) what she would have paid for the necessities
of the flesh if I were still alive'.

At this point, much disturbed by what he had told me,
I said, 'What has happened to Pedro da Jaca, our fellow
citizen, who died not long ago? Please say if you know
anything about him.

[Sancho] replied, 'The works of mercy he frequently,
but very generously spent on the poor at the time of the
last famine have assigned him to the repose of the blessed
and made him a participant in eternal life'.

Since I had heard him answer me so quickly and
easily, I added, 'And do you know anything about Berer,
another fellow citizen of ours, who likewise died a short
while ago?'

[Sancho] said, 'He is in the power of Hell because,
when he was feudal lord of this estate, in charge of breaking up and putting an end to disputes by passing judgement
[on them], he often made unjust decisions because he
had been bribed by gifts or a favour, and because on
one particular occasion he was not afraid to impound a
poor widow's pig and so cruelly remove any life-support
[she had]'.

This made me much more eager to ask more important [questions], and so I said, 'Have you been able to find out anything about King Alfonso who has been dead for a few years?'

To this, another individual, who was sitting on the window which was immediately above my head, replied, 'Don't ask him about that, because he doesn't know. His recent arrival in our region hasn't let him know this yet. But I've been lingering with spirits of this kind for five years, since the day of my death, and this means I have more knowledge than he has. What you're asking about the King has not remained unknown [to me]'.

But I was astonished a second time to hear a new voice behind me and, wanting to see where the voice was coming from, I turned my eyes to the window and, helped by the brilliance of the moon whose light was then illuminating the whole house, I caught sight of a man sitting on the window-sill and noticed he was dressed the same way as [Sancho].

I asked, 'Who are you?'

He said, 'I'm a companion of the man you're looking at, and I'm on my way to Castile with him and many others'.

'And did you say you know something about King Alfonso?' I asked.

'I know where he has been', he replied, 'but I don't know where he is now. He was tortured by severe torments for some considerable time among the sinners until he was taken away from them by the monks of Cluny. What happened to him after that, I really don't know'.

After he had said this, he turned to his companion who was sitting near the fire and said, 'Get up! Let's be on our way again. Look! The army which was behind us has filled all the roads within and outwith the town.

Many of them have gone past us at top speed, and we ought to press on and follow them quickly'.

At these words, Sancho got up and, in a tearful voice, repeated what he had asked [me] before.
'Master, I entreat you not to forget me and I beg you to take care to urge my lady, your wife, to make good for my wretched soul what she owed my body'.

With these words, they both suddenly disappeared. I called out and woke my wife who was sleeping next to me in the bed, and before I began to tell her what I had seen and heard, I asked her whether she owed any wages to Sancho, who was servant to both of us. She replied that I could not have heard that from anyone except the dead man, for she still owed Sancho eight shillings. I could have no further doubt at all in the complete trustworthiness of something the dead man's narrative and my wife's corroboration were both telling me. When morning arrived, I took eight shillings from my wife, added an appropriate amount of my own, and distributed them to the poor for the salvation of the man who had appeared [to me]. I also added payment for Masses to be said, at my earnest request, for the more complete remission of his sins.[15]

The dead Sancho appeared to the original narrator in very particular circumstances. It was 'about' midnight. In the absence of clocks, of course, estimation of the time would be approximate (although it was possible to tell the time from the position of the moon and stars when they were visible), but midnight was a significant expression from the Bible, for on the one hand it was at that time God killed the firstborn of the Egyptians and that death was most likely to remove people from life, but it was also a Biblically designated time for prayer – hence the usual monastic hour for the first service of the day: an hour of potential danger at which one should be wakeful. It was also the point at which people's 'first sleep' ended. During the Middle Ages and the early modern period, people's sleep-patterns were different from ours. There were two of them, broken by a period of wakefulness, the first ending at about midnight and the second beginning an hour or two later.[16] There is therefore no need to suppose that Peter the Venerable's narrator was dreaming when he saw his two ghosts. Nor does the account give, as such accounts usually do, any indication that the man was in that curious state of half-sleeping and half-waking, when paranormal incidents are sometimes alleged to happen. Firelight, it may be claimed, creates a strange play between light and shadow, but not, surely, enough to create two male figures whom the narrator treats as though they were as real as himself. In any case, we are told the room was brilliantly clear with moonlight, and so the narrator's immediate question to Sancho – 'Who are you?' – is perhaps not so much evidence of genuine ignorance as of fearful astonishment in the face of a phenomenon which was obviously preternatural.

The ghost appears in physical form, recognisable as an individual once he has turned his face from the fire to look at the narrator, and is able to interact physically with his surroundings, since he can pick up a stick or a poker and turn over coals in the fireplace. We may say of him, therefore, that he is lifelike in appearance; that there is no sense in which he is transparent or fuzzy; that he is seen by two natural lights –from the fire and the moon – not by his own luminosity; that he can make sounds and thus interact in a perfectly natural way with the narrator; and that once the narrator's initial astonishment is over, interaction between him and the ghost is entirely natural, that is to say, without any further manifestation of the ghost's being a non-human entity. Thus far the ghost is typical of those which are narrated or discussed in many medieval sources. Nevertheless, one may notice certain differences between this and the narratives with which we began. The group of knights who appeared to Otloh of St Emmeram's brothers were standing in mid-air; and the ghosts in Boccaccio's story, while able to interact with those who saw them, were actually repetitive, performing exactly the same actions over and over again, as though they were part of a programme running in a loop. The matter-of-factness which characterises Peter the Venerable's anecdote suggests that the importance of the story lies elsewhere, not in the details of the apparition, but in the conversation between him and the narrator.

This purveys information the narrator either says he does not know – such as his wife's still owing Sancho eight shillings in wages – or which he could not discover by other means – such as the post-mortem fates of Pedro da Jaca and Berner; and acquiring information this way, information which subsequently turns out to be accurate, is one sign that the apparition is to be trusted and is therefore not a lying demon. We are also reminded hereby that people who have done wrong in this life will be punished for it in the next until reparation has been made, a common enough theological cliché in the mouths of the living, but an admonition of startling immediacy when spoken by the mouths of the dead. The narrator's wife is actually in debt to Sancho, but in paying his final wages to relieve the poor she not only assists them and relieves the state of his soul, but relieves herself also of a small injustice (however inadvertent it may be), and thus restores balance to her own moral life as well as helping to do the same for Sancho. The point about the value of charitable works is then underlined by the ghost's information about Pedro da Jaca. He is in repose with the blessed – again we have the notion of death as a kind of sleep or rest – and enjoys eternal life because he was generous, and more than generous, to the starving poor while he was still alive. The late Berner, on the other hand, is damned not only because he was a corrupt judge, but also because he was cruel to a poor widow. 'Widow' like 'midnight' carries Biblical resonances. 'You shall not afflict any widow, or fatherless child' (*Exodus* 22.22); 'thou shalt not pervert the judgement of the stranger, nor of the fatherless; nor take a widow's raiment to pledge' (*Deuteronomy* 24.17); 'oppress not the widow, or the fatherless, the stranger, nor the poor' (*Zachariah* 7.10). So the underlying message of the anecdote so far is conventional enough: the fate of the dead depends largely on their former relationship with the poor.

We may also note the separate fates of the three dead men Sancho, Pedro, and Berner. Berner is in Hell, Pedro in Heaven, and Sancho in some kind of curious state which is neither. He and his army companions seem to be back on earth, returning to the region in which their final sins were committed to make reparation there. It is a curious requirement. Is Purgatory this hinterland between the spiritual and material worlds? If so, it is quite different from the geographical concepts we have noted before. The three men's estate is reminiscent, *mutatis mutandis*, of a medieval Jewish belief that every Sabbath the wicked, who spend the rest of the week expiating their sins in torment in Gehinnom, are released to pass the day roaming the earth, free from pain.[17] Peter the Venerable's military horde, however, is not wandering so much as going on pilgrimage as an act of penance, in very similar fashion to the way its several members could have behaved in life. Returning to the scene of their crime is interesting. A frequently recorded aspect of many ghosts is their appearance and reappearance in certain places: Boccaccio's ghosts are two such examples, and Caesarius's convent girl another. Is Sancho's explanation that he and his companions are returning to Castile to do penance a rationalisation of this looping behaviour, or is there again a Biblical echo, 'Then shall the slayer return, and come unto his own city, and unto his own house, unto the city whence he fled' (*Joshua* 20.6)?

Ghosts are usually dressed – a slightly peculiar point in itself. As Hilary Evans observes, 'If they are truly spirits from another world, there should in principle be no reason for them to wear clothes at all. Whereas clothing is important to us living persons, whether to help us cope with the climate or to conform to social requirements, this would not seem to apply to those who have moved to another world... Yet naked ghosts... are extremely rare. Ghosts are apparently as mindful of Earthly propriety as are the living'. To explain this, Evans quotes from a 1950s book, *The Boy Who Saw True* by Cyril Scott, in which a boy with second sight records:

> I thought I'd ask Grandpa [that is, his grandfather's ghost, who frequently visits him] why he wasn't naked, or why all spirits aren't naked. He said, 'Do you think of yourself as going about naked?' So I said, 'No, I didn't.' Then he said, 'Well, neither do we. We look as we think of ourselves. That is why people over here wear such a lot of different sorts of clothes, and why even I wear clothes that aren't the fashion any more with you in your world.'[18]

We also have the observation of a woman who saw her dead husband one day:

> One forenoon about eighteen months after my husband had died after a prolonged fight against emphysema, I left the CAB office where I did voluntary work twice a week. It had been quite a busy session and I was glad to get into the spring sunshine. I decided to cross the Abbey churchyard and so avoid the town centre with

its narrow crowded streets. I had just passed the Abbey when directly opposite at the further end of the path I saw my husband approaching smoothly and rapidly. But he was visible only from the armpits down, as if I could see only what he could see of himself as he looked down. Although he was some little distance from me, I could see each detail clearly as if he were but a yard away. Whilst he appeared to walk, I had the impression that his feet did not actually touch the ground. He was dressed in a double-breasted suit long out of fashion, and was wearing equally unfashionable shoes in the style of about forty years ago. He seemed supremely happy, and I felt he was reliving a period of his life when he had been very happy'.[19]

The two ghosts of Peter the Venerable's anecdote, however, are naked except for a small scrap of cloth concealing their private parts. Since both are part of the dead soldiery on its way back to Castile, we have to ask ourselves what is the significance of this nakedness, because the immediate expectation might be that they would be clothed either as they were in life or as they were in death – that is to say, wrapped in a shroud. – for this is how medieval ghosts commonly appeared. Are we meant once more to hear a subliminal voice from the Bible, 'Naked came I out of my mother's womb, and naked shall I return thither' (*Job* 1.21)?

The narrator's interchange with Sancho's ghost thus has many of the elements of an encounter which has some, but not all, the marks of what Schmitt called an *exemplum*, a story with moral and doctrinal purposes. But it also seems to be shot through with memories of Biblical texts – not surprising, since Peter the Venerable's source was a man who later became a hermit, and the version we are reading is that of a Cluniac abbot. But then comes the second ghost, and

with him we find one or two curious details which are not
those of the 'standard' exemplum.

He resembles Sancho in as much as he appears suddenly, is
both visible and audible, is naked except for a modesty-cloth,
and interacts with the narrator in a quite natural fashion.
What stimulates his appearance, however, is the narrator's
question about the late King Alfonso, essentially a supererog-
atory question stemming from idle curiosity. The previous
questions involved people the narrator knew or to whom
he had some kind of connection. They were *concives*, fellow
citizens. King Alfonso is quite another matter, and with this
somewhat improper query the story takes on an interestingly
unusual turn. The narrator addresses Sancho, but it is the
second ghost who answers, first as a kind of disembodied
voice from behind and above the narrator who has then
to turn round to see who is speaking. Now, the sequence
of the narrative's appearances – Sancho seen and addressed:
second ghost heard and then seen – may be no more than
an extended chiasmus, a rhetorical device in which the order
of words (or in this case, actions), in one part of the story
is inverted in the other. But the curiosity of having the
second ghost make his entrance as a voice behind the narrator reminds one of *Apocalypse* 1.10 and 12, 'I was in the spirit
on the Lord's day, and heard behind me a great voice... And
I turned to see the voice that spake with me'.

The ghost's answer to the narrator's question contains certain unexpected pieces of information. The place or state
of the dead is called a 'region', but the Latin *partes* is actually plural, implying that the region is made up of several
parts or distinct areas. Sancho does not know the answer to
the narrator's question because he has not been dead long
enough to learn it, whereas the second ghost has. The dead,
therefore, acquire knowledge from each other and elsewhere
after death. Even so, the second ghost's knowledge is incom-

plete because although he knew King Alfonso was rescued
from Purgatory by the prayers of the monks of Cluny – a
detail which turns this part of the narrative into a *miraculum*,
a story intended to enhance the reputation of a particular
religious establishment – the King's present whereabouts are
unknown to him. Surely if the King had been released from
his torments by the prayers of the living, he would now be
in Heaven since this is the natural destination of sinners who
have completed their purgation? But the ghost does not
know, and thus it seems that there are further things to be
learned, even by those who have been dead for five years.

So Peter the Venerable's second-hand account of two
revenants is not an easy story for us to read and judge. If
we try to 'explain' it, the interest dissolves before our eyes.
Does the detail about the unpaid wages, for example, indicate cryptomnesia on the narrator's part and indicate that he
although he actually did know at some point in the past the
wages had not been paid, his conscious mind has forgotten
it, and now makes the information appear in a strange and
somewhat disturbing form? If so, one must say that it would
be very odd for so trivial a matter to surface in such a way,
especially since it was not the narrator's fault his servant
went off to war without his last pay packet. The person
who should be having the Sancho-experience should surely
have been the wife. Or is the incident an example of the
working of some kind of super psi? This is an hypothesis
which suggests that the full capacities of the human mind
are not known to us, and that the unconscious, using little
understood powers of telepathy, clairvoyance, and so forth,
is able to scan the universe, winnowing all the knowledge
of past and present, which is still lingering there in some
form or another, and using what it considers relevant to any
given situation to create pseudo-spirit entities which are real
enough in every detail to convince the person who sees or

hears them that they are genuine, independent personalities. As a notion, this may have its attractions, but Hilary Evans sounds a needful note of caution:

> The concept of super-psi has been welcomed by those who, whether or not they have a personal belief in survival, are unconvinced by the evidence [for it]. It is not really a theory, because it has no specific tenets: it is simply a recognition that, since there are no known limits to the capabilities of the mind, we cannot exclude the possibility that the creativity of the subconscious is capable both of creating apparitions and of investing them with information content of which no living person is aware. The weakness of the super-psi concept is that it explains nothing: it simply states the possibility that an explanation for certain phenomena may be found without requiring us to take on board the notion of survival. By contrast, the various survival hypotheses explain the matter much more simply and straightforwardly.[20]

A third explanation for what the story says happened to the narrator is that he actually did see and hear two ghosts. The *form* taken by the narrative, however, is a matter different from its content. Ostensibly, the two visitors were revenants, that is, human beings who were once alive but have now returned to the living, although 'return', of course, begs the question of whether they left in the first place. The amalgamation of *exemplum* and *miraculum* is meant to appeal to a medieval attention, not to a modern one, and if reconsidered in this light, makes a number of notable impacts on the reader or listener. It engages its audience by its unexpectedness, reinforces their notions of a tripartite afterlife, reminds them that what we do in this life resonates in the next, evokes their fellow-feeling for the poor, comforts them with the assertion that the prayers and good works of the living can and do benefit the dead, and intrigues them by letting slip details they did not know about the otherworld, or which they were unlikely to have suspected, or which represent popular as opposed to learned or clerical opinion on the subject. Most powerfully, it shows them that the living and the dead are separate parts of a single community (as, for example, Scots and French are different nations but members of one Europe), and that the usual divide between them may be bridged without warning and the two interact without fear or hostility.[21]

Unexpected visitations happen in a variety of ways, of course, and there are some people credited with what Scottish Gaelic calls 'two sights' – an ability to see the living as though they were on their way to being dead, appearing as it were in a transitional state between two worlds. The phenomenon was described by a late seventeenth-century traveller in the Western Isles, Martin Martin:

The seer knows neither the object, time, nor place of a vision, before it appears; and the same object is often seen by different persons, living at a considerable distance from one another. The true way of judging as to the time and circumstance of an object, is by observation; for several persons of judgement, without this faculty, are more capable to judge of the design of a vision, than a novice that is a seer. If an object appears in the day or night, it will come to pass sooner or later accordingly. If an object is seen early in the morning (which is not frequent) it will be accomplished in a few hours afterwards. If at noon, it will commonly be accomplished that very day. If in the evening perhaps that night; if after candles be lighted, it will be accomplished that night; the latter always in accomplishment by weeks, months, and sometimes years, according to the time of night the vision is seen. When a shroud is perceived about one, it is a sure prognostic of death. The time is judged according to the height of it about the person; for if it is not seen above the middle, death is not to be expected for the space of a year, and perhaps some months longer; and as it is frequently seen to ascend higher towards the head, death is concluded to be at hand within a few days, if not hours, as daily experience confirms. Examples of this kind were shown me, when the persons of whom the observations then made enjoyed perfect health.[22]

This ability to see the living-as-dead, however, is by no means a modern phenomenon. It is recorded of the native inhabitants of the Isle of Man in the mid-fourteenth century that, 'Frequently the natives of that place see people who have died, even during the day, and they are with or without their heads according to the manner of their death. In order to see this, those born elsewhere, or visitors, place their feet on top of the islanders' feet, and thus they will be able to see what the islanders see'. Nor is the ability confined to Celtic countries, for in the Netherlands, Denmark, and the Balkans, male children born with a caul can see ghosts and foretell deaths in their community; and in his survey of Man nearly 350 years later, William Sacheverell noted that

an ancient man, who has been long clerk of a parish, has affirmed to me that he almost constantly sees [death lights] upon the death of any of his own parish; and one Captain Leathes, who was chief magistrate of Belfast, and reputed a man of great integrity, assured me he was once shipwrecked on the island, and lost great part of his crew; and that when he came on shore people told him he had lost thirteen of his men, for they saw so many lights going toward the church, which was just the number lost.[23]

But if second sight represents the ability of certain living individuals to act as involuntary channels of communication anent what is happening in the realm of the dead, or about to happen in that of the living, the practice of necromancy represents a deliberate attempt on the part of the living to manipulate the dead for their own purposes. The English word has shifted its meaning somewhat. Nowadays it can be used simply to refer to ritual magic; but it was in its proper sense of raising and consulting the dead by magical means that it was well-known (although forbidden) in both Biblical and Talmudic times. According to Jewish belief, the dead could be raised (in spirit) only during the first twelve months after death, and even then not on a Sabbath. Various methods could be employed: (1) using a magical incantation; (2) spending the night on the grave, ritually clothed, and burning sweet-smelling substances until one heard a very faint voice coming out of the grave; (3) a man and a woman placing themselves at the head and foot of the grave, striking a rattle, and reciting an invocation; and (4) invoking the dead by the use of angelic names. A late Talmudic source, *Sefer Ha-Razim*, gives a procedure for this fourth method. The operator had to stand facing a tomb, holding a small glass bowl containing oil and honey mixed, and pray to Hermes, guardian of the boundary between the living and the dead. The prayer directs the deity to raise up a particular ghost – the operator is to name the dead person he wishes to consult – so that it may be questioned without fear. When the ghost arrives, it is to be offered the oil and honey and then, after the operator has finished and wants to dismiss the ghost, the instructions are to strike the spirit three times with a branch of myrtle which the operator has been holding. Myrtle is significant. It was especially associated with Aphrodite and, in connection with the Eleusinian Mysteries at any rate, symbolised life and sexuality. Carried by the necromancer, it would therefore act as a wand of power, temporarily transmitting a vivifying energy to the dead person and thereby enabling him or her to interact with the living.[24]

In vivid contrast to these procedures, however, stands the tradition of revivifying the dead with blood. The clearest example comes from Greek fiction. In the eleventh book of Homer's *Odyssey*, the eponymous hero is under instruction to consult the dead seer Tiresias and so digs a pit into which he pours honey mixed with milk, and wine and water. He sprinkles white barley over them and then cuts the throats of a ram and a black ewe, allowing their blood to cascade into the pit:

> Then the spirits of those who had died began to gather out of Erebos: brides and unwed youths, and old men who had borne much misery, and tender young girls with a heart still new to sorrow, and many who had been wounded with bronze-tipped spears, men killed in war, still wearing their armour stained with gore. Large numbers of them began to roam to and fro, back and forth around the pit on every side, uttering a dreadful wailing shriek. Pale fear seized hold of me (*Odyssey* 11.36-43).

Among the many ghosts Odysseus recognises and with whom he converses is one of his dead companions, Elpenor. The two know each other immediately and are able to converse, which means not only that Elpenor could be seen and heard, but also that he was able to interact with his living friend. But when Odysseus sees the ghost of his mother, something prevents a similar interaction. It is not until Odysseus allows her to drink some of the blood from the pit that she suddenly recognises him and begins to speak to him. Yet he and Elpenor had been able to talk without

Elpenor's drinking any blood. These ghosts are described as *psykhai*, a word essentially meaning 'breath', an indication of the presence of life, and it is clear that the blood in this particular ritual has been used as if it were an elixir to restore semblance of life to the spirits. There is, however, an important difference between Elpenor and Odysseus's mother. Elpenor had not yet been given his due funeral rites. He therefore still had his body (which had not been burned in accordance with Greek custom), and so the blood which would restore a temporary substance to the dead individual was not really necessary in his case. Elpenor, as a spirit still tied to his unhonoured corpse, was lingering upon the threshold of the otherworld and able to function in some manner akin to the way he had functioned in life. Odysseus's mother, on the other hand, had received every due rite and therefore depended on the blood for any revivification of her living powers. Not until Odysseus permits her to drink is she able to see him and recognise him and converse with him. Even so, she is still an insubstantial spirit, for when Odysseus tries to embrace her, she flutters from his arms 'like a shadow or a dream'.[25]

Roman necromancy followed more or less the same pattern, and we have already noted the second most famous episode in Classical literature, that involving the female magician Erictho in Lucan's *Pharsalia*. Just as in Odysseus's rite, it is the blood which brings a dead person back to extremely limited life. The difference is that Odysseus was speaking to insubstantial spirits; Erictho has revivified a corpse. Both examples are literary, but there can be no doubt that such rituals were carried out in real life. Lucan's gruesome narrative is, in fact, based on an historical event, and Cicero, fifty years earlier, recorded that high-ranking Romans were happy enough to dabble in the practice. So prevalent did it remain, indeed, that two fourth-century AD Emperors,

Constantius II and Valentinian I, felt obliged to issue edicts prescribing the death penalty for those who continued to go out at night and make necromantic sacrifices, prohibitions which had limited effect, because people within the Empire were still practising necromancy nearly a hundred and fifty years later.[26] In Christian Europe, the dead continued to be resurrected – by prayer, not blood, and for curative not predictive purposes – by virtue of the power transmitted from the Apostles in accordance with *Matthew* 10.8: 'Heal the sick, cleanse the lepers, raise the dead, cast out devils'. St Front de Périgueux and Martial de Limoges, for example, are each credited with resurrecting a dead person with the help of 'St Peter's staff', a clear variation on the stem of myrtle carried by pagan necromancers. But the prevalence of necromancers continued to worry the Church and drew forth many a discussion on the witch of Endor, seeking to show that the dead Samuel was merely an illusion created by the Devil, or some kind of clever trick. Fraud, certainly, was by no means unknown during the Middle Ages, and Johannes Nider tells us he heard about a man in the city of Bern who persuaded people that, for a price, he could converse with spirits of the dead. By the fifteenth century, however, 'necromancy' – or 'nigromancy' as it was sometimes spelt from the early twelfth century, probably because a dozing copyist misheard 'necromancy' – had begun to extend its meaning from raising the dead to working ritual magic in concert with demons. So references to necromancy in later medieval and early modern texts need to be examined carefully in case one misunderstands them.[27]

A double tradition was thus inherited by the Middle Ages from the antique world. Ghosts might be insubstantial spirits or the revived bodies of the dead, although sometimes the two seem to overlap, as in the case of the ghost which appeared to Gawain and Guinevere. The day became as dark as midnight

– that significant time again – when suddenly from a nearby
loch appeared a flame in the shape of Lucifer:

> Bare was the body and black to the bone,
> All be-clagged in clay, uncomely clad.
> It cursed, it wailed like a woman,
> But neither on hide nor in complexion did it have any
> clothing.
> It stammered, it was stupefied, it stood as a stone;
> It was bewildered, it muttered, it grumbled like a
> madman.
> All glowing as an ember the ghost there glides,
> Surrounded in a cloud of dark clothing;
> Circled with serpents that sat to the sides –
> To tell the toads thereon would be very tedious for my
> tongue.[28]

Apparition or resurrected body? It is difficult to tell. The
ambiguity was part of the late medieval conception of the
dead, a conception which seems to have been influenced
by the immense catastrophe of the Black Death in the mid-
fourteenth century. After so many deaths, so many villages
wiped out, so many piles of cadavers to be disposed of, the
physical aspect of the dead began to receive more and more
attention, in art as well as in literature; and to this histori-
cally specific conception we must add the long-standing
belief that the dead would eventually be resurrected, body
and soul. It was a belief inherited from Judaism, for confidence in one's own and others' resurrection was regarded in
some quarters at least as indispensable to being considered
a member of the Israelite community, although the Talmud
records divided opinion about whether those living outwith
the land of Israel will be resurrected or not. *Kethuboth* 111a,
for example, has Rabbi Eleazar saying they definitely will

not, whereas Rabbi Abba ben Memel was equally sure they would be. When it came to Christian burials, the corpse was regularly placed with its feet to the east in anticipation of resurrection, when he or she would rise bodily to meet Jesus who would be appearing in the east. Such a resurrection is important, for it vindicates the lives of the righteous and literally embodies the individual's transformation from transient to immortal life; and, as Odo of Ourschamp makes clear, every part of the body will be involved:

> The question arises if everything which belongs to the sum of the human body such as nail-cuttings, shorn hair, milk teeth, circumcised foreskins, and so forth are to be reunited with it. The Gospel says, 'All your hairs are numbered' (*Matthew* 10.30); and the commentary says, 'They are like money which is counted so that it may be saved'. From this it seems that all these things are saved so that, at the resurrection, they may be restored to the body.

It is not surprising, therefore, that the Middle Ages, and the thirteenth century in particular, saw a growing and persistent debate about the exact relationship between the soul and the body, especially in the afterlife, and began to see death as the absolutely defining moment in a person's existence, fixing the immediate fate of both soul and body in that instant, so that Purgatory and the time spent in it, suffering in ways which are always described in vivid physical terms, are determined almost by the quality and nature of one's final breath, although mitigated or exacerbated by the life which preceded it. Belief in ultimate physical resurrection, then, must surely have had an effect on the belief that if the dead rose and appeared before their appointed time, they would be likely to do so in physical form and thus be tangible as well as visible and audible.[29]

The dead could be resurrected by saints – and medieval literature is full of such examples – but also by Satan, as Thomas of Cantimpré tells us in an anecdote about a virgin from Nivelles, who was confronted in church one evening by a corpse the Devil had revivified. Terrified but brave, the young woman seized a staff with a cross on top of it and whacked the dead man hard on his head, thus felling him to the ground, after which she was troubled no more. Violence, then, worked when other, less vigorous remedies did not, as can be gathered from an incident of about 1150 when a Welsh corpse was disinterred and sprinkled with holy water to stop it from moving and frightening people. The holy water, alas, had no effect, and the locals were obliged to chase it back to its grave and there remove its head, an action which produced the effect they wanted.[30] One of the common forms for such entities to take was that of a *vrykolax;* a zombie or vampire. The roots of these traditions, as one might expect, go back to ancient times. Assyrian religious texts speak of seven malevolent spirits who have a particular liking for human blood; in a play of the fifth-century BC Greek tragedian Aeschylus, *Choephoroi,* the chorus consists of vengeful spirits who embody the curses of a murdered victim and seek in return the blood of the man who had killed him; an Ethiopic charm prays that God will drive away 'all demons and evil spirits who eat flesh and drink blood, who crush the bones and seduce the children of men'; and in Jewish folklore, the *estrie* was both evil spirit and human female who sustained herself on a diet of human blood. The vrykolax – principally a figure from Orthodox Christian traditions – is both vampire and resuscitated body: not the pale, recognisable corpse of one's dead relative or neighbour, but a bloated caricature of itself (one Greek word describing it is *tympanaios,* 'drum-like'), with dark skin, a blood-red face, and staring eyes. Its limbs are supple, its hair, beard, and nails have grown, and it stinks appallingly. A sixteenth-century author, Leone Allacci, was eye-witness to the discovery of a vrykolax in Chios during the opening of a tomb.

> On top of the bones of other men there was found lying a corpse perfectly whole; it was unusually tall of stature; clothes it had none, time or moisture having caused them to perish; the skin was distended hard, and livid, and so swollen everywhere that the body had no flat surfaces but was round like a full sack. The face was covered with hair dark and curly; on the head there was little hair, as also on the rest of the body, which appeared smooth all over; the arms by reason of the swelling of the corpse were stretched out on each side like the arms of a cross; the hands were open, the eyelids closed, the mouth gaping, and the teeth white.[31]

But how were such creatures made, or how did they come into being? Folklore gives a variety of explanations. In parts of Eastern Europe and the Balkans, it was said that a child born with teeth would die and become a vampire, returning to kill its relatives so that it might have company in the land of the dead; in Greece, a still-born infant had to be disposed of properly or it would come back as a vampire; in northern Germany, children who turned again to the teat after being weaned were more likely to turn into vampires; and in Chios, it was sufficient for a cat to jump over a corpse to cause the latter to change its nature into that of a vrykolax. The body of someone who died excommunicate could not decay, either, but remained whole and became swollen and black. Vrykolakes and vampires were almost entirely hostile to human beings. Not only did they kill them, they caused epidemics and storms, and destroyed crops and livestock, too. Even if they were not quite so murderous, they spread terror among the communities they visited. William of Newburgh records two such: a dead man from the county of Buckingham, who came back to sleep with his living widow, nearly crushed her to death with the immense weight of his body; and another from the town of Berwick ranged over the surrounding countryside pursued by phantom dogs barking and howling at him. The only way to deal with such creatures was to kill them again – hence the stake through the heart, or decapitating, or removal and burning of the heart, or chopping up the body and burning it on a pyre.[32]

The legacy of ghosts passed on by the Middle Ages was thus one in which the dead came back to the living either as apparitions or as apparently substantial beings in order to ask their help to right a wrong, or to warn the living to reform their lives. They also brought information about the afterlife, especially about Purgatory, from which many of these dead had been released temporarily in order to communicate with the living, although the impression of Purgatory we gain from their various accounts is both complex and confusing. It seems to be at once a geographical area and a state of being, the latter not always a condition of purgative fire, but certainly one of pain, often amounting to torment. Increasing emphasis on the body's physical decomposition and corruption allied itself to a long-standing tradition of reanimated bodies, resurrected either by their own malevolent condition, or by the power of Satan, or through human agency by means of necromantic rituals. No wonder, then, if the dead were treated with the utmost care, even being buried with the consecrated Host (although this was forbidden by a series of Church Councils), to protect them against evil spirits who might seek to resurrect them before their time. Perhaps no European practice, however, was as strange as that of the Incas of Peru, where the mummified bodies of their kings were not only fed, but had their clothes laundered, and lifted whenever their attendants had the feeling they wanted to pee.[33]

III

EARLY MODERN GHOSTS:
PERSISTENT APPEARANCES, STAGE
PHANTOMS, AND POLTERGEISTS

St Dunstan heard the souls of the dead singing in Canterbury Cathedral. For him and for his contemporaries there was no surprise in such a phenomenon. The living and the dead existed cheek by jowl, and the living were happy to use their local churchyard where their dead rested (but not always in peace), for such diverse purposes as shopping – because cemeteries carried the right of sanctuary, they were also exempt from taxation and thus popular with trades-people – dancing, strolling, playing games, and public entertainment such as juggling or playing music. Bonfires were lit and church bells rung on All Souls' Day (2 November) at the beginning of winter to comfort the dead and welcome their return; and 'years-minds', anniversaries on which the funeral rites were repeated, provided a spur to the living to renew or to double their prayers for the souls in Purgatory. Necromancy was practised even in the most exalted circles. Abbot Trithemius, for example, was asked by the Holy Roman Emperor, Maximilian I, to conjure a vision of his dead wife, Mary of Burgundy, and succeeded in doing so, for the Emperor recognised her by a mole on the nape of her neck. So our survey of ghosts and the afterlife thus far gives the impression that for most people the images of the dead and the otherworld had not altered a great deal since Classical times. The one big change had been the emergence of Christianity, with an official body of doctrine which sat not so much uneasily as slightly askew almost everyone's deep-seated convictions, including those of priests and monks and nuns. After all, as we have seen, ghost stories could be and were commonly told in order to convey certain desirable messages: the importance of the Church's sacraments, the hope of forgiveness for sins even after death, and the real assistance the living could afford the dead through alms-giving, Masses, prayers, and indulgences.[1]

But all this depended to a greater or lesser extent on the doctrine of Purgatory, and with the advent of the various reformation movements during the sixteenth century Purgatory came under sustained attack, with reformers issuing either denials or at least serious doubts that it even existed. Luther, for example, was not sure at first. In 1522 he took a wary stance –'Dear God, if this soul is in a state so that it can still be helped, I pray that you would be merciful to it' – but by 1528 he found himself able to write, 'Nor have we anything in Scripture concerning Purgatory. It too was certainly fabricated by goblins', although he continued to admit that God was perfectly capable of passing souls through some kind of purgative process after death. But if the dead went straight to Heaven or Hell upon their demise, what was to be said about their state in between death and the Last Judgement? Reformers were not sure. A kind of long sleeping, or a period of waiting in 'Abraham's bosom' were two not very happy suggestions, along with one which Hobbes called 'mortalism', the idea that the soul sleeps between the individual's death and the Last Judgement, during which time it is aware of nothing. The new theology therefore can be seen as promoting a rift in the community of the living and the dead by maintaining that, as the fate of the dead is fixed and there is nothing anyone can do to alter it, they and their bodies should be moved to lie beyond the social boundaries within which interaction and thus change are possible. This can be seen with particular clarity in the case of the Scottish Kirk which deliberately sought a physical distance between the living and the dead by objecting to burial within the church itself since, in the egregiously vivid phrase of one burial inscription, it was considered unseemly to defile Christ's kirk with carrion.[2]

The problem tended to be resolved by the logical suggestion that if the dead either did not or could not move from their post-mortem state, then ghosts in the sense of spirits or souls of the dead could not exist. Consequently, if anyone experienced what seemed to be a ghostly visitation, the apparition must be either an angel or an evil spirit taking on the guise of a dead person. Luther, for example, explained that Satan would conjure a ghost in order to deceive people and that he had, indeed, been doing so throughout the Catholic world. So when a blacksmith's young apprentice came to him with a story about a ghost which had pursued him round the streets at night, asked him questions to determine whether he was a Catholic or a Protestant, and then threatened to break his neck if he returned to the blacksmith's house, Luther advised him not to believe everything he was told and cautioned him against telling lies. The Protestant Ludwig Lavater, too, argued that Samuel's appearance to Saul at the behest of the witch of Endor was a demon in Saul's shape – an explanation which, as I have mentioned before, had much earlier precedents and, as West observes, 'Among believers in the manifestation of spirits the foremost question about an apparition in the likeness of a dead man was not as to its substantivity but as to its further nature. Was the phantasm representative of a separated soul or of a demon? If of a demon, good or evil? If of a soul, was it from the Christian havens of the dead, or was it an earth-bound vestigial personality after the pagan doctrine?' The whole subject of ghosts therefore became a bone of contention between the various reformists and Catholic writers who, naturally, defended the Church's teaching on Purgatory.[3]

These confessional splits within Christendom reveal very clearly the accuracy of John Newton's observation that 'differing readings of ghosts in the sixteenth and seventeenth centuries represented a clash of different theologies, or interpretative orders, the ghost being read from within the perspective of the tradition to which the interpreter belonged'. The meaning of one's experience is thus not derived entirely from one's personal reaction to a visitation, but is filtered through the circumambient religious (or non-religious), social, and cultural networks which inform the individual's understanding both of the present world and of the world to come. Without the belief in Purgatory, Protestants' reaction to ghosts was liable to be tentative. Ghosts in their view were troubling since, theologically speaking, they should not have been able to break the confines of Heaven or Hell to make an appearance. Not that Protestants argued this was impossible. God could, obviously, do as He chose. But they saw no reason why God should allow the dead to return and therefore leaned towards the proposition that He did not do so. Indeed, without Purgatory and the need for the help of the living which it generated, why should the dead return to contact the living; and if there was no interaction, but merely an appearance, that appearance was the more disturbing in as much as it seemed to be inexplicable. Hence Protestants turned to the inscrutable 'Providence of God' to account for the unaccountable. Ghosts either became omens and prodigies, a part of that host of signs, portents, and wonders which had existed in Classical times and which filled the Bible with warnings of God's wrath, and acted as manifold calls to repentance or as harbingers of the Last Days; or they were condemned as fraudulent tricks and impostures, hangovers from the superstitious days of Catholic supremacy. 'All these brainless imaginations of... house-haunting and the rest', fulminated Samuel Harsnett in his *Declaration of Egregious Popish Impostures* (1603), 'were the forgeries, cozenages, impostures, and legerdemain of crafty priests and lecherous friars.'[4]

And yet, and yet: Protestant writers could still report a ghost story which might just as well have been recounted by a Catholic source two or three hundred years before the reformation. Thus, in 1623 there was published *A Strange and Fearfull Warning to All Sonnes and Executors*, which relates the dreadful time suffered by a Wiltshire tailor, John Barefoote, at the hands of a poltergeist. The pamphlet makes it clear that Barefoote is the target of the preternatural activity because he failed to execute his father's will, and misappropriated property his father had left to John's sisters; and the ghost is overtly designated 'God's angel', sent to punish Barefoote's sins. Nor did radical changes in theological thinking automatically find their way into popular practice. Protestants in Germany, for example, continued to treat the dying and the dead in ways very similar to those of their Catholic neighbours. They would open a window to let the soul escape; read a blessing as soon as death occurred, to prevent ill-intentioned persons from rousing the dead and asking him or her questions which the corpse would be obliged to answer. They rearranged the furniture to confuse the ghost should it try to come back, and set a place for it at the funeral feast. In other words, popular Protestant as well as Catholic practice was divided between placating the dead and preventing their return. As Robert Scribner puts it, 'Such customs reflected the notion that the deceased had merely altered his state but was still present as a "living corpse" (*lebender Leichman*) who could see, hear, think, walk, experience emotions, and above all, because of his super-natural liminal state, could protect or bring harm'.[5]

But people were well aware that not every account of a ghost might be entirely reliable. Erasmus's dialogue of 1524, *Exorcismus sive Spectrum*, for example, tells the story of Polus who, merely for personal amusement, spread the rumour that a country bridge was haunted by a soul in torment, and on another occasion persuaded a priest to exorcise a spirit which did not in fact exist because Polus had invented it. The charge of faking ghosts was thus a useful Protestant stick wherewith to beat Catholics, and it was a common accusation that priests and monks and nuns had counterfeited apparitions to deceive and impose upon simpletons. Yet Protestants themselves were not above playing on popular acceptance of the reality of ghosts, and faking appearances. So, a number of disaffected individu-als in the parish of Radwynter in Essex, who wanted to rid themselves of the incumbent vicar, tried to scare him away by manufacturing ghosts in the churchyard; and one Henry Church found himself in front of the Court of Star Chamber in 1621 for trying to trick a widow out of her money by counterfeiting the ghost of her late husband with a view to frightening her into yielding up her inheritance. Fraud, then, was known to be one explanation for ghosts: error was another. A Bolognese chronicle relating to 1504 records a simple mistake:

> Still another amazing thing appeared in the so called 'Sala' fields twelve miles from Bologna. At midday in those

fields several shadows were seen from afar which, caused by meteorological impressions, seemed to be eighteen or twenty men dressed in white, red, and black, and they seemed to be fighting among themselves. And when anyone approached to try and see them at close range, they saw nothing at all; and to those who remained far away it seemed as if those who had approached were conversing with ghosts, which appeared for a good many days, during which many curious citizens went to see them.

The Capuchin Noel Taillepied gave consideration to whether a ghost might be merely something imagined, but rejected the notion on the grounds that in the many cases in which several people saw the same apparition, it was unlikely all would have been similarly deceived simultaneously; while, on the other hand, the Jesuit, Martín Del Río, became incandescent at the very thought of those who denied the possibility that the dead, with God's permission, might return to the living, calling them atheists and heretics, false brethren and the offspring of vipers. But he goes on to record a number of other opinions about the non-reality of ghosts:

> Certain of their number are of the opinion that those who claim to have seen spirits are suffering from madness, have lost their minds, are delusional, and ought to be referred to doctors for a course of hellebore. Others announce that all anecdotes of this kind are superstitious and the idle dreams of insane old women.[6]

But it should not be thought that either the Middle Ages or the early modern period had a uniform view of or explanation for spectral phenomena. The whole subject, indeed, became matter for intense debates about related questions such as the nature of materiality, the workings of the imaginative faculty, and the very reason for any ghost's making an appearance in the created, physical world. On this latter point West sums up the difference between the two leading confessional contenders. The central question of the dispute between Catholics and Protestants on ghosts was the place of ghosts in God's providence, and this not so much as to their nature – for both sides held that no return of souls could be conceived save as a miracle, a special act of God – but as to their reason. Protestants denied that there was any reason for souls of the dead to return; Catholics named many reasons, all of them valid within the scheme of Catholic theology and some not altogether without the pale of the reformed theology'. These reasons included a demonstration of God's power (thus redounding to the greater glory of God), a mercy from God in allowing the dead to issue a warning to the living, and an evidence of God's justice striking at sinners through the dead.[7]

The Protestant position, of course, might lead to the abandonment of more than just ghostly appearances. Sadducism – scepticism about any explanation of the world which expressed itself in terms of supernatural conceptions at all – emboldened by such doubts and encouraged by the flood of new knowledge appearing in the works of many natural philosophers, threatened to bring to the fore a great deal of latent scepticism which had long lain not altogether dormant in ordinary folk, while Descartes's round assertion that 'there exists nothing in the whole of nature which cannot be explained in terms of purely corporeal causes' might be seen as banishing God to a realm of His own, and leaving the machine of nature, which He had created, to run itself under the watchful eyes of human beings. The tendency in some Protestant thought on ghosts can be gauged from the

Englishman Howard who actually accepted the existence of
spirits and their ability to do things beyond human powers,
but suggested they did so through illusion, and that Satan's
purpose in encouraging belief in ghosts was to weaken correct belief relating to life after death.

> I conclude that neither souls nor bodies can appear to
> conjurors but by a figure or a shadow of illusion, so far
> as it may take a seeming colour, by the practice of our
> enemy... [The Devil], by nourishing a false conceit in the
> minds of simple and unlearned men that the souls of the
> faithful are harboured in rest, but wander up and down,
> I cannot tell how many years... before they can arrive in
> their desired port, he giveth check to the doctrine of the
> Gospel touching Heaven and Hell.

No wonder, then, that learned men cried 'Atheism!' at
any suggestion which sought to decry the supernatural or,
indeed, preternatural, and looked to ghosts and witchcraft
to supply proofs that this mechanistic philosophy was mistaken. Thus, Henry More wrote in 1681:

> I look upon it as a special piece of Providence that there
> are ever and anon such fresh examples of Apparitions and
> Witchcraft as may rub up and awaken their benumbed
> and lethargic Mindes into a suspicion at least, if not an
> assurance that there are other intelligent Beings besides
> those that are clad in heavy Earth or Clay: In this, I
> say, methinks the Divine Providence does plainly outwit
> the Powers of the Dark Kingdom, in permitting wicked
> men and women and vagrant spirits of that Kingdom
> to make Leagues and Covenants one with another, the
> Confessions of Witches against their own Lives being so
> palpable as Evidence (besides the miraculous feats they

play), that there are bad Spirits, which will necessarily open a Door to the belief that there are good ones, and lastly that there is a God.[8]

A large and varied range of responses to the phenomenon of ghosts was thus given voice during the early modern period. Nevertheless, while theologians, doctors, and natural philosophers might argue and propose from their different intellectual eyries, a majority of people still continued to experience and report all kinds of spectral experiences, even if these were often mediated via the pens of intellectuals. Girolamo Cardano, for example, recounts an incident which happened to his father. One night, while in a state of wakefulness, he says, 'I [*that is, his father*] felt someone put his thumb on the crown of my head... He put his index-finger on top of my head, then his middle finger, and then the rest in such a way that his little finger stretched almost as far as my forehead. It was the hand of a ten-year old boy, to judge by the size, and seemed to come out of the pillow... Finally it came to my mouth. It had already thrust the tips of its index finger and middle finger inside when I had a presentiment of something evil, and to prevent the whole body from attacking me, I pushed it away with my right hand'. Even more physical was a revenant or vrykolax from Breslau, the ghost of a shoemaker who had committed suicide by cutting his throat. His widow had had the corpse washed and wrapped in secret, out of embarrassment, but the burial then took place with full Christian rites. But after rumour had started to spread that he was, in fact, a suicide, the shoemaker began to appear to people, by day as well as by night. He would lie down in people's beds and almost smother them, and if he squeezed them, his fingers left highly visible marks. It was decided to exhume his body. This was found to be bloated, but otherwise little changed from what it had been while he was alive, and it was only when the corpse was burned to ashes that the ghost ceased from his violent hauntings.[9]

Such corporeal ghosts are seen above all, rather than heard, and this illustrates a point made by Barbara Lewis that 'early modern religion was still intensely visual; seeing was believing, far more than hearing, and much more so than the private mental discipline of absorbing information from a written text', which was the particular emphasis of the various Protestant confessions.[10] This visuality may be illustrated by the remarkable vogue for bringing ghosts on to the stage in theatrical performances. Between 1560 and 1610 twenty-six surviving plays provide us with as many as fifty-one ghosts, and that refers to the English stage alone. Some appear to offer comfort, others are conjured by necromancy, some tell the audience the plot, some are comic characters; but most are connected in some way or other with revenge or appear to prophesy doom to the persons who killed them. This last is the function of the ghost in Shakespeare's *Julius Caesar*, who exchanges a few words with Brutus, his principal assassin.

> Brutus: How ill this taper burns! Ha, who comes here?
> I think it is the weakness of mine eyes
> That shapes this monstrous apparition.
> It comes upon me. Art thou any thing?
> Art thou some god, some angel, or some devil,
> That mak'st my blood cold and my hair to stare?
> Speak to me what thou art.

> Ghost: Thy evil spirit, Brutus.

> Brutus: Why com'st thou?
> To tell thee thou shalt see me at Philippi.
> [Act 4, scene 3]

Flames were believed to become dim or turn blue in the presence of a ghost or evil spirit, so both Brutus and the audience know instinctively that the figure which has just walked on the stage, or on to one of the stage's upper balconies – conventionally the place representing mid-air when required – or risen through a trap set in the apron stage, is not of this world.

At first Brutus wonders whether he is experiencing some kind of hallucination. Then he asks if the apparition is substantial, that is, has physical form. Finally, he turns to the current Protestant hypothesis: that ghosts may be angels or demons in disguise, the former coming with a message from God, the latter seeking to mislead an unwary human to his destruction. The command to speak is important. Not all ghosts do so. When Banquo's ghost appears twice to Macbeth, on neither occasion does it interact vocally with its murderer. It simply occupies Macbeth's place at table and stares at him. Inevitably this raises certain general questions quite apart from the exigencies of the dramatic situation which has been written for it. Does a ghost not speak because it is unable to do so? Are we to understand thereby that it is capable of translating itself into the material world by means of visual but not aural terms? Or is it merely that speech is unnecessary because the visual message alone is sufficient to make itself understood? In the case of Banquo, for example, sight alone is clearly enough. But when Caesar's ghost says something, the fact that it answers is alone significant, and its reply confirms Brutus's worst fears. For the reply is ambiguous. We may hear it as 'I am your guilty conscience made manifest'; but it is equally possible (and perhaps more likely in a sixteenth-century context), to take the words at face value and hear, 'I am your personal attendant evil spirit', an interpretation which would confirm the view that the ghost was of diabolical origin. One is reminded of an interchange between Elizabeth Leakey and her dying mother-in-law with whom she seems to have been at variance. Old Mother Leakey threatened she would come again after her death, to which Elizabeth replies, 'What, will you be a devil?' and receives the answer, 'No, but I will come in the Devil's likeness'. Brutus's demand that the apparition speak is in accord with Catholic advice, for the Capuchin Noel Taillepied observed, 'It is quite true that we are actually affrighted and startled in some degree at any such appearances or at a ghost, and our hair will rise and prickle on our heads, nevertheless even if it be a spirit of evil and malignant aspect, who upsets tables and chairs and jolts furniture... do not fear any the more, nor tremble and shake, but boldly say, "If thou art of God, speak; if thou art not of God, begone"'.[11]

Now, demons and ghosts on the sixteenth-century stage often had to cope with the requirement that they appear and disappear suddenly, as non-human entities were wont to do. This could be done in several ways. There were mechanical devices such as doors, traps, and screens; and there were verbal clues to the audience that a figure they saw on stage was either not yet supposed to be visible, or was meant to have disappeared from view. When Banquo's ghost vanishes the second time from the stage, for example, the time allowed by the text for its exit is so short that it suggests the ghost's disappearance was achieved by his sinking through a trap-door set in the floor of the apron stage; and Mummers' plays regularly contain such lines as 'In comes I...' as a sign to the audience that the person speaking is now meant to be visible. It is a convention of willing audience co-operation in seeing and not-seeing which is common to other theatres, too: one thinks of scene shifters and manipulators in Chinese theatre, or the puppeteers in Balinese shadow-plays.[12] This co-operation argues a certain sophistication in the audience, and we can note other examples of people's being alert to the clues they were being given by the playwright. Steve Sohmer, for example, has pointed out that just before the ghost in Hamlet first appears in stage, the text of the play is thick with significant words and phrases intended to help the audience interpret the moment. It is pitch dark and cold. The time is between midnight and one in the morning. One character's reference to 'yon same star that's westward from the pole' can plausibly be identified as Deneb in the constellation known to English Christians as 'the Northern Cross', a reminder of death and resurrection and hence of the region or state between these two. The name of one of the characters on stage, Marcellus, is reminiscent of St Marcellus whose feast day falls on 30 October. This was the first of three successive nights on which the ghost, we are told, has walked already. Since he is now to walk for a fourth time, the date of the opening action of the play must be 2 November, All Souls' Day, the climax of that short period of the year during which ghosts traditionally leave their graves in some form or other, and seek out the living for assistance or revenge. We therefore do not need the ghost to tell us (as he does later), that he has come from Purgatory. We were able to deduce as much from the conversation between the guards on Elsinore's walls before he ever appeared.[13]

Ghosts on the sixteenth-century stage thus emphasised the physicality of the dead and undercut the thrust of Protestant theology which argued that, since there was no such place or state as Purgatory, apparitions must be demons or angels or tricks, or emanations of the brain arising from illness, over-heated imagination, or drunkenness. Perhaps, then, it was no accident that the early seventeenth century began to see an outburst of poltergeists who began to enter the ghostly canon in increasing numbers at this time. These spirits of the dead who cause objects to move, and generally behave in a destructive manner which may be perceived in many ways as part of a continuum from 'mischievous' to 'terrifying', do not seem to have been part of the regular Classical repertoire, although the Roman playwright Plautus does exploit for comic effect disembodied knocking at a door, which the *dramatis personae* attribute to a poltergeist. This kind of ghost was known in the Middle Ages, of course – Geraldus Cambrensis, for example, recounts a story of two haunted houses in which objects were thrown around and clothing ripped, and Otloh of St Emmeram tells us about a drowned monk who returned from the dead to give a dishonest cellarer a sound flogging – but the sixteenth and seventeenth centuries seem to have taken a greater interest in recorded instances of this type of violent spirit-activity. The Jesuit Martín Del Rio described them as follows:

> Sometimes [these spectres] are content just to annoy and disturb, doing no bodily harm, like that throwing of which Guillaume de Paris writes, which disturbed his sleep with the clattering of pots and hurling of stones, and, having pulled away his mattress, turned him out of bed; and the devil of Salamanca, who attacked people indiscriminately with large stones which struck them with a blow both empty and harmless. Marcus Magnus in Psellus says this is characteristic of subterranean demons... By what arrangement demons can throw stones and perform other things which seem to require hands and physical instruments, the Scholastics are in dispute. I myself agree with those who say these things are done by a demon substantially present in that place, who moves the air next to the stone by a command of will.[14]

Several of these activities, and Del Rio's suggested explanation of their source, turn up in one of the most detailed accounts of poltergeist activity of the seventeenth century, from someone of apparently unimpeachable trustworthiness and veracity, François Perreaud, a French Calvinist minister, and his narrative may serve to illustrate the genre as a whole. Before we begin to look at it, however, it is worth noting how extraordinary a case this is. In their study of poltergeists, Gauld and Cornell made a list of sixty-three characteristics drawn from a study of 500 cases of poltergeist activity ranging from the sixth century AD to the nineteenth, and taken from all over Europe and North America. These characteristics include the length of time the phenomena lasted, the movement of objects, variety of sounds, whether there were apparitions or not, breakages, disarrangement of objects, assaults on the person, ringing of bells, and so forth. If one measures each of these 500 cases against the sixty-three characteristics to see how many each case exhibits, one finds that the Mâcon incident comes out top of the list by quite a large margin – eighteen out of sixty-three, as opposed to its nearest rivals, Italy 1696 (thirteen), Scotland 1695 (twelve), and the USA 1679 (also twelve).[15]

François Perreaud cannot be counted as one of the great luminaries of the European reformation. Certainly he was a pastor much respected by his ecclesiastical equals and superiors and had what appears to have been a long and honourable career, dying amid general plaudits at the age of eighty-five in 1657. But had it not been for this one slight, though intriguing, claim to fame, his death would have wrapped him in permanent obscurity. As it is, he claims our attention because in 1612, soon after he had arrived in Mâcon to start his ministry, both he and his household were subjected to a series of almost unremitting attacks from a ghost or evil spirit which plagued them in poltergeist fashion from mid-September to 22 December that same year. Perreaud then wrote an account of his experience, *L'Antidemon de Mâcon*, which he showed to various people but left unpublished until 1658 when it appeared from a press in Geneva, to be followed by translations into English (1658), Dutch (1665), and Welsh (1681). Having created something of a brouhaha, however, the book went out of print and has remained so ever since. Nevertheless, the Mâcon episode is still quoted in accounts and discussions of poltergeist activity, although it is now known mainly by repute. For Perreaud's book is scarcely read, its accompanying *Demonologie* largely ignored, and his reasons for writing both simply not considered. It will be useful, therefore, to redress that neglect a little and acquaint ourselves with both the man and his visitation.

He came from a respectable Burgundian family which seems to have converted to Protestantism very early. His grandfather, Pierre de Perreaud, had gone to Geneva in 1537 and was there turned to the reformed faith by none other than Calvin himself. Pierre had three sons, two of whom became Protestant ministers, and it was the eldest, Abel, who was the father of François. Abel served the Reformed Church in the Pays de Vaud, a region notorious for both witches and werewolves, and there in 1572 (or, according to some accounts, 1577), his third son, François, was born. It seems that François, in the burgeoning family tradition, decided at an early age that he would become a minister, and the rest of his life was spent in the service of various churches in Burgundy and the Pays de Gex. He was thirty-five or forty when he arrived to take up his post in Mâcon and had married the previous year Anne Farci who, in due time, gave him three sons. When the poltergeist incident broke out, however, apart from one somewhat malicious remark by the demon, we hear nothing about a child; so either Anne was pregnant at the time, or the Perreauds had not yet started their family.

Commendations of François's character and service to the Church were attached to the printed versions of his book in 1653. Part of the approbation given him by the Synod of Burgundy in October 1651 is worth recording.

We, pastors and elders of the reformed churches of the province of Burgundy... certify to all that M. Perreaud, minister of the holy ministry in this province for the space of fifty years... in all that time, and in all churches, doing the office of a good pastor and a faithful servant of God, both in doctrine and in life, of which he had an especial testimonial given him by the church of Mâcon in the last synod of the province... and he has the like from the church of Thoiry... to which we add that altogether it has pleased God to bring him into many, and some very extraordinary trials, especially when he served the church in Mâcon: yet the same God has strengthened him with a constant health of his body and godly tranquility of mind, and has endued him with virtue to bear and overcome all his afflictions. We therefore beseech the Lord daily to fill his servant with more and more strength in his old age, and that after he has finished his course, he may depart in peace and obtain the crown of glory reserved for those that will persevere faithful to the end.

Clearly François was a man held in high esteem for his probity and in consequence he was able to receive a reformed *nihil obstat et imprimatur* for his venture into the otherwise suspect territory of witchcraft, demons, and malignant spirits. Perhaps more importantly, his readers were thus able to feel they could read his book with impunity of conscience, since it had been approved by such estimable moulders of public opinion. But it was not merely local Protestant ministers who were prepared to express their conviction that, however extraordinary a tale M. Perreaud had to tell, his word might be believed. His account could also be regarded as legitimate evidence for scientific investigation into manifestations of preternatural phenomena, for in 1644 Sir Robert Boyle, a future member of the Royal Society and someone whose interests encompassed more than one of the occult sciences, was spending time in Geneva and there met Perreaud from whom he heard an account of the Mâcon episode and was given a chance to read the as yet unpublished manuscript. Boyle was greatly impressed both by what he read and by the character of its author, and when he came to correspond with Joseph Glanvill on the question of the reality of witchcraft, he chose this story as the one fully corroborated and verified account with which he was acquainted. He therefore sponsored its publication in English, which finally appeared not long after the first French edition. Its preface makes clear why Perreaud had at last been persuaded to go into print. He was, said the translator, 'compelled to it by the many various and therefore some false relations of that story which were scattered abroad'.

What appeared in translation, however, was only the *Antidemon*. The *Demonologie* which precedes it, and to which it fulfils the office of introduction or prefatory sermon-cum-explanation, was quite ignored. But, in order to understand Perreaud's full message, it is necessary to see what he has to say about witchcraft and demonology in general; and therefore it is to the *Demonologie* we must turn first to sharpen our attention for the personal memoir which follows.

Perreaud begins with a short preface in which he explains that in 1652 he visited Bern for the first time for fifty years and there congratulated the city on passing a law against witches, which declared its intention henceforth to investigate charges of witchcraft with a due measure of thought, lengthy deliberation, and ripe regard for the attendant circumstances and ramifications thereof. This reminded Perreaud, he says, of three things: first, an older but similar ordinance published by Venice, which curbed the abuse of allowing those who accused others of witchcraft of benefiting from their escheated goods; secondly, the attacks he himself has suffered at the hands of Catholics who have drawn attention to the large number of witches burned in the Pays de Vaud, and infer therefrom that reformed religion is to blame for the infestation (to which Perreaud replies that if Satan was bold enough to attack Adam and Eve in Eden, he was quite apt to do as much in places where the pure Gospel was preached); and thirdly, his experiences in Mâcon when he arrived there to take up his ministry. He believes it is possible to show that all these incidents are not unconnected and so, stimulated by his visit to Bern and the judicious Witchcraft Act of its city council, he has decided to make available his treatise on demonology 'wherein', he says, 'I have tried to explain by reasonable grounds and principles what one must believe, the strength and weakness of evil spirits, and the proper remedies and safeguards one may undertake against them'.

The treatise is divided into twelve short chapters and reads like an extended sermon. Perreaud begins by addressing himself to the problem of those people who do not believe in the existence of angels, good or bad. There are two ways of proving something, he says: the Word of God and experience. He then furnishes the usual examples from Scripture to show that both good and bad angels exist, and then makes the observation that just as a secular state needs executioners and people to carry out the ordinances of justice, so demons are necessary to punish sin and test the faith of believers. Experience, too, confirms the existence of these entities. Houses and châteaux all over Europe have been abandoned because they are infested with evil spirits whose numbers are so vast, they cannot be counted. Perreaud then adds the unexpected comment: so why is there only one Devil? Because, he answers, 'Devil' is a collective noun ('ce mot "Diable" est un mot collectif').

This procedure of appeal to Scripture and experience is followed throughout the remaining chapters. Perreaud goes on to argue that witches and sorcerers undoubtedly exist and that maintaining their non-existence is simply one of Satan's tricks. (Here he takes a side-swipe at Montaigne, who actually did not question the existence of witches so much as suggest that one must be quite convinced of the possibility of the reality of their crime before one burned them for it). Satan imitates God, says Perreaud, by sending visions to his witches as God sent visions to His prophets; and the Devil's marks are the equivalent of circumcision among the Jews or baptism among Christians. Nevertheless, it is as dangerous to be over-credulous as it is to be unbelieving. Certain phenomena may have a natural explanation. Deliberate fraud must not be discounted. Misunderstanding by the ignorant should be taken into account. Malicious accusation is always possible, as when an evil spirit suddenly began to make appearances at night in the city of Tours. The citizens called him *le Roy Hugon* or *Huguet*, and Protestants in the city were henceforth known as *Huguenots* because they held their meetings only at night under the aegis of this evil spirit.

Popular belief that witches can raise hailstorms and tempests is both wrong and impious. Only God can do such things. Certainly the Devil does have great power on earth and in the air, but neither he nor his evil spirits can do anything except by God's permission and licence. If storms do occur, they are more likely to be signs of God's anger at our sins, and it should be a consolation to us to know both that calamity comes either from God or from Satan acting under God's directions, and that God will not permit us to be tested beyond our endurance.

The word *demon* means 'someone who knows', says Perreaud – (actually, it does not, but no matter) – and demons are possessed of two qualities: the power to know and the power to act. Demons apparently know what is going on in the present, for they can enter people's minds and read their unspoken thoughts, although only God can *really* know what is going on in someone's mind. (If that is not altogether clear, it is because Perreaud himself seems confused about this point). Demons can also predict the future, not because they know it, but because they are immensely skilled both at reading signs and drawing correct inferences from the past, and these they use to give what appears to be an extraordinary accurate forecast of the future.

Nevertheless, demons work principally through illusion and they may persuade people to believe their illusions ether by working upon the individual imagination or upon the exterior senses of sight and sound. As an example of the former, Perreaud refers to the story of a man who refused to sit down because he believed his buttocks were made of glass and that if he rested them on a chair they would crack in pieces. Such mistaken beliefs, he says, are caused by melancholy, an excess of black bile in the system, which causes fumes to rise from the stomach to the brain where they interfere with the natural spirits resident there and so produce something akin to hallucination. Hence, says Perreaud, witches merely imagine they fly to their Sabbats and nocturnal assemblies, while Satan also makes use of their melancholic proclivities to manufacture illusions in their brain. Demons, in fact, are expert conjurors and can deceive the eye and ear, either by creating illusions themselves or having magicians and witches create them on their behalf.

But demons can also do things impossible to humans. For example, they can use other bodies for their own purposes – the corpses of those who have been hanged are a common choice – or manufacture false bodies from congealed air. Once in the new body they can make it speak by striking the air so that it vibrates through the corpse's lungs and mouth and so reaches the ear of the listener, so that it appears as though real speech and real articulation are taking place. This, says Perreaud, is how the poltergeist at Mâcon was able to speak and he and his friends were able to hear an apparent voice. Demons can use human bodies because their own are so much lighter, and lighter things have power over heavier. Thus they can carry witches through the air, as a wind carries objects heavier than itself. Therefore a demon's ability to throw stones or domestic utensils, ring bells, and create other noises should not be regarded as strange or unlikely. Nor are such manifestations illusory. Satan's repertoire of tricks is immense and aimed entirely at achieving a single goal: the destruction of humanity. He misleads people through idolatry (for example, via the Church of Rome or, even worse, by means of those who claim to effect cures by means of popular magic); through heresy and false doctrine, perfidy and atheism, murders, duels, religious wars, debauchery, and the corruption of justice. The end of the world is not far off; therefore Satan is constantly inventing new stratagems to ensnare and destroy the faithful. What, then, can one do to protect oneself against him? He is not to be restrained by superstitious means such as crosses, relics, holy water, and exorcisms. A strong faith in the mercy of God, prayer, vigil, and fasting are the appropriate weapons with which we must fight, and if we live our lives as in the presence of God, we may be assured of God's protection from ultimate harm.

While the logical progression of the argument of the *Demonologie* may not be altogether coherent, the main thrust of Perreaud's disquisition is clear.

1 Evil spirits do exist and are capable of doing harm to human beings. They operate, however, only with permission from God and cannot go further in malignancy than He allows.

2 Much of what they do is sheer illusion. That it appears real to us is simply because evil spirits exist on a more subtle plane and have a much greater knowledge of and control over nature than we.

3 Having been fettered by God for a thousand years, Satan has now been released and is working havoc against humanity. With the advent of true religion in Europe, he is making even greater efforts to ruin human souls.

4 That said, we must not allow ourselves to fall into superstitious over-credulity and see demonic activity where there is none. A judicious vigilance and a constant trust in God will see us safely through any demonic nightmare.

There is nothing here which is in the least novel or unorthodox. Indeed, there is very little which is distinctively Protestant, apart from a few shafts drawn against Catholicism. Demonologies by Catholic and Protestant writers from the late sixteenth century onwards had been saying more or less the same things as each other. Girolamo Menghi, for example, suggested that 'the most powerful remedies against these diabolical nightmares are a sorrowful and tearful contrition for one's sins, confession, and the Lord's prayer devoutly said, holy communion, devotion of the holy cross, exorcism… meditation on Christ's passion, giving alms, fasting, pilgrimage, and prayer to the saints' [*Fustis Daemonum* (1586), chapter 17]. *Mutatis mutandis*, the emphasis here is upon contrition for sin, prayer, and fasting, all of which Perreaud would have been happy to approve. Both parties tended to refer to the same authorities with an almost tedious regularity, and Protestants quoted Catholic authors quite cheerfully as magisterial texts worthy of absolute credence. Any differences between them tended rather to lie in their illustrative details, often contemporary anecdotes, which might lend themselves to confessional manipulation and which could be used for sectarian purposes to underline a desired doctrinal point; while another source of difference could be found in the remedies and safeguards the writer recommended. Catholics had an immense repertoire of what Protestants called 'counter magic' to range against the Devil and his servants. Protestants, on the other hand, were forced to rely principally on prayer and steadfast hope, gritting their teeth, like Job, and waiting patiently until the storm had passed: an austere, even bleak, advice which not everyone could like or follow.

As an example of the demonological genre therefore, Perreaud's book is limited. As a prefatory sermon, setting the tone and ambience for his poltergeist account, however, it is both interesting and novel, and if we treat it, not as an intellectual discussion but as a personal document, an exhortation to faith and trust in God by someone who had particular need of both, it takes on the air of a personal conversation between Perreaud and the reader, a warning of the dangers from preternatural forces which may spring unexpectedly into anyone's daily life, and a reassurance that however disconcerting or frightening these may be, they are not beyond our courage or our endurance.

The title page of the poltergeist book reads: 'The Antidemon of Mâcon, or, the particular and absolutely true story of what a demon did and said at Mâcon several years ago in the house of M. Perreaud, resident at that time in the said town. In contradiction of several falsehoods which have become common currency'. The first Perreaud knew something was amiss was when he returned home on 19 September 1612 after an absence of five days, to be greeted by his wife and her maid who were in great distress. On the evening he left, they said, his wife had gone to bed and fallen asleep. Suddenly the bed-curtains were pulled violently aside. The maid, who was sleeping in the same room, got up to see what was wrong but could find nothing. Next evening the two women slept in the same bed. Something drew back the coverlet and the maid was thrown out of bed. Making her way down to the kitchen, she found she could not get in as the door appeared to have been bolted from the other side. But there was a great deal of noise, as though pots and pans were being thrown down on the floor. Rousing the house-boy who slept at the front of the house, the two of them went back to the kitchen. The boy opened the door without any difficulty, and the maid saw that there were kitchen utensils all over the place. The same thing happened the following night.

'I was astonished', says Perreaud, 'but not inclined to believe them too readily. Women are by nature timid and I thought it might be some tearaway playing a prank'. So before he went to bed, he searched the house thoroughly, locked all doors and windows, and closed the shutters. He then said prayers and went to bed, while his wife and the maid sat by the fire with their distaffs. There was a lighted lamp on the table.

Suddenly a great racket started in the kitchen: rolling, knocking, scratching, and thumping on the wooden partition. Plates, trenchers, and other utensils were thrown at the wall. Perreaud listened carefully, then got out of bed, took his sword, and entered the kitchen, the maid going in front of him with a lighted candle. There was no one there. Perreaud went back to bed. The same thing happened again. Again he searched and found nothing. 'It was at that moment', he says, 'I realised it must be an evil spirit'.

His reaction next day was to consult the elders of his church, who rallied round and from that day forward kept him company each evening until midnight or even later. Perreaud also told François Tornus, who was a local notary and a Catholic, and he too joined the assembly of watchers. Henceforth Perreaud was subject to a series of minor violences. On one occasion, for example, between 1pm and 2pm, Dr Connain, a local physician, came to see Perreaud. Together they went into one of the bedrooms and found bedclothes scattered all over the place. The maid came and put them back in order, but no sooner had she done so, and while both Perreaud and Dr Connain were in the room, the bed disarranged itself again. Perreaud's books in his study, and his hour-glass, were thrown on to the floor. On one occasion, while he was trying to read, the spirit made the sound of a fusillade of muskets under the floorboard. Nor did it confine its activities to the house. It went out into the stable where it twisted the mane and tail of Perreaud's horse, and turned his saddle back to front.

Then at 9pm on 20 November, it started to whistle three or four times, especially in front of Tornus. Next, it spoke. Its voice was hoarse and kept repeating, '22 deniers, 22 deniers', no more than three or four paces away, followed by, 'Minister, minister!' Perreaud exclaimed, 'Get thee behind me, Satan', and added, 'Yes, I am a minister and servant of the living God before whose majesty you tremble': to which the spirit replied, 'I'm not contradicting you'. It then began to recite mangled versions of the Lord's Prayer and the Commandments, sang part of Psalm 81, and revealed all kinds of personal details about Perreaud's family, including the fact that his father had been poisoned, the name of the murderer, and the place where the deed was done. Perreaud indicates that all this was true, but unfortunately we have no further details about what must have been quite a scandal whenever it happened.

The spirit said it had come from the Pays de Vaud – significant, perhaps, because of the area's association with witchcraft – and, disguised as a man on a poor, exhausted horse, had called on Perreaud's elder brother (a detail Perreaud says he later confirmed as true), and recounted an incident when it (the spirit) had raised a sudden wind which had nearly drowned Amos Perreaud and his guests as they boated on a nearby lake. Then it spoke of those who had lived in the house before Perreaud. The wife had murdered her husband by pushing him downstairs after a quarrel, and several people present with Perreaud thought this might well be true.

But the spirit spoke to others as well as to Perreaud. It revealed incidents supposedly private to Claude Rapai, a launderer, who was a regular member of the watching company, and likewise to Philibert Guillermin, another launderer. A third man had his secrets revealed and Michel Rapai, who often came with his father, became the object of the spirit's attention for a while, as the spirit repeated a private conversation between Michel and one of his friends, and mimicked the voice of Michel's mother. This louche sense of humour seems to have been characteristic of the spirit. One evening it began to blaspheme, and when Perreaud reproached it, said it wanted to see the curé of St Etienne so that it might confess its sins, adding, 'Don't let him forget to bring holy water so that he can exorcise me'. Next it told the story of how it had been present at the recent attack on Geneva, saying it jumped down from the walls into the moat and tried to run away. Then it croaked like a frog. Some of these details are puzzling. Are they merely the spirit's peculiar sense of humour, or are they the memories of a revenant who is mixing incidents from his past, human, physical life with inanities intended to annoy or provoke?

The relationship between the spirit and the Perreauds' maid was particularly odd. She came from Bresse and spoke only the local dialect. The spirit used to joke with her and she would giggle back, quite unperturbed. On one occasion, it snatched a candlestick out of her hand, leaving her with only the lighted candle. On another, it took her clothes and draped them around the bedposts, and disarranged rooms after she had tidied them. But there came a point when she had had enough and wanted to leave the Perreauds' service. They hired a girl in her place, and for a while the two young women were together in the house – presumably while the maid from Bresse worked out her notice or trained her successor – and indeed shared the same bed. But the spirit took exception to the new arrangement and eventually got rid of the newcomer by beating her soundly and throwing water over her when she tried to sleep. Perreaud was highly suspicious of the maid from Bresse. She was, he says, suspect of witchcraft and came from a suspect family. (How interesting, therefore, that he was prepared to hire her as a servant in the first place). A number of people suggested to him that she was the case of his trouble, and to a certain extent he was inclined to agree. Nevertheless, true to his principle of caution, he did not commit himself to this explanation before, as we shall see, giving due consideration to others.

The games this spirit seemed to play with its audience were subject to frequent changes of mood and tone. One evening it said it was not itself at all. 'He' had gone to Chambéry to take part in a court case and wanted to make 'his' will. The spirit now speaking was the other one's valet. At this, one of Perreaud's regular visitors rushed to the place whence the voice was issuing, but found nothing there save a few old rags and a bottle. The spirit laughed and said, 'I always heard you were stupid. Of course I'm not in the bottle!' Still in its character of valet, the spirit complained of being poor, badly dressed, and cold, and asked Perreaud for charity. This Perreaud refused. The spirit retorted that the voice they had heard the previous day had not been his after all, but that of one of its friends. The 'friend' and the 'master' were now on their way to Chambéry, it said. Perreaud now pauses to inform us that a spirit did indeed turn up in the house of a famous lawyer in Chambéry, saying it came from Mâcon and demanding exotic food for its 'master'. The spirit-voice had then apparently broken into rude songs, followed by imitations of the fairground cries of quack doctors, cardsharps, and the hallooing of people at a hunt.

Its last verbal assaults on Perreaud and the company took the form of tempting their greed by saying that six thousand écus were hidden in the house and asking if they would like to find them. It then promised to appear in any shape they might choose; but Perreaud rebuffed all such advances, whereupon the spirit became angry, burst into insults, and then in a last change of mood slyly tried to imply it was actually the soul of a woman who had died in the house not long before the Perreauds moved in, and who had sworn on her deathbed to do them such harm as she could. Finally, it prophesied disaster for the Huguenots, the birth of a daughter for Mme Perreaud, and an early death in three years for Perreaud himself. Then, on 25 November, it fell silent and never spoke again. Nevertheless, it continued its physical assaults not only within Perreaud's house but elsewhere, too. It rang small iron bells in the house, in the street, and in the fields furth of the town. A friend of Perreaud's, Abraham Lullier, said he heard them in his house and several people complained the spirit was making the sound come from their purses. One day, while Perreaud was visiting Lullier, the spirit caused a gold ring to vanish from the table and half an hour later made it fall from the air on to a nearby workbench. Then it knocked two or three times on the eaves. Next evening Lullier came to sit with Perreaud, and at about midnight went home with Claude Rapai. As they were on their way, they saw a prostitute dressed in an unusual fashion, braiding her hair in the moonlight, but as they approached, she vanished.

The end came in mid-December. During the last fortnight of its visitation, the spirit threw stones (one of which weighed more than three pounds), all over the place within the house non-stop from morning till night. On one of these days, the Catholic François Tornus visited Perreaud. A stone landed at his feet. He picked it up, marked it with a coal from the fireplace, and threw it furth at the rear of the house. Almost immediately it was cast back within the house, recognisable by its mark. Tornus, who picked it up, said it was warm. Finally, on 22 December Perreaud's neighbours caught a large snake which was coming out of his house and paraded it through the town. 'Here', they said, 'is the Devil from the minister's house.' The local apothecary identified it as a viper, a type of snake rare to the neighbourhood, according to Perreaud. Whether by coincidence or the providence of God, from that moment all poltergeist activity ceased and neither Perreaud nor his neighbours were ever troubled again.

Was Perreaud's experience typical of that sort of phenomenon generally known as 'poltergeist'? The word means 'noise spirit', and a definition provided by the sixteenth-century Jesuit demonologist Martín Del Rio is as clear as one could wish:

Sometimes [these spectres] are content just to annoy and
disturb, doing no bodily harm, like the throwing of which
Guillaume de Paris writes, which disturbed his sleep with
the clattering of pots and hurling of stones and, having
pulled away his mattress, turned him out of bed; and the
devil of Salamanca, who attacked people indiscriminately
with large stones which struck them with a blow both
empty and harmless. Marcus Magnus in Psellus's [book]
says this is characteristic of subterranean demons... By
what arrangement demons can throw stones and perform other things of kinds which seem to require hands
and physical instruments, the Scholastics are in dispute. I
myself agree with those who say these things are done by
a demon substantially present in that place, who moves
the air next to the stone by a command of will.[16]

Clearly by this definition there can be no doubt that Perreaud
thought he was suffering the attentions of a poltergeist,
but we should, I think, be aware of how extraordinary a
case this is. Referring back to Gauld and Cornell's studies of poltergeists, from this point of view alone therefore
Perreaud's account is highly significant and worthy of closer
examination.[17]

Modern investigators of psychic phenomena usually
divide poltergeist cases into those which are centred on
persons and those centred on places. The Mâcon case clearly
belongs to the former category since although the phenomena were largely concentrated within Perreaud's house,
they also happened elsewhere and to other people, and by
and large we must regard Perreaud himself as the principal
magnet, although whether he was also the trigger is another
question. It is something of a cliché that poltergeist activities
tend to happen in the presence or in the general locality of
a disturbed adolescent whose neurosis acts as a precipitat-

ing factor in the outburst; but as so often the cliché turns out to be true only in part, and caution is required before one attributes a single explanation to what is a series of highly complex phenomena. A modern case will illustrate the point. In early summer 1989, a workshop and retail shop in South Wales were subject to poltergeist haunting which was still continuing in 1991. In many ways what happened then is similar to what happened in Mâcon. Small stones or coins, apparently coming from nowhere, would strike the walls and floors and occasionally hit people without, however, doing them any harm. A paint scraper which had gone missing suddenly reappeared and was found to be hot to the touch. Small objects materialised out of nothing; large stones crashed on to the roof; a diary disappeared from a drawer and was later found on the roof of a nearby building; planks of wood and other objects were thrown about the workshop and retail shop while customers were present; and on several occasions, when someone threw a stone into that corner of the shop which seemed to be the focus of activity, it was thrown back almost at once to land by the side of the person who first threw it. A large number of people witnessed these attacks or were subject to them, and all were thoroughly questioned by investigators who finally came to the conclusion that they were entirely reliable and that no one was playing tricks. Most noticeably, as they remarked, no adolescents were involved. We cannot be sure there were any in Mâcon, either. It is possible, of course, that the maid was quite a young girl but we have no indication of her age and therefore had better not jump to any misleading conclusions.[18]

In view of the immediate scepticism with which such phenomena may well be greeted, almost automatically, by many modern *bien pensants*, the comments of the principal investigator of this Welsh case are worth recording. 'As a psychologist, observation of my own frame of mind during the course of each investigation was almost as interesting as the investigation itself. Each time I witnessed phenomena and noted not only the physical behaviour but also the emotional reactions of other people present, I felt that normal explanations could safely be ruled out. However, on thinking things over afterwards, my rational mind would always intervene and insist that some rational explanation there *must* be. The result was I would fix on any possibility, no matter how absurd, rather than stay with the conclusions produced by actual observation...This is of course not an uncommon response. The parapsychological literature is full of examples of investigators who have initially been convinced by their experiences, only later to doubt the evidence of their own sense. In its way, this is as unscientific as the opposite extreme, that of gullibility'.[19] Interestingly enough, this is exactly the point Perreaud himself makes in chapter 3 of his treatise on demonology: that it is as dangerous to be unbelieving about such matters as it is to be too credulous.

But what did Perreaud himself think was going on? He addressed himself to this problem and offered a number of possibilities. First he observed that sometimes demons are held in restraint by God and at other times released. 1612, he thought, was a time when they were loosed, and he appealed to the experience of Pierre de Lancre, a French advocate and writer on demonology and witchcraft, whose book, *Tableau de l'inconstance des mauvais anges et demons*, had been published only a few months before the Mâcon phenomena. In that same year, too, a demon had used the body of a hanged woman to visit a man in Paris, while at Mâcon the prisons were full of men and women accused of witchcraft. These, adds Perreaud, appealed against their sentences to the Parlement de Paris, and while they were being conveyed thither they met someone who looked like 'un homme de justice'. The mysterious stranger promised them they would come to no harm and, sure enough, says Perreaud, they returned to Mâcon, their sentences quashed and void. Mâcon also witnessed the phenomenon of a young girl who noticed her maid was often absent at night and questioned her about it. The maid confessed that she attended a meeting of witches. Fired by curiosity, the girl agreed to accompany her to the next meeting and was borne up in the air by a demon. While they were flying over the monastery of the Capuchins, however, the girl automatically made the sign of the cross and found herself precipitated into the garden whence she was rescued and taken home by the startled monks. At the same time, demons created havoc in various places in and around Mâcon, especially in the neighbour-hood of two churches, St Etienne and St Alban. There could be no question, therefore, in Perreaud's opinion, that 1612 had seen a great deal of demonic activity, particularly in Mâcon, and that it was at least possible God was permitting this to happen.

Nevertheless, this was only one possibility. Some people, thought Perreaud, thought the trouble lay in his wife's maid, the woman from Bresse, who, as we have noted already, was suspected of being a witch and came from a suspect family. Perreaud himself wondered whether she might not be guilty of witchcraft, but he does not pursue the point, nor does he seem to agree that she was the agent of the demonic or poltergeist activity. But he did note that his experience began very soon after he had arrived in Mâcon to take up his ministry. Perreaud had not liked the first house he lived in and petitioned the government to let him move into another, not altogether the kindest request to make, since someone else would have to be displaced to make way for him. Perreaud records that the aldermen and notables of Mâcon were very much opposed to his moving, and says that many of them became highly emotional and abusive. One, indeed – the pupil of a well-known magician, as Perreaud darkly observes – warned him to expect trouble, and the demonic attacks began that very day. The previous owner of the second house, a woman, had had to be dispossessed by judicial judgement in order to make way for the Perreauds, and naturally she was resentful. Unable to bend or persuade the law to her point of view, it seems she took matters into her own hands, for Perreaud tells us she was discovered one day, kneeling beneath the chimney, calling upon the Devil to do harm to him and his family. Perreaud thereupon made a formal complaint and the woman was ordered to appear before the authorities and explain herself to them. This she did, and it is interesting to notice that they did no more than bind her over to keep the peace. This may indicate a customary lenience in the local magistrates, or it may be a sign that Perreaud's action in moving house had not gone down well with certain sections of the town. But the episode ended with a coincidence. The date of the woman's court appearance was 22 December, and on that day all poltergeist activity ceased for good. 'In my opinion', says Perreaud, 'this woman was the most likely cause'.

His opinion should not come as a surprise. He has signalled something of the kind right from the start, for the title of his account is significant. *L'Antidemon de Mâcon* is unusual because of that word 'antidemon'. At first glance, an antidemon should mean 'someone opposed to a demon', just as 'Antichrist' is an entity opposed to Christ. In this case the most likely antidemon of Mâcon would be François Perreaud himself. But this is too bizarre an explanation and we must surely turn to the other meaning of the Greek preposition *anti*, 'standing in place of'. This, I think, makes sense. Someone standing in place of a demon seems to indicate that Perreaud suspected a human agency behind the demonic acts and, as he says at the end, the woman ejected from her house to make way for him is a very good candidate. We should not, however, jump to any premature conclusion that because Perreaud is pointing the finger at a human being, he is therefore implying the whole thing was a fraud. This is completely to misread his convictions. Nothing could be more likely, according to contemporary belief, than that a woman with a grudge should have turned to harmful magic to right what she saw as her wrongs, and there is no reason for us to doubt that Perreaud made every effort to leave us an accurate record of what he saw and heard and thought he knew; and what he saw and heard and thought he knew was that for more than twelve weeks at the end of 1612, a prolonged operation of maleficent magic had been directed against him and his household, either by Satan at the behest of God as a test of their faith and endurance, or by some malign spirit acting under the control of a non-demonic agent whose identity might be guessed but was not known for certain.

Perreaud's experience, reluctantly published so long after the event, thus provides a reminder of early seventeenth-century Protestant attitudes towards preternatural phenomena. It supports traditional Protestant views on possession and witchcraft, for it acknowledges that Satan's power is real but limited, and that his attacks are part of God's plan for humanity which must suffer them, like Job, with prayer and exemplary patience. It gives an edifying account of Protestant piety, thereby affording what he would have regarded as a useful counterbalance to Catholic works on the same subject, which suggest that only the Catholic Church can provide an effective panoply against diabolical assault; and because Perreaud was considered to be truthful and reliable, and because his account contains few details which might be regarded as overblown or fantastic, his book gained a respectful readership, particularly in England, which might otherwise have dismissed its narrative altogether.[20] Curiously enough, it also foreshadows in certain ways the experience and opinions of John Wesley and his family. During the winter of 1716–17 their household was subject to a type of haunting characterised by Samuel Wesley as the visitation of an evil spirit. The disturbances lasted for about two months and then abruptly ceased. Emily Wesley gave her opinion that they had been caused by witchcraft, since a year previously the neighbouring town had been disturbed by witches.[21] John Wesley, who meditated on this episode for a considerable time, then produced his famous dictum that 'the giving up of witchcraft is in effect giving up the Bible', an assertion which mirrors Perreaud's earlier opinion that 'those who deny devils and witches tacitly deny God, Heaven, and Hell'. It was a logical consequence of faith in the literal truth of Scripture, which helped to keep alive a tradition of belief in these particular preternatural phenomena well into the so-called age of enlightenment.

IV

THE SEVENTEENTH CENTURY:
BOLSTERING RELIGION,
PARTNERING WITCHCRAFT

If there had never been a single over-arching explanation for the appearance of the dead to the living, that diversity of opinion was perhaps particularly noticeable during the seventeenth century. Two events in England, whose consequences spread elsewhere as the decades wore on, were the temporary establishment of the Commonwealth, which permitted (or suffered) a remarkable explosion of radical dissent from what had hitherto been relatively entrenched notions: and the creation of the Royal Society whose function was to investigate and report on natural phenomena of every kind. Protestant denial of Purgatory and subsequent identification of ghosts as largely either illusions or evil spirits tended to merge ghosts with demons, and therefore explanation of how ghosts were at all possible, with demonological theory which did the same for evil spirits. The two, it was thought, stood or fell together, and once the bases of demonological theory came into question so, inevitably, did those of ghosts. The attraction to and eventual triumph in learned circles of the mechanical philosophy which, by its very nature, precluded any such thing as a substance which was not physical; and its proposition that Nature was governed by immutable laws meant that unexpected interventions such as the marvellous works of demons or the reappearance of the dead were deemed impossible. Any occult phenomena were therefore attributable to the workings of Nature herself, and if one did not understand immediately how such things were done, one could be confident that, in time, after due investigation and experiment, Nature's hidden operations could and would be brought to light. Statistical laws and theories of probability formulated by European mathematicians – Girolamo Cardano, Pierre Fermat, Christian Huygens, Blaise Pascal, Jacques Bernoulli, Abraham de Moivre – contributed to the notion in learned circles that Nature had no room for chance, and that what appeared to be chance or fortuitousness was simply an event whose causes were not yet known. Old models, old explanations, old authorities were now redundant and, as the Restoration poet, John Oldham, wrote, men 'Make God at best an idle looker-on, / A lazy monarch lolling on his throne'. Even the Catholic Thomas White was prepared to say anent ghosts and haunted houses that 'most of our stories... if they were examined to the bottom would be found to proceed from the frequent cogitation and passionate affection of the living towards their departed friends'.[1]

Experience, meaning 'experimentation', became the watchword of the period. Hence it was thought that evidence of the afterlife might be acquired by deliberate manipulation of events. Joseph Glanvill, for example, relates one such instance. A Dr Dyke was asked to come to attend a sick child and was accompanied thither by his cousin, Captain William Dyke. The two men were obliged to spend the night in the house of the patient and were put up in the same bed (a common enough practice).

After they had lain a while, the Captain knocked and bids the servant bring him two of the largest and biggest candles lighted that he could get. Whereupon the Doctor enquires what he meant by this. The Captain answers, 'You know, cousin, what disputes my major and I have had touching the being of a God and the immortality of the soul. In which points we could never yet be resolved, though we so much sought for and desired it. And therefore it was fully agreed between us that he of us that dyed first should the third night after his funeral, between the hours of twelve and one, come to the little house that is here in the garden, and there give a full account to the survivor touching these matters: who should be sure to be present there at the set time and so receive full satisfaction. And this', says the Captain, 'is the very night and I am come on purpose to fulfil my promise'.

The doctor tried to dissuade him, pointing out that the Devil might take advantage of the situation to deceive him, but the Captain refused to listen and insisted on pressing ahead. The doctor, he said, could come with him if he wanted, or stay where he was and go to sleep.

But for his own part he was resolved to watch that he might be sure to be present at the hour appointed. To that purpose, he sets his watch by him and as soon as he perceived by it that it was half an hour past eleven, he rises and, taking a candle in each hand, goes out by a back door, of which he had before got the key, and walks to the garden-house where he continued two hours and a half, and at his return declared that he had neither seen nor heard anything more than what was usual. 'But I know', said he, 'that my major would surely have come had he been able'.

About six weeks later, the Captain went to Eton to enter his son as a scholar there, and the doctor accompanied him. The two men stayed for two or three nights, not together this time, but in separate bedrooms.

> The morning before they went thence, the Captain stayed in his chamber longer than he was wont to do before he called upon the doctor. At length he comes into the doctor's chamber, but in a visage and form much differing from himself, with his hair and eyes staring and his whole body shaking and trembling. Whereat the doctor, wondering, presently demanded, 'What is the matter, cousin Captain?' The Captain replies, 'I have seen my major'. At which the doctor, seeming to smile, the Captain immediately confirms it, saying, 'If ever I saw him in my life, I saw him but now'. And then he related to the doctor what had passed, thus. 'This morning after it was light, someone comes to my bedside and suddenly drawing back the curtains calls, "Cap! Cap!" (which was the term of familiarity that the major used to call the Captain by). To whom I replied, "What, my major? To which he returns, "I could not come at the time appointed, but I am now come to tell you that there is a God and a very just and terrible one, and if you do not turn over a new leaf" (the very expression as is by the doctor punctually remembered) "you will find it so".' The Captain proceeded, 'On the table by, there lay a sword which the major had formerly given me. Now, after the apparition had walked a turn or two about the chamber, he took up the sword, drew it out, and finding it not so clean and bright as it ought, "Cap, Cap", says he, "this sword did not use to be kept after this manner when it was mine." After which words he suddenly disappeared.'[12]

These compacts or covenants are not altogether unusual. In 1578 Chonrad Stoeckhlin and his friend Jakob Walch were talking about death and the afterlife, and agreed that whichever of them should die first would return (if God permitted), and tell the other what it was like. Eight days later, quite without warning, Jakob died and after another eight days appeared to Chonrad while Chonrad was out in a wood, cutting down a fir tree. This is Chonrad's evidence to magistrates after he had been arrested on charges of witchcraft, and it can be paralleled by many other instances from the Middle Ages and the early modern period. In the cases of Stoeckhlin and Captain Dyke, the ghost appeared to the person who had made the contract with the living friend. This does not always happen, as we can see from a nineteenth-century case recorded by Edmund Gurney. The speaker is Arthur Bellamy, and the date 1874.

> When at school my wife made an agreement with a fellow pupil, Miss W., that the one who died first should, if Divinely permitted, appear after her decease to the survivor. In 1874 my wife, who had not seen or heard anything of her school-friend for some years, casually heard of her death. The news reminded her of her agreement, and then, becoming nervous, she told me of it. I knew of my wife's compact, but I had never seen a photograph of her friend, or heard any description of her. A night or two afterwards, as I was sleeping with my wife, a fire brightly burning in the room and a candle alight, I suddenly awoke and saw a lady sitting by the side of the bed where my wife was sleeping soundly. At once I sat up in the bed and gazed so intently that I can still remember form and features. I was much struck with the careful arrangement of her coiffure, every single hair

being most carefully brushed down. How long I sat and gazed I cannot say, but directly the apparition ceased to be, I got out of bed to see if any of my wife's garments had by any means optically deluded me. I found nothing. Hallucination I rejected as out of the question, and I doubted not that I had really seen an apparition. I lay till my wife some hours later awoke and then I gave her an account of her friend's appearance, all of which exactly tallied. 'But was there any special point to strike one in her appearance?' 'Yes,' my wife promptly replied, 'we girls used to tease her at school for devoting so much time to the arrangement of her hair.' This was the very thing which so much struck me.[3]

This is one of many cases Gurney, who was honorary Secretary of the new Society for Psychical Research, reported as part of his endeavour to furnish scientific evidence for telepathy. Why, then, did the telepathy, if that is what it was, miss its mark in this instance? Perhaps, as Hilary Evans observes, because the husband was more receptive to the message, or the wife was in some way resistant to it.

But with increasing pressure among intellectuals during the seventeenth century to abandon a God-centred view of creation in which the Deity played an active role in the historical process both of nations and individuals, and in which the attendant realms of angels and spirits were either denied or disregarded, it is hardly surprising that cries of 'Atheism!' were bandied about. Robert South, preaching in Westminster Abbey in 1667, attacked the Royal Society in cutting style.

The persons here reflected upon are of such a peculiar stamp of impiety that they seem to be a set of fellows got together and formed into a kind of diabolical society for the finding out new experiments in vice... and, scorning to keep themselves within the common, beaten, broad way to Hell by being vicious only at the low rate of example and imitation, they are for searching out other ways and latitudes and obliging posterity with unheard of inventions and discoveries in sin, resolving therein to admit of no other measure of good and evil but by the judgement of sensuality, as those who prepare matters to their hands allow no other measure of the philosophy and truth of things but the sole judgement of sense... Such, as by a long, severe, and profound speculation of Nature have redeemed themselves from the pedantry of being conscientious, and living virtuously.[4]

'Atheism', however, is not necessarily a simple word to understand in this particular context. All kinds of considerations governed learned pronouncements, and a man might say somewhat different things depending on the company he was keeping. The astronomer David Halley, for example, found himself caught between his private investigations of the history of the earth, which he conducted independently of Scriptural authority, and the neuroses of the Anglican Church after 1688, which felt itself threatened by the new political establishment and in consequence tended to view unorthodox opinions of whatever nature as possible covert, or even overt, attacks on both its position and theology. Hence Halley's failure to obtain the Chair of Astronomy at Oxford, a professorship which was under the effective control of the Archbishop of Canterbury and the Bishop of Worcester. Halley, the Bishop was told, was a sceptic and a banterer of religion, both of which epithets were quite enough to have him called an atheist; and Halley did himself little good (if contemporary reports can be believed), by promising the Bishop that he was a good Christian and avowing to someone else that he did not believe in Christianity at all.[5] By the 1690s, too, religion and 'atheism' had become identified with political parties. Tories were Christians, Whigs were atheists, as far as the new Tory establishment was concerned, and the use of reason unaided by Scriptural authority or the light of God's providence was condemned as 'atheistic' per se.

The second half of the seventeenth century, then, can be seen as a period in which major shifts in religious and scientific thought were taking place, with the latter increasingly viewed as inimical to the former. The occult sciences – various types of magic, astrology, alchemy – and their attendant world views which made room for angels and demons and spirits of the dead began to fall out of favour in those circles wherein they had once represented the cutting edge of intellectual research and experimentation, and were relegated to the back rooms of 'superstition' and 'Papist fraud'. But the occult sciences have a way of reasserting themselves in the teeth of denial and argument and 'experience', and the radical sects which flourished during the Commonwealth eagerly promoted them all, complaining bitterly, for example, that Oxford and Cambridge were neglecting both natural magic and astrology. The so-called 'Family of Love' had links both personal and philosophical with astrology; some followers of Jakob Boehme, a German mystic, supported alchemy as an outward symbol of inward regeneration; and many magical treatises were now translated into English, so great was the demand for the kind of wisdom they contained.[6] All this gives some notion of the persistence of modes of thought among many educated men and women (and therefore hints at a similar unbroken persistence among the generality of citizens), which a small urban, and especially metropolitan, élite was busy rejecting; and we should be on our guard against applauding this élite as fellow 'modernists' and consigning the rest to the gloaming of Reaction or Superstition. Identifying with figures or groups in the past is a dangerous business, since the past is not so easily resolvable into Those Like Us and Those Not Like Us. That way lies Disneyfication of historical understanding.

Ghosts, then, remained and flourished, vigorous symbols of the reality of non-physical worlds or states of existence, and useful weapons to flourish in the faces of those 'atheists' and their fellow-travellers who, it was alleged, were seeking to reduce creation to a Godless, or at least a God-forsaken, mechanism. That the general public remained fascinated by ghosts and continued to experience them in one form or another as frequently as ever before can be gauged from an early English newspaper, the *Athenian Mercury*, which was published twice weekly between 1691 and 1697. Its purpose and scope are best seen in its full title – *The Athenian Gazette, or Casuistical Mercury, Resolving all the most Nice and Curious Questions proposed by the Ingenious*. The questions ranged widely, as a selection of the contents of the fourth volume shows. 'What testimonies find ye in history (the Sacred Writ excepted) that can give us assurance of such a person as our Saviour and His miracles? Whether a Dissenter is a schismatic? Whether bees make that humming sort of a noise with their mouth or with their wings? Whether interrupting discourse by repeated kisses be not rude and unmannerly?' – and were interspersed with anecdotal information: 'There being a strange story of an apparition' or 'It hath been my misfortune to be seduced'. But many questions were related to life after death – 'Do the deceased walk? Where are the souls of men to remain to the Last Day?' – and one of the journal's issues was devoted entirely to this kind of query. The editors, explaining that this issue was intended not only to give satisfactory answers to these questions, but also to reduce 'the many proselytes

of Sadducism and Hobbism amongst us', carefully published
it in All Souls' night, 1691.[7]

It is interesting, then, that after 1660, in a reaction against
the Heaven or Hell doctrine of Calvinism in particular,
attempts were made among certain Protestants to argue
for an intermediate state for the souls of the dead – in
effect an effort to re-establish Purgatory, or something
like it, under a different name. The effect, of course, was
to offer (or rather re-offer) an explanation for a persistent phenomenon which popular belief and opinion was
stubbornly reluctant to abandon, especially in the light of
its frequent and convincing experience, and to direct this
experience of ghosts in the direction of moral reform.
One says 'direct' because while the reporting of ghostly
visitations may have been made in many instances by
members of the public, the recording of them was largely
done by a much smaller group of educated individuals, many
of them clergymen such as Joseph Glanvill, who in 1681
published *Saducismus Triumphatus, or A Full and Plain Evidence
concerning Witches and Apparitions*, and Richard Baxter, author
of *The Certainty of the Worlds of Spirits* in 1691. Apparitions
provided not only proof of the afterlife and of its attendant
judgement of souls and their ultimate destinations of Heaven
or Hell, but also a leaven of vitality in what was all too
often the dull stodge of a workaday sermon. Moral exhortation could be enlivened by appeals to a not uncommon
experience whose very weirdness furnished its own sense
of verification. As Sasha Handley observes, too, this 're-
appropriation of ghosts by a cross-section of Protestant
divines in 1690s England was a pragmatic response to a
changing climate of religious belief and, potentially, a site of
confessional and social unity that could help to heal the
internal divisions of an increasingly fragmented Protestant
church'.[8]

Not every ghost, however, is the spirit of a dead person. Sometimes the living appear in a kind of bilocation. Richard Baxter records one such, relating to 4–5 June 1691.

Mary, the wife of John Goffe of Rochester being afflicted with a long illness, removed to her father's house at West Malling, about fourteen miles distant. There she died. The day before her departure she grew very impatiently desirous to see her two children whom she had left at home in the care of a nurse. Between one and two o'clock in the morning she fell into a trance: the widow Turner who watched with her that night thought her to be in a fit, and doubted whether she were dead or alive. The next morning Mary told her mother that she had been at home with her children. 'That is impossible, for you have been in bed all the while'. 'Yes, but I was with them last night when I was asleep'. The nurse at Rochester affirms, and says she will take her oath on it before a magistrate, that a little before two o'clock that morning she saw the likeness of the said Mary Goffe come out of the next chamber (where the elder child lay on a bed by itself), and stood by her bedside for about a quarter of an hour. The younger child was there lying by her. Her eyes moved and her mouth went, but she said nothing. The nurse, moreover, says that she was perfectly awake. She sat up in her bed and looked steadfastly upon the apparition, and a while after said, 'In the name of the Father, Son, and Holy Ghost, what art thou?' Thereupon the appearance removed and went away. She slipped on her clothes and followed, but what became on it she cannot tell. She confidently affirmed, "If ever I saw her in all my life, I saw her this night'.

It may be significant that Mary was in a trance-like state and about to die, for this peculiar condition could have loosened the bond between her body and 'something other' – her soul, her spirit, her doppelgänger – which would then have freed this 'something other' to move temporarily beyond its usual limitations. Homer seems to have been of the opinion that human beings exist in a double form, the body and the *eidolon*, a kind of image of the individual which co-exists with the body and is set free from it by death, and a similar notion can be found elsewhere in the folklore of Europe, especially that relating to mirrors. In Germany, for example, one must not put a corpse in front of a mirror or look at the corpse therein because that will produce two images, and the second foretells another imminent death. This is why mirrors are veiled while there is a corpse in the house – a very widespread European practice – and also because the soul of the deceased can, under certain conditions, be seen in the mirror, and if the image of a living person be reflected along with it, the soul of the dead may carry the living away.

But perhaps the most obvious example of a ghost, or ghostly figure, which is not necessarily that of a dead person is the poltergeist. We have already looked in detail at one case, but let us look at another to see what the two cases have in common, in what ways they may be different, and whether the passage of nearly a century had any notable impact on the way people responded to a poltergeist experience. This second narrative is recorded in great detail, almost in the form of a diary, so that we can follow very clearly what was happening from day to day, and in some instances almost from hour to hour. The account is given by the local minister, Alexander Telfair, and witnessed as true by the signatures of no fewer than fourteen people, five of whom were local clergymen.[9] Between February and the beginning of May 1695, we are told, extraordinary events troubled the household of Andrew MacKie on his farm in the parish of Rerrick, a coastal town in the south of Kirkcudbrightshire. Internal evidence tells us that the house had a thatched roof, with walls possibly made of wattle and daub, and an open fire fed by peat. The house was not old. It had been built in 1667, and there had been at least two previous owners, one whose Christian name has not been preserved, but whose surname was MacNaught, the other a Thomas Telfair. Andrew kept sheep and cattle, the black cattle and small sheep with coarse wool which were common in Galloway, but was actually a mason by trade. In view of what the minister recorded, it is interesting to see what was said about the people of the parish a hundred years later:

All ranks, both in their appearance and manner of living, make a very different figure from their immediate fore-fathers. The same reasons that account for similar changes that have taken place all over the country will no doubt apply here, these alterations being nowise peculiar to the inhabitants of this parish. The people here, in general, are peaceable, humane, and hospitable; have a lively sense of decorum and character; and many of them give indubi-table proofs that their minds are deeply influenced with rational piety. As an evidence of their sobriety and tem-perance, there are not two men in the whole parish who are so far enslaved by a habit of drinking as not to provide for their families, notwithstanding the many temptations they are exposed to from the variety and abundance of foreign spirits illegally imported on the coast, and (what is perhaps the cause of a still more general debauchery), the cheapness of whisky. In respect both of civil and ecclesiastical matters, the inhabitants may justly be said to be a people who 'meddle not with them that are given to change'. The farmers here, as well through the country at

large, are a set of civilised, conversible, and well informed
men, far superior to those in the same station in many
other places of the kingdom. Their line of business, being
chiefly in the cattle branch, by which they are often led
out into the world, and frequently into the company of
gentlemen who, here, are all either speculative or practical
dealers in cattle, gives an illumination to their minds and
a polish to their manners which those in a mere grain
country are absolute strangers to.[10]

This patronising, but not necessarily inaccurate account of
MacKie's community paints a picture which tells us that
their very different forefathers − of whom MacKie, of
course, was one − are likely to have been somewhat less
than sober (in both senses of the word) and less religiously
devout than the Kirk would have liked. But there is no
reason to imagine that MacKie and his contemporaries
were feckless or far gone in drink, or that they might be
unreliable in their reports of personal experiences. MacKie
himself is described by his minister as 'outwardly moral'
− a slight caveat, perhaps, but not one which affects the
story as it unfolds − and 'honest, civil, and harmless, beyond
many of his neighbours'. Rumours and reports about his
case had apparently been circulating, which is why, just as
François Perreaud had been alarmed at the distortions intro-
duced into reports of his experience and therefore wrote his
Antidemon to put the record straight, Mr Telfair undertook
to write an authenticated account of what MacKie had
suffered, not alone or in the privacy of his family, but in full
view of Alexander Telfair himself and many others.

MacKie's case was preceded by certain events which
throw an interesting light on a late seventeenth-century
Scottish village. Rumour had got about that when MacKie
'took the mason word', he devoted his first child to the

Devil. There is evidence that there was some kind of craft lodge or incorporation including masons in Kirkcudbright as early as 1691, and 'taking the mason word' is a Scottish expression meaning to be initiated into and take part in the rituals of a lodge. So it looks as though the secrecy attendant upon lodge practices had given rise to the foolish notion that Satanic rites were celebrated in the lodge, somewhat akin to the assumption that if witches met, they worshipped the Devil and offered children to him.[11] The minister, however, says that MacKie never joined the lodge and knew nothing about Craft rituals. But he and his family did have a distant brush with someone the minister calls 'a woman *sub mala fama*', which may mean simply that she had a bad reputation, but is likely to imply that there were those who believed she practised magic. This woman left some clothes bundled up in a sack with the MacKies for safe keeping and died before she could recover them. Gossip said MacKie and his wife kept some of them, a slander the MacKies denied entirely. Ill-natured tittle-tattle, then, had not passed by a respectable family, but the minister appears to have been satisfied that there was nothing more to it than spite.

By contrast, a previous owner of the MacKie's house does seem to have had deliberate dealings with a witch. Neither he nor his mode of business were doing well, so he sent his son to a witch who was living in Irongray, a parish about twenty-five miles as the crow flies north-east of Rerrick and therefore at least twice that distance on the ground, to find out the cause of his declining fortunes. It is interesting that he should send so far and that he should choose to inquire of someone at such a distance. Since it is unlikely there was not a magical practitioner of some kind living closer at hand, we may speculate that this woman had a reputation for being particularly skilled in detecting preternatural causes of apparently natural events, and that it was therefore well worth the effort and expense of undertaking a round trip of perhaps a hundred miles to consult her and get her diagnosis and advice. The son arrived, had his consultation, and received an answer; but on his way home he fell in with some foreign soldiers and went off to Flanders with them, and it was not until a number of years had passed that he met someone from the same parish, who was able to take back the witch's answer.[12] Why did the young man's father (recorded only as 'MacNaught' in the minister's text), not send to the witch again in the meantime? Perhaps he was too poor, or had no one to send, or died; for we are told that when the messenger got back, he found that MacNaught was dead and his wife had gone elsewhere. So it was not until the MacKies began to suffer from the poltergeist that the witch's diagnosis was reported, and even then, it was reported to the minister, not the MacKies. But knowledge of what she had said came to the ears of Thomas Telfair – perhaps a relative of the parish minister – who owned the house before Andrew MacKie, and it was he who came and searched under the threshold and found something resembling a tooth. This was evidently the kind of thing the witch had said was causing MacNaught his trouble – a *maleficium*, an instrument of hostile magic – and so Telfair threw it on the fire where it burned like a lump of tallow.

Was this the end of the matter? By no means. Telfair had actually never suffered any trouble or reversion of fortune while he had lived in the house, and since the *maleficium* had been destroyed, it cannot have been that which stimulated the poltergeist into action. The minister, having prefaced his account with this notice of what appears to be an unrelated incident of witchcraft, but which turns out to be relevant later, now enters upon a detailed report of the MacKies' poltergeist experience. It began in February 1695 with animals apparently breaking free from their tethers during the night, and a creel full of peats in the house being shifted to the middle of the room and set on fire. On 7 March, stones started raining down all over the house, a phenomenon which was to continue until the end of the whole haunting in May. It could not be discovered whence they came or what or who was throwing them, but they were thrown more frequently during the night than during the day, and more often on Sundays during time of prayer than on other occasions. Many were aimed directly at the minister. On 13 March, for example, the stones were small and did not hurt, but on the 18th they were larger and hurt when they hit him. On the 21st he was struck on his sides and shoulders with a big stick, an assault also suffered by members of the family and by neighbours who came to visit them and pray with them. On 4 April two ministers, Andrew Ewart and John Murdo, came to the house and spent the night in fasting and in prayer.

> But it was very cruel against them, especially by throwing great stones, some of them about half a stone weight. It wounded Mr Andrew Ewart twice in the head, to the effusion of his blood. It pulled off his wig in time of prayer, and when he was holding out his napkin betwixt his hands, it cast a stone in the napkin and therewith threw it from him. It gave Mr John Murdo several sore strokes, yet the wound and bruises received did soon cure.

On 6 April the poltergeist threw stones and fireballs both inside and outwith the house, and cast a stone on to the bed in which the MacKies' children were lying, a stone so hot it burned a hole in the bedclothes and remained too hot to handle an hour and a half later.

The incident of the burning peats in the creel which happened right at the start was also the first of many similar attempts to set the house on fire, although these did not really get underway until 4 April when the poltergeist threw a glowing peat among those who had gathered for prayer in the house. Next day the spirit set fire to some thatch straw which was piled in the yard, and threw the fireballs and the hot stone we have just noted. On the 7th it set fire to the house twice; on the 14th to straw in the yard; on the 19th straw in the barn; on the 27th the house again twice; on the 29th the house; and so frequently did it keep doing so on that day that Andrew MacKie 'put out all the fire that was in the house and poured water upon the hearth'. Yet still fire kept breaking out. The final episode in the whole haunting took place on 1 May, and that was destruction by fire of a little sheep-house, after which the phenomena ceased for good.

Stones are by no means unusual in poltergeist cases, as can be seen from François Perreaud's experience, but they also appear in cases of alleged bewitchment, and it is these which may prove to be of particular interest here. Joseph Glanvill, for example, records the trial of an Irish witch, Florence Newton, in September 1661, during which one John Payne gave evidence that the previous January, Mary Longdon, one of his servants, 'was much troubled with little stones that were thrown at her wherever she went, and that he hath seen them come as if they were thrown at her, others as if they dropped on her, and that he hath seen very great quantities of them, and that they would, after they had hit her, fall on the ground and then vanish, so that none of them could be found'. Fire-raising, on the other hand, *is* a somewhat unusual feature, since it is not normally part of the poltergeist phenomenon. Richard Baxter in 1691 noted one incident from *c.*1660, but the majority of others belong to the nineteenth and twentieth centuries; so we may take it that this poltergeist's fire-raising – and especially its frequency – is a noteworthy aspect of the case.[13]

The Rerrick poltergeist's throwing of stones, however, is not the only example of apportation. The door-bar and other things (not specified) 'would go through the house as if a person had been carrying them in their hand, yet nothing seen doing it', a spade was thrown at Andrew MacKie, and a meal-sieve was tossed about all over the house. Andrew MacKie tried to take hold of it and at last managed to get a firm grip. But the poltergeist's grip was even stronger and at last the mesh was torn from the rim, rolled up, and thrown at Thomas Airds, who was visiting the house. The poltergeist also threw mud at people, a missile preferable, perhaps, to the faeces which were thrown by a German poltergeist in Dortmund during May 1713.[14] Violence was offered to individuals and to people who happened to be gathered in the MacKies' house: not only were they liable to be struck by stones. On 22 March the poltergeist beat people with staves, poked Andrew MacKie several times on the shoulder, and then grabbed him by the hair. Others it dragged up and down the house by their clothes, lifted bedclothes off MacKie's children while they were asleep and slapped them on their hips so hard that the smacks could be heard all over the house. On 10 April it gripped and handled some people's legs, and made others fall to the ground by lifting their feet as they stood. It did the same kind of thing for the next three days. Andrew Tait from Torr came to spend the night with the family and brought with him a dead bird – presumably as an offering for the pot – but the poltergeist beat him with it, as it did three other young men who came in and settled to prayer. One of these, Samuel Thomson, 'it also gripped by the side and back, and thrust as if it had been a hand beneath his clothes, and into his pockets', thereby terrifying him so much he became ill at once.[15]

So far we may say the poltergeist was behaving more or less in the classic mode of its kind, except for the frequent fire-raising. But there are two peculiar incidents in this case which relate it much more closely to hostile magic and a form reminiscent of demonic possession. On 5 April the house was full of neighbours. Andrew MacKie's wife – (one cannot say 'Mrs MacKie' because Scottish women kept their own names after marriage and we do not know what Andrew's wife was called) – went out to bring in some peats for the fire and found a big stone loose under her foot. It had not been loose before, so next day she lifted it up and found seven small bones wrapped up together with some fresh blood and a lump of meat in a dirty old piece of paper. Nothing could have been clearer. This was a *maleficium*, an instrument of malevolent magic, and since the blood was fresh and the covering stone noticeably loose, the packet could not have been placed there more than a day or two earlier. Somebody was therefore either seeking to multiply the MacKies' problems by seeking to scare them with this device, or by intensifying the poltergeist phenomena with the help of deliberately malicious witchcraft. Andrew MacKie's wife then did something which at first glance may seem rather odd. Instead of calling her husband, or burning the packet – an obvious way to destroy its magical effects – she put it back under the stone and ran a quarter of a mile, in some distress, to the house of one 'Colline', that is, 'Collin', the name of an estate in south Kirkcudbrightshire. Now, one of the witnesses to the poltergeist is recorded as a Charles MacLellan of Collin, a 'landlord' (that is, an owner of some land). It was common practice for a landowner to be referred to simply by the name of his property as well as by his full title, so it seems reasonable to presume that

MacLellan was the man of whom MacKie's wife sought help. MacLellan came back with her, to find that the phenomena had been worse than ever: stones, fireballs, a burning hot stone flung into the children's bed, a staff thrust through the house wall above their heads and shaken over them. MacLellan started to pray at once, without removing the packet, and the phenomena continued remorselessly. But then he picked up the packet and they ceased immediately. He handed over the packet to Alexander Telfair, the minister, and two days later all those still alive who had lived in the MacKies' house since it was built were summoned by the local magistrate and, in the presence of several witnesses including the minister and Charles Maclellan were required to touch the bones 'in respect there was some suspicion of secret murder committed in the place'. Had anyone present done such a murder, it was believed, the bones would have given some indication of his or her guilt, such as bleeding or making some movement. Nothing, however, happened; but as the bones were clearly components of a magical device rather than the remains of unlawful violence, this was only to be expected.

Why did Andrew MacKie's wife go to MacLellan? He was not a clergyman or a magistrate, although he did own property and therefore had some standing in the community. Was it on the advice of her husband? If so, why did he not go instead of her? The narrative gives the impression she ran to MacLellan's house in a panic after discovering the *maleficium* without pausing to talk to anyone, and the implication is surely that she instinctively went to the person she thought could deal with this magical problem. If this be so, the further implication is that Charles MacLellan was an *unwitcher*, that is, someone known to have the power to lift or banish enchantment. We are told he 'went to prayer' upon arriving at the house. What kind of prayer did he use? Was it some kind of exorcistic formula, or a prayer used with exorcistic intention? It is significant that he did not remove the *maleficium* before he prayed. Are we to understand that his prayer was said over the packet in an attempt to deprive it of its power before it was lifted and handed over to the clergyman? The possibilities are various, but if MacLellan was indeed an unwitcher, then his status in the community and his acceptance by the clergyman and the magistrate as a respectable person speaks volumes about the place of magic in people's lives at the time.

While we are on the subject, it is also worth noting an incident which happened very near the start of the haunting. One Saturday the adults were out of the house and the children came in to find what they thought was someone sitting by the fireside with a blanket thrown over him. Naturally they were afraid, but the youngest boy, aged about nine or ten, plucked up courage and said to the others, 'Why are you afraid? Let us bless ourselves and then there is no reason to fear it'. He then blessed himself, pulled the blanket away, and found the figure to be nothing more than a four-foot stool turned upside down. It is the blessing which catches one's attention. The word used in the text is *sain*, which means 'to protect from harm or evil by a ritual sign or act, especially by making the sign of the cross'. Now, it is not really possible to suggest that the MacKies were Catholics, because their parish minister describes the whole family in terms of satisfaction with their conduct, something he is not likely to have done had they not belonged to the Presbyterian Church. So if the boy did make the sign of the cross on himself, it suggests that this gesture had lost its specifically Catholic associations but had lingered on as a ritual act to be performed in the face of preternatural danger – an essentially magical gesture in a context suggesting the presence of ghosts or evil spirits.

1. The *ba* visits the dead person. Tomb picture. New Kingdom period. The *ba* was the essential substance and vitality of a human being, which was able to move about, and enter into an image and so vivify it. It was commonly represented in funerary pictures as a bird, since a bird is free to move all over the place, even in the air, which a human being cannot do.

2. One of the judges of the dead. Egyptian papyrus. In many religions, the dead are obliged to undergo a judgement of their actions while they were alive. Ancient Egypt envisaged one supreme judge, Osiris, and forty-two assessors. If the dead person failed this examination, he or she was handed over to a monstrous being known as 'The Devourer', and suffered a second, total death.

Viro Nobilissimo. Excellentissimo, Domino DAVIDE THOMAN. &c. Consiliario Prov. Au
gustana Primario. Sebaldecha meritis. &c. Artium Fautori. Æstimatorem magno

3. Necromancy. The witch of Endor raises the spirit of Samuel for King Saul. At a
critical juncture in the reign of King Saul, he went to a female necromancer and asked
her to raise the spirit of the prophet Samuel who had recently died. Reluctantly she
did so, and the dead Samuel warned Saul he was about to die in battle. Controversy
over this episode was very long-lasting. Was the ghost real, or a trick, or an illusion
created by Satan?

4. One common method of communicating with the dead was through automatic writing. In this, an individual opens him or herself to act as a channel through whom a deceased person can move a pen and so convey a message. This message, attributed to the Mediaeval theologian Peter Abelard (1079-1142), says, 'All we who have taken part in Adam and have been led into deception by the serpent have died through sin, and have been restored to salvation through the heavenly Adam and have been brought back to the wood of life whence we are cut off by the wood of shame'.

Opposite: 5 Necromancy. Edward Kelley and an assistant raise a corpse for the purpose of asking it questions. From Grillot de Givry, *Le musée des sorciers, mages, et alchimistes* (1929). Francis Barrett gave clear advice on necromancy in *The Magus* (1801). 'Those who are desirous to raise any souls of the dead ought to select those places wherein these kind of souls are most known to be conversant ..... Churchyards, places devoted to the executions of criminal judgements, places where there have been so great and so many public slaughters of men, a place where some dead carcass that came by violent death is not yet expiated nor was lately buried'.

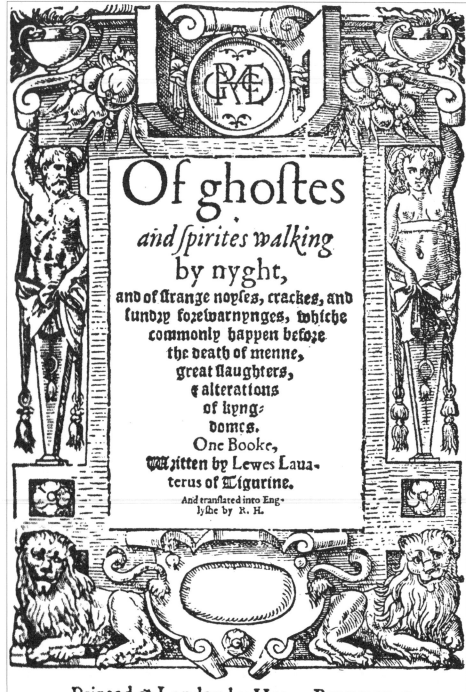

Of ghostes

and spirites walking
by nyght,

and of strange noyses, crackes, and
sundry forewarnynges, whiche
commonly happen before
the death of menne,
great slaughters,
& alterations
of kyng-
domes.
One Booke,
Written by Lewes Laua-
terus of Tigurine.

And translated into Eng-
lyshe by R. H.

Printed at London by Henry Benneyman
for Richard Watkyns, 1572.

7. The demon drummer of Tidworth. From Joseph Glanvill, *Saducismus Triumphatus* (1681). In 1661 a Mr Mompesson confiscated the drum of a demobilised Parliamentarian who then went away full of anger. From April that year until mid 1663, Mompesson's house and household were subjected to the full range of poltergeist activities – drumming, scraping, odious smells, personal assaults, and so forth. The case is interesting because the drummer was still alive. In fact, he was arrested and tried on a charge of witchcraft, based on these events in Tidworth. Found guilty and sentenced to transportation, he managed to evade the court officers and was never found again.

Right: 8. Ghost accusing the defendant in the middle of a court room. Daniel Defoe, *Secrets of the Invisible World* (1738). Defoe changed his mind about ghosts. After recording the case of Mrs Veal in 1706, fifteen years later he denied the possibility that the dead can return, although he continued to believe in the reality of spirits, saying that these can take on human shape for purposes of their own.

Opposite: 6. Frontispiece to the English translation of Ludwig Lavater's *Ghosts and Spirits Walking by Night* (1572). Lavater (1527-86) was a Swiss Protestant clergyman working in Zurich. In this book he gives four signs to help his readers distinguish good spirits from bad: (1) they are frightening at first, but then soothe and comfort our fear; (2) the form under which they choose to appear is a clue to their nature; (3) so is their tone of voice; and (4) a good spirit acknowledges and laments the sins it has committed.

9. Tombstone from Logiepert in Angus, showing the dead rising at the Last Day to the sound of the resurrection trumpet. The figure of Death is particularly sinister because he has a goat's legs and feet. These inevitably associate him with Satan, or at least an evil spirit. The spear or dart he holds may be a sign of comfort if the onlooker remembers *Psalm* 90.6 (Vulgate), 'Thou shalt not be afraid for the terror by night, nor for the arrow that flieth by day'.

10. Thomas Perks raising a spirit with dire consequences to himself. From 'Raphael', *The Familiar Astrologer* (1832). According to the Reverend Arthur Bedford, minister of the Temple Church in Bristol in 1703, Thomas Perks, a young man of twenty, consulted him on the lawfulness of summoning spirits and, against Bedford's advice, proceeded to an invocation which proved successful. Emboldened by this, he continued the practice, but one December night found he had summoned demons he could not send away. This frightened him so much that he fell into an illness from which he never recovered.

11. The resuscitated corpse. Nineteenth-century interpretation of an ancient fear. So great was the terror of some people during the nineteenth century in particular that they might be buried alive, that they arranged for warning devices to be enclosed in the coffin with them, such as a length of string attached at one end to a finger and at the other to a bell which could be rung in case of need. The picture is reminiscent of a twentieth-century Russian charm which includes the lines, 'I grab the hand of one deceased, who passed last year, who stumbled in the summer war'.

Marley's Ghost.

12. Marley's ghost visits Scrooge. From Charles Dickens, *A Christmas Carol* (1843). The famous sentence, 'Old Marley was as dead as a door-nail', came from a remembered dream Dickens had during a summer visit to Broadstairs. Dickens, like so many of his contemporaries, was fascinated by the preternatural, and his close friend John Forster once noted that 'such was his interest in things supernatural that, but for the strong restraining power of his common sense, he might have fallen into the follies of Spiritualism'.

13. Examples of automatic writing. Nineteenth century. From T. Flournoy, *Esprits et mediums* (1911). Mrs Verrall, a lecturer in Greek at Newnham College, Cambridge, described her experiences of automatic writing. The words, she said, came to her as single things and seemed to vanish as soon as she had written them. She perceived a word or two, but never understood whether it made sense with what went before. Although she was aware at the moment of writing what language her hand was using, when the script was finished she often could not say what language had been used. She was sometimes very sleepy during the production of the writing, and more than once momentarily lost consciousness of her surroundings.

14. A ghost almost entirely enveloped in its shroud, an image well-known in the nineteenth century from appearances of the dead during Spiritualist séances. Russian engraving. Ghosts dressed in their shrouds have been known since the Middle Ages, but the high point of perceiving them thus was the mid-nineteenth century. Good examples of the type can be seen in photographs by Édouard Isidore Buguet, taken between 1873 and 1875. Convicted of fraud in June 1875, Buguet fled to Belgium to avoid serving his prison sentence, and continued his spirit photography there.

15. Malay vampires. From Montague Summers, *The Vampire in Europe* (1929). In c.1902, Walter Skeat was told about certain Malay vampires. '[My informant told me] that he was walking down the main street of the town when he was stopped and asked if he wished to see some skulls. He had the presence of mind to reply in the affirmative, and was taken outside the town and there shown two skulls which had been feeding, it was alleged, upon the soul of a Malay woman. I myself then went to see them, and bought the two skulls for a couple of dollars, and brought them home'.

16. The fates of the dead. Nineteenth-century Catalan engraving. The wicked dead
are ushered into a kind of oven by a demon carrying a meat-fork whose blades are
pointing ominously in their direction. They go to the sound of drum beats, as though
they were condemned prisoners on their way to execution and, curiously enough,
carry their belongings with them – a case, perhaps, of you can take it with you.

PHANTASMAGORIA,
THIS and every EVENING,
AT THE
LYCEUM, STRAND.

17. Nineteenth-century advertisement for a phantasmagoric performance. The style of the poster goes back to the sixteenth century. It shows a necromancer raising a shrouded ghost, but the designer has made one serious mistake. The circle on the floor is meant to protect the necromancer against any danger from the spirit, yet here the ghost is shown standing inside the circle, which means that the necromancer is wide open to psychic or even physical attack.

DRACULA

6d.

BY

BRAM

STOKER

6d.

WESTMINSTER

Archibald Constable & Co Ltd

2 WHITEHALL GARDENS

18. Dust jacket for Bram Stoker's *Dracula*. Stoker made notes from a very wide variety of sources as part of his research into vampires. These include a cutting from the *New York World* of 2 February 1896 about New England belief in vampires, and cuttings about the vampire bat. He also found, in a book about goblins and Welsh folklore, references to a bat which terrifies the creatures of a marsh, and he probably read Sir Richard Burton's book, *Vikram and the Vampire* (1870), with its cast of blood-sucking demons and other horrors.

19. Illustration from Bram Stoker's *Dracula*. This picture summarises many of the peculiar fantasies of the late nineteenth century, combining sex and death and horror. A half-naked woman wrapped in a shroud-like sheet; the vampire fresh from feeding on her neck; a triumphant demon rising behind him; heavy chains hanging from the bed-end, symbolic of sado-masochism; a young man sprawled in a state of trance or terror or death; and the bed itself floating on clouds, as though to indicate that the whole episode is a nightmare which, to judge by the position of his body, the young man is partly in and partly out of.

20. 'Beth-Oni' in Tackley, Oxfordshire, scene of ghostly disturbances between 1905 and 1908. Ada Sharpe, who published an account of her experiences in the house, remarked, 'I have noticed, and it seems to me rather a cruel thing to do, that in houses where one room is known to be specially haunted, that room is reserved for visitors. I positively shrink form being put into the "Visitors'" room myself from the knowledge of this fact. After three years' incessant nerve strain to which I was subject day and night, I do not pretend to have regained anything approaching my earlier nerve power, or feel unprepared for unlimited shocks'.

Two days after Andrew MacKie's wife had fetched MacLellan to deal with the *maleficium* she had discovered, it was Andrew MacKie's turn to find something disconcerting in his yard. It was a letter, written in and sealed with blood. On the back it said, 'Three years thou shalt have to repent a[nd] put in good order', and within was written, 'Woe be to thee, Scotland. Repent and take warning, for the door[s] of Heaven are already barred against thee. I am sent for a warning to thee to flee to God. Yet troubled shall this man be for twenty days a[nd] three. Repent, repent, opent [*sic*] Scotland, or else thou shall'. There are several mis-spellings in this text, but the meaning is clear enough. Since the warning is addressed to Scotland, it seems as though Andrew MacKie was being used merely as a demonstration of preternatural power – the 'twenty days and three' bring us to 1 May when the phenomena did indeed cease – and since much of the poltergeist's violence against the person was directed at people engaged in prayer, we may assume that the apocalyptic tone of the message was aimed more at the community in general than at Andrew MacKie in particular. But it is an intervention which seems to have little to do with the rest of the incident. The poltergeist concentrated his activity on the MacKie's house and immediate surroundings, and upon anyone who happened to be there; and the violence against prayer is typical of an instance of demonic possession, if it can be said that an evil spirit possesses a location rather than an individual. Unlike the *maleficium*, the letter makes no sense in the context, and one is therefore tempted to dismiss it as somebody's attempt either to muddy the waters or to drive up the emotional temperature for purposes of his or her own.

So far we have concentrated on the poltergeist's violence. But this sprang from an entity who was neither invisible nor silent. The visibility, however, is odd. It happened on 21

March at night when the minister was in the MacKie house
at prayer. 'I felt something pressing up my arm', he wrote in
his report. 'I, casting my eyes thither, perceived a little white
hand and arm, from the elbow down, but immediately it
vanished'. He was leaning against the side of a bed at the
time, so could it be that this was no more than one of the
children who reached briefly from beneath the bedclothes,
perhaps in sleep, and touched his arm by accident? This
appears to be a rational explanation but actually leaves one
unsatisfied, since it is difficult to believe that a grown man
and (dare we say it without being patronising), an educated
one, should have mistaken so evident a child's hand for a
preternatural manifestation. No other sighting took place
during the whole incident, It was not until 30 April when
the haunting had nearly ceased that Charles MacLellan and
others who were in the barn at prayer 'observed a black thing
in the corner of the barn; and it did increase, as if it would fill
the whole house. [MacLellan] could not discern it to have
any form but as if it had been a black cloud'. This 'thing' is
clearly identified with the poltergeist, as the minister goes
on immediately to say what 'it' did next – throwing chaff
and mud, and gripping people hard round their waist.[16]

Most notable, however, this poltergeist spoke and spoke
intelligently for the most part, interacting with human
beings first in a series of noises and single words, then by
means of sentences or exchanges. It did not begin to speak
until the night of 2 April when it cried, 'Whisht! Whisht!'
(*shut up, shut up*) at the end of every sentence in a final
prayer, and then whistled so realistically that the MacKies'
dog ran to the door as if it had been called. On 3 April it
did the same and then fell silent until 6 April, that significant
day on which the *maleficium* was discovered and Charles
MacLellan came in answer to the pleas of Andrew MacKie's
wife, when 'it thrust a staff through the wall of the house

above the children in the bed, shook it over them, and groaned'. Once more it became silent until the 15th when it whistled, groaned, and cried, 'Whisht! Whisht!' during prayers, interruptions it repeated next day along with saying, 'Bo, bo!' and 'Kick, cuck!' *Bo* is a contemptuous expression directed at a man. The noun *kick* means 'dismissal, rejection', and *cuck* is probably *kukk*, that is, 'cow shit'. On the 20th it went on whistling and saying, 'Whisht!' but now added a sentence directed at the person it was beating – either, 'Take that till you get more', or just 'Take you that' – a growth of verbal confidence which finally erupted on the 26th into direct communication.

What happened then is best given in the words of Alexander Telfair's record.

The 26th, it threw stones in the evening and knocked on a chest several times, as one to have access, and began to speak and call those who were sitting in the house witches and rooks [*big, disagreeable women*], and said it would take them to Hell. The people then in the house said among themselves, if it had any to speak to it, now it would speak. In the mean time Andrew MacKie was sleeping. They wakened him, and then he hearing it say, 'Thou shalt be troubled till Tuesday', asked, 'Who gave thee commission?' To whom it answered, 'God gave me a commission, and I am sent to warn the land to repent. For a judgement is to come if the land do not quickly repent'. And commanded him to reveal it upon his peril; and if the land did not repent, it said it would go to its father and get a commission to return with an hundred worse than itself, and would trouble every particular family in the land. Andrew MacKie said to those who were with him, 'If I should tell this, I would not be believed'. Then it said, 'Fetch betters. Fetch the minister of the parish

and two honest men upon Tuesday's night and I shall
declare before them what I have to say'. Then it said,
'Praise me and I will whistle to you. Worship me and I
will trouble you no more'. Then Andrew MacKie said,
'The Lord who delivered the three children out of the
fiery furnace deliver me and mine this night from the
temptations of Satan'. Then it replied, 'You might as well
have said, Shadrah, Meshah, and Abednego'. In the meantime, while Andrew MacKie was speaking, there was one
James Telfair in Buittle, who was adding a word, to whom
it said, 'You are basely bred, meddling in other men's
discourse, wherein you are not concerned'. It likewise
said, 'Remove your goods, for I will burn the house'. He
answered, 'The Lord stop Satan's fury and hinder him of
his designs'. Then it said, 'I will do it, or you shall guide
well'.

Several things about this exchange are immediately striking: (1) the exchange happens at all; (2) the poltergeist is
coherent but not always grammatically correct, almost as
though it were speaking a foreign language (although it is
always possible the oddities are the result of the minister's
transcribing the abbreviated notes he may have made on the
spot at the time); (3) the subject-matter is related to that
of the letter written in blood, which suggests, perhaps, that
the entity was making an appeal for Scotland to repent of
its sins, by demonstrating its power over a group of people
chosen more or less at random for the purpose – an implication which would have its effect on how we regard the
letter in blood, which would then take on an air of preternatural authenticity rather than one of human fraud – or
that the person responsible for the letter was playing some
part in providing the script for this ostensibly non-human
warning; (4) it is not an exchange with one person which

could perhaps have taken place internally, but one which a number of people could hear and in which they were able to participate. Now, most of these points are those almost more appropriate to a case of demonic possession than a poltergeist haunting. In their review of 500 poltergeist cases mainly dating from before 1800, Gauld and Cornell found that while voices, groans, whistles and similar noises were present in twenty-six per cent, a demon communicated in only two per cent.

But I say 'almost' more appropriate because, of course, no one in this incident gives evidence of actually being possessed. The poltergeist remains an entity separate from anyone else's body. What are we to make of these exchanges between humans and the non-human? We could put them down to imagination. Was everyone present making them up? This suggests conscious and indeed collective fraud, for which there is no evidence; and we should in fairness admit that since the minister, Alexander Telfair, vouches for the honesty of Andrew MacKie, his parishioner, whom he must have known well, it would be somewhat perverse to insist that Andrew and the other witnesses were simply liars. Were those present experiencing a collective hallucination, or a series of individual hallucinations which became one in the minister's account? 'Hallucination' is a favourite recourse of materialists when presented with this and similar reports. It is well to remember that there is no single theory of hallucinations, so resort to this attempted explanation will need to define what it means by the word. Moreover, simply saying 'hallucination' in connection with these phenomena explains nothing. As Hilary Evans points out, the word merely points to some type of mental process which seeks to come to terms with something which could be a *simple hallucination* – that is, a perception of a non-physical being which has no separate existence other than that provided by the person who sees it – or an *hallucination* + *content* – that is, a perception of a non-physical being which does have an existence, an existence separate from its viewer.[17]

Simple sounds such as whistling or groaning are easy to make and therefore easy to fake or mistake. A whole conversation is different. There were several people in the house when the poltergeist decided to break into dialogue. It focussed its efforts on Andrew MacKie himself, but was prepared to enter into an exchange with James Telfair when he interrupted. Can we consider the likelihood of ventriloquism? It is technically possible for someone to throw his or her voice so that it seems to be issuing from somewhere other than the actual agent, but it is not a technique which can be used successfully by anyone, nor can it be used successfully without a good deal of practice. So if we posit ventriloquism as an answer to the poltergeist's ability to speak, we also imply either that someone in this small Scottish parish discovered he or she had the gift, practised and honed it over a period of time before it was required, took advantage of the poltergeist's activity to try it out with a few single words and whistles from time to time, finally used it to exchange coherent sentences with two people on 26 April, and then never used it again. (We can say this last, because there is no evidence from anywhere that any similar speaking poltergeist appeared in the area during the possible life-span of a Rerrick ventriloquist). Was such a ventriloquist a fraud – someone intending to trick his or her neighbours into believing what the poltergeist was saying? If so, are we to connect the monitory letter with this same person? If such a person was so concerned for the moral welfare of Scotland, why did he or she want (as the ventriloquist evidently did), to remain anonymous? Are we to claim, too, that he or she was responsible for all the poltergeist's other physical phenomena, and if so, how do we account for the mechanics whereby they were done? Or are we to assume that a ventriloquist who had never before given evidence of his or her gift suddenly found an opportunity of exercising it because, by a happy coincidence, a poltergeist became active in her or his community and thereby offered an unexpected chance for someone who had been nurturing an apocalyptic message and happened to possess the gift of a secretly honed ability to cast her or his voice to intervene in the poltergeist episode for her or his personal gratification? The more we try to rationalise the situation, especially without being in possession of all the relevant contemporary facts, the more absurd our attempts at explanation become.

Comparison with the episode at Mâcon shows that the two incidents have a great deal in common. They were largely concentrated within the environs of a single household – spreading somewhat further afield in Perreaud's case – and focussed attention on a single individual, François Perreaud or Andrew MacKie. Objects were thrown; both poltergeists whistled, groaned, spoke individual words, and had coherent conversations with the principal target – one in the case of MacKie, several with Perreaud. Religion was mocked and prayers were interrupted. In each place there were several witnesses to the various manifestations, and in each case witches played some role, either directly or indirectly as part of the general context in which the poltergeist experience was happening. There were a few differences, but these are not especially significant. Fires were started in Rerrick but not in Mâcon; there was no visual apparition in Mâcon, and in Mâcon the poltergeist developed an amicable relationship with a woman of the household. The similarities, which outweigh the singularities, however, are noteworthy. It may be suggested, of course, that someone in Rerrick had read Perreaud's book which appeared in

English translation in 1658, but this raises difficulties, most of which cannot be resolved because of our lack of information. Was the book available in Scotland at this time? Where did the supposed human agent for the poltergeist get hold of a copy? Why did he or she want one? Reading the book presupposes an ability to read, so was the supposed agent an educated person? Why, having read Perreaud's book, pick on Andrew MacKie and his family as targets? There is no evidence he was on bad terms with the minister or his neighbours, so spite does not seem to be an adequate explanation of this particular episode. Then there is the more general question: if the 'poltergeist's' aim was to bring about reform in Scotland as a whole, why choose to bully one obscure family in the far south of the country?

If we are to go down this 'rationalising' path, however, we must also take into consideration the poltergeist haunting of Gilbert Campbell, a weaver in Glenluce, from October 1654 until some time past the following September. Here the poltergeist is tacitly identified with the ghost of a beggar, Alexander Agnew, hanged for blasphemy, who was known to have borne a grudge against Campbell and threatened to harm his family. Stones were thrown, fires raised, the contents of chests strewn around, and Campbell's daily quota of work ruined. There was a single visual manifestation – a naked hand and arm from the elbow down, just as in MacKie's case – and several coherent verbal exchanges between the poltergeist and the local minister. The minister and several 'gentlemen' were suspicious of the spectral voice, so '[they] arose and went to the place where the voice seemed to come from, to try if they could find anything; and after diligent search, nothing being found, the gentlemen began to say, "We think this voice speaks out of the children" – for some of them were in their beds'. Notice that the men are puzzled, search for a hidden source, find nothing, and *then* try to rationalise the phenomenon by suggesting the voice came from the children. But as the voice continues at top volume and the theory about the children is not raised again, it looks as though the notion was mooted briefly and then dismissed in the light of further experience.

The incident was recorded by Henry More in a continuation of Joseph Glanvill's *Saducismus Triumphatus* (1682) and by George Sinclair in *Satan's Invisible World Discovered* (1685). Are we to wonder whether the Rerrick agent had read either or both of these works too? Gauld and Cornell also draw attention to the very close parallels between the Rerrick incident (1695) and one which took place in Naples (1696–7), and ask rhetorically whether it is likely that a copy of Alexander Telfair's account could have reached Naples – and presumably have been translated out of his highly idiomatic Scots – in time to allow some Neapolitan hoaxer to imitate MacKie's experiences in remarkable detail.[18] In the absence of any likelihood that the various supposed human agents were dependent on reading poltergeist accounts for their inspiration, it seems we must be willing to treat the incidents as separate from each other, and the similarities as springing partly from the basic nature of the poltergeist experience and partly from the ambience of heightened religious anxiety attended by consciousness of witchcraft or at least some kind of magical activity in the background.

As we have seen, the seventeenth century generated particular forms of unease. Foremost among those relevant to our subject-matter is the disintegration of demonological theory among some of the educated classes, which took with it ghosts, ghouls, poltergeists, and spirits of all kinds, including those of the dead, and raised the possibility that God, having created the universe, took no further interest or part in it, but left it to run itself like some complex machine, a theory which could be and was said to produce 'atheism' by many for whom traditional beliefs and explanations of the workings of creation still held good. As Nigel Smith points out, 'To be regarded as an atheist in the seventeenth century did not require a denial of the existence of God, but the denial of a divine economy of rewards and punishments, in heaven and hell; [and] in the writings of extreme religious radicals... forms of speculation were developed concerning the organisation of existence that located the divine and the hitherto transcendental in the natural world, or that construed the divine in terms of very basic human identities and processes'.[19] But if witches and spirits and ghosts really existed, then so did the structure of the universe upon which that existence was posited; so defence of the former, with attested evidence of their various activities, became an invaluable weapon in the hands of both churchmen and conventionally Christian scholars. In the words of an anonymous letter addressed to Henry More and published with the second edition of *Saducismus Triumphatus* in 1682, 'Too many deny witches because they believe there are no spirits, and they are so persuaded because they own no Being in the world but matter and the results of motion, and consequently can acknowledge nothing of a God'.[20] Perreaud's and MacKie's poltergeists, by contrast, roared out the reality of God and of their own existence, and thus established for those who would hear a most irrefutable set of arguments against any who might wish to deny them.

V

THE EIGHTEENTH AND NINETEENTH CENTURIES:
UNNERVING THE PUBLIC, INTRIGUING SCIENCE, PHOTOGRAPHING SPIRITS

There is something unavoidably histrionic about poltergeists. While other ghosts makes themselves seen or heard
for some specific purpose such as having a wrong righted or
exercising an innate malice towards the living, either of which
may be seen as solemn or at least serious in its intention,
poltergeists, while often frightening because of the violence
of their activities, nevertheless appear to have little more
motive for their stone-throwing or verbal abuse than sheer
naughtiness, in spite of what they themselves may sometimes
claim. In consequence, it is not really surprising to find that
– the ghost of Hamlet's father or of Julius Caesar apart – the
most common vehicle for representation of preternatural
beings during the late sixteenth and seventeenth centuries
was the theatre, and pantomime theatre at that. As E.J. Clery
has pointed out, 'the prototype spirits of the age were... the
devils of Marlowe's *Doctor Faustus*, with their fireworks and
grisly practical jokes'.[1] So audiences were accustomed to see
the manifestations of their deepest fears not only embodied
but also guyed in a kind of charivari which released their
tensions at the same time as it plated upon them. This was

a tradition which continued, *mutatis mutandis*, in eighteenth-century theatre. The effect can be gauged from a description of David Garrick's performance as Hamlet, which was seen by a German visitor to London in 1775.

> Hamlet appears in black... Horatio and Marcellus, in uniform, are with him, and they are awaiting the ghost; Hamlet has folded arms under his cloak and pulled his hat down over his eyes; it is a cold night and just twelve o'clock. The theatre is darkened, and the whole audience of some thousands are as quiet and their faces as motionless, as though they were painted on the walls of the theatre; even from the furthest end of the playhouse one could hear a pin drop. At these words, Garrick turns sharply and at the same time staggers back two or three paces with his knees giving way under him; his hat falls to the ground and both his arms, especially the left, are stretched out nearly to their full length, with the hands as high as his head, the right arm more bent and the hand lower, and the fingers apart; his mouth is open; thus he stands rooted to the spot, with legs apart, but no less of dignity, supported by his friends, who are better acquainted with the apparition and fear lest he should collapse. His whole demeanour is so expressive of terror that it made my flesh creep even before he began to speak. The almost terror-struck silence of the audience, which preceded this appearance and filled one with a sense of insecurity, probably did much to enhance this effect.
>
> At last he speaks, not at the beginning, but at the end of a breath, with a trembling voice: 'Angels and ministers of grace defend us!'
>
> The ghost beckons to him; I wish you could see him, with eyes fixed on the ghost, though he is speaking to his companions, freeing himself from their restraining hands,

as they warn him not to follow and hold him back. But at length, when they have tried his patience too far, he turns his face towards them, tears himself with great violence from their grasp, and draws his sword on them with a swiftness that makes one shudder, saying, "By Heaven! I'll make a ghost of him that lets me!" That is enough for them. Then he stands with his sword upon guard against the spectre, saying, "Go on, I'll follow thee", and the ghost goes off the stage. Hamlet remains motionless, his sword held out so as to make him keep his distance, and at length, when the spectator can no longer see the ghost, he begins slowly to follow him, now standing still and then going on, with the sword still on guard, his eyes fixed upon the ghost, hair disordered, and out of breath, until he is lost to sight'.[2]

What this meant in other visual terms is to be seen in the art of the Swiss painter Johann Füssli (Fuseli) who painted several scenes from London performances of Shakespeare during the 1780s and 1790s. Deeply influenced by Garrick's style of acting, he combined the techniques of traditional theatrical portraits with those of reportage recalled in the studio to produce *Gertrude, Hamlet, and the Ghost of Hamlet's Father* (1793), which shows Hamlet illuminated by a light emanating from the tall, still, armoured figure of the ghost partly lost in shadow. His hair stands on end, his eyes are fully wide and staring, the fingers of his right hand spread open in the traditional acting gesture of horror. The light has drained all colour from his face and neck, so that he appears to be more bloodless than the ghost, and his pose is one of interrupted flight, his right leg well advanced and turned away from the ghost, his left foot resting only upon its toes. Gertrude sees only Hamlet, and her gesture of fright and astonishment arises from what she discerns of his terror. The painting is thus both a record of contemporary acting technique and an interpretation of the effect this was intended to have on its audience. Such performances, of course, trod a thin line between genuine horror and unintended comedy or farce. Note, for example, the ludicrosity of the following speech from Matthew Lewis's extremely popular play (not a comedy but a 'drama'), *The Castle Spectre*, first performed at the Theatre Royal, Drury Lane, on 14 December 1797. 'Had I minded all the strange things related to this castle, I should have died of fright in the first half hour. Why, they say that Earl Hubert rides every night round the castle on a white horse; that the ghost of Lady Bertha haunts the west pinnacle of the chapel tower; and that Lord Hildebrand, who was condemned for treason some sixty years ago, may be seen in the great hall, regularly at midnight, playing at football with his own head'.[3]

But the emphasis on the physicality of ghosts (which did not replace the conception of them as non-material beings but ran parallel to it in popular imagination), may also have owed something to changes in attitudes towards dead bodies, which were evidenced in the growing popularity of dissection as both a public entertainment and a source of specialised instruction. Not for nothing was the place of such demonstrations called an anatomy 'theatre'. People were accustomed, of course, to watch human bodies being ripped apart during public executions which were often conducted in a festive atmosphere. As Arlette Farge observed of eighteenth-century France, 'Because society at that time was so visual and mannered, it was customary to interpret much on the basis of the body's signs and signals; for, before it is anything else, and least of all a public spectacle, the body is a language. Naked and dying, it was both language and spectacle. Its appearance and constitution afforded the spectators a vast amount of information and nothing was considered unworthy of comment or lengthy interpretation'. This could equally well be said of dissections a hundred or two hundred years previously. But the earlier interpretation rested upon slightly different presumptions; for the human form was then considered to be representative both of the created universe and of everything within it. Thus, to dissect a human body was to look more closely into the deeds and intentions of God the Maker, and so the dissector was performing a religious as well as an intellectual set of actions; and, as Jonathan Sawday points out, 'Throughout the sixteenth and seventeenth centuries, in the texts of French, English, German, Venetian, and Dutch anatomists, the injunction that to know oneself was to know God was continually repeated'. It is not surprising, then, that churches were often used as anatomy theatres.[4]

Deeper and more intimate examination of the body, however, had perhaps unforeseen effects. As anatomy formulated itself more and more along what we should call 'scientific' lines of inquiry, it gradually began to divorce itself from the theologically ordered universe, and therefore we may start to see a separation of the dead from their traditional geography and a tendency for the living imagination to dwell upon the physical horrors of dissolution, both of which affected the way ghosts were perceived intellectually and visually. It was a situation reminiscent of what Del Rio found particularly objectionable in 'those philosophers who are too wedded to the flesh. As St Augustine puts it very well "In a carnal human being, the whole system of understanding amounts to the custom of seeing with his or her own eyes". These people believe nothing unless they see it, and in consequence actually believe nothing at all'. This sense of separation also showed itself, among the learned, in the growth of a notion garnered from Classical studies, that death was little more than an everlasting sleep and therefore did not require the intense emotional preparation which both Catholic and non-Catholic societies had long insisted was essential, and in the new attitude of doctors that when death came it should be accepted, by the dying as well as by his or her death-bed attendants, as an ineluctable *medical* fact and thus endured with the kind of stoic resignation demanded by the new secularised philosophy.[5]

A symptom of the disjunction in the community of the living and the dead was lamented by 'A ruling elder of the Church of Scotland' in 1767:

> Our forefathers chose to have their houses as near to churches as possible, in order to have easy access to perform their religious duties in public, as also to keep them daily in mind of their own mortality, by having the church-yards under their eye, and more particularly the sepulchres of their ancestors; in which they hoped to be gathered unto them, and not to find a grave in a foreign land. But we their degenerate offspring, far wiser in our own conceits, and more polished in our manners, must have the parish-churches, if nigh to our seats, removed out of our sight as so many eye-sores, especially if they stand in the way of our delineated plan of policies. We will have them razed from the foundation, and rather than be thwarted in our desecrating inclinations, we will build others at a distance upon our own proper charges: And then the floor of the old church and the church-yard must be turned into a part of an avenue, or a bowling-green, into stables, or cow-houses, if not, perhaps, into a kennel for dogs! whose paws may scratch up the bodies, and their voracious teeth gnaw the bones of the dead! Shocking thought, enough to make one tremble![6]

It may be noted that 'a ruling elder' was observing and lamenting the behaviour of the gentry among many of whom fundamental changes of outlook had taken and were still taking place. If the Reformation had abolished Purgatory and thus, at least in theory, left the dead with no other apparitional role except as hallucinations, or illusory emanations from a disturbed or sick constitution, or as actors in tales told by an uneducated peasantry: the ideas of Descartes, Newton, Hobbes, Bayle, and Locke had combined to produce an intellectual milieu which elevated reason above authority, and an anti-metaphysical empiricism above traditional intuitive belief, and thus on the one hand encouraged scepticism with regard to all things supernatural and preternatural, and on the other an access of condescension and ridicule. David Hume expressed the new attitude in his essay on superstition and enthusiasm:

> The mind of man is subject to certain unaccountable terrors and apprehensions, proceeding either from the unhappy situation of private or public affairs, from ill health, from a gloomy and melancholy disposition, or from the concurrence of all these circumstances. In such a state of mind, infinite unknown evils are dreaded from unknown agents; and where real objects of terror are wanting, the soul, active to its own prejudice, and fostering its predominant inclination, finds imaginary ones, to whose power and malevolence it sets no limits. As these enemies are entirely invisible and unknown, the methods taken to appease them are equally unaccountable, and consist in ceremonies, observances, mortifications, sacrifices, presents, or in any practice, however absurd and frivolous, which either folly or knavery recommends to a blind and terrified credulity'.[7]

This may sound sceptical and enlightened enough for anyone. Nevertheless, we should not be misled into accepting 'the enlightenment' on its own propagandistic terms. The eighteenth century called itself 'enlightened' in contrast with the 'dark' Middle Ages, priding itself on having emerged from an age of superstition into one of scientific rationality. In fact, the eighteenth century provides us with as many examples of credulity as it does of rational thinking, and it is easy to forget or overlook the fact that a notable stimulus for the self-congratulation of the period's educated élite was the anti-Catholicism and anti-clericalism rife in both French and British societies of the time. Thus, for example, the 1765 preface to Walpole's seminal Gothic novel, *The Castle of Otranto*, suggests that Italian priests were deliberately working against the 'progressive' ethos of the period in order to 'confirm the populace in their ancient errors and superstitions' – a typical affirmation of the time, whose subtext presents to the reader a number of suggestive contrasts: 'modern' England/backward, superstitious Italy; English/foreigners; Anglicanism or deism/Catholicism; 'progress'/retrogression – while Matthew Lewis's novel *The Monk* (1795) opens in a church of the Capuchins where the bell has been tolling to signal the time for Mass. 'Do not encourage the idea', says Lewis, 'that the Crowd was assembled either from motives of piety or thirst of information... In a city where superstition reigns in such a despotic way as Madrid, to seek for true devotion would be a fruitless attempt.' An English version of the Characters of the fourth-century BC Greek philosopher Theophrastus, published in 1774, redrafts Theophrastus's 'Superstitious Man' as a Catholic:

> The superstitious man, oppress'd
> With fears that rob him of his rest...
> Suppose him of that church where laymen
> Clinch ev'ry Popish lie with Amen', etc.

In France there were complex reasons for changes in public attitudes towards Christian commitment, especially perhaps as evidenced in the way it regarded death, which pointed to an increasing internalisation of religious belief, particularly during the second half of the century, and thus to a separation between orthodox faith and its requirements anent belief and behaviour, and the new spirituality which rejected official religious systems in favour of personal choice and feeling.

The eighteenth-century German *Geistergeschichte*, by comparison, was not nearly so parochial in outlook, even though the German public was as keen on the genre as its British counterpart. But the ghost and vampire stories of the French Benedictine, Augustin Calmet, *Dissertations sur les apparitions des anges, des démons, et des esprits, et sur les revenants de Hongrie, de Bohème, de Moravie, et de Silésie* (1746), reflected a deep-rooted anxiety about the dead, one characteristic of the eighteenth century when it came to serious consideration of the topic, and one in which the dead were viewed with repulsion rather than awe or compassion. The stories also mirror the period's preoccupation with distancing the dead from the living, with premature burial, and with the link between vampirism and madness, which demanded that both the vampire and the lunatic be confined out of sight in a secure cell from which he or she should be sure never to escape.[8]

But the more some writers poured doubt or scorn on such subjects as ghosts, magic, demons, witchcraft, and other manifestations of the preternormal, the more others hastened to air a different point of view.

'We no longer believe in ghosts?' wrote Gotthold Lessing on 5 June 1767, 'Who says that? Or rather, what does it mean? Does it mean we are so advanced in our knowledge that we can prove the impossibility of ghosts? Does it mean that certain incontrovertible truths which contradict belief in ghosts have become so widely accepted, are so insistently and invariably present in even the most ordinary person that everything which conflicts with them must of necessity seem to him ridiculous and absurd? No, it cannot mean that. The statement 'we no longer believe in ghosts' can mean only that in this matter, concerning which almost as much can be said for as against, which has not been finally decided and cannot be decided, the prevailing mode of thought has tilted the scales in favour of disbelief. Some people do hold this opinion, and many want to give the impression they do. These produce all the arguments and set the fashion. The majority keep silent, they express no firm opinion, they cannot make up their minds. During daylight hours they listen with approval when ghosts are ridiculed but in the dead of night they shudder as they listen to tales about them'.[9]

Actually, what we see during this period is a continuation of the confessional battles of the sixteenth and seventeenth centuries pursued in different terms. Whereas before the argument had been between Catholic and Protestant (both sides appealing to scepticism and belief according to the needs of their debate), the late seventeenth and eighteenth centuries set what they called rationalism against irrationality, and empiricism against belief, with advocates of the latter adducing continuing manifestations of the preternatural as proof of its validity and thus, most importantly, as defences of the Christian religion against the attacks of its rationalisers and detractors. Hence, for example, John Wesley's great and particular interest in various manifestations of occult phenomena, especially ghosts. The Wesley family, indeed, had personal experience of a poltergeist, and while some contemporaries tried to explain it as no more than a series of pranks played by servants and a disgruntled cunning man whom Samuel Wesley had denounced in a sermon, John was quite sure the ghost had been sent by Satan to punish Samuel for a fault committed some fifteen years before. Other personal experiences will have served to confirm him in his positive attitude to the occult. On 1 November 1724 he wrote to his mother from Oxford: 'Three gentlemen of our college were in September last walking in the fields near Oxford about half an hour after six, of whom the foremost was named Barnesley, who, going to cross the path, of a sudden started back and turned as white as ashes, but being asked by the others what ailed him, answered, 'Nothing'. The second man coming up to the same place seemed presently more frightened than he, and bawled out that he saw one in white shoot across the path as swift as an arrow. Mr Barnesley, hearing that, told him he had seen it just before; and both of them describe it to have been like a man or woman in light grey, but of so thin a substance that they could plainly see through it. They had likewise another accident the same evening'. [10]

Whatever the views of the learned, too, popular beliefs continued to be happy, even eager, to have themselves confirmed by accounts of preternatural happenings. Thus, chapbooks catering for popular taste came off the presses, giving accounts of ghostly apparitions, vouched for as 'full' and 'true', complete with illustrations, while pamphlets in large numbers took journalistic pains to claim the truth of their narratives in extensive title pages, as for example, *An authentic, candid, and circumstantial narrative of the astonishing transactions at Stockwell in the county of Surrey, on Monday and Tuesday, the 6th and 7th days of July, 1772, containing a series of the most surprising and unaccountable events that ever happened, which continued from first to last, upwards of twenty hours, and at different places*. What were these extraordinary events? Mrs Golding, an elderly woman living at Stockwell, apparently suffered the attentions of a poltergeist which caused china, glasses, and plates to fall down from their kitchen shelves and break on the floor. Then various other objects elsewhere in the house fell down and broke, to such an extent that kindly neighbours arranged for Mrs Golding's property to be removed in case of further damage and loss. These precautions, however, proved useless and breakages continued. Suspicion began to gather about the maid, 'a girl of about twenty years old, an age when female timidity is too often assisted by superstition', according to the pamphlet. The grounds of suspicion were simply that she appeared to be restless but otherwise remarkably calm in the presence of phenomena which left her mistress fainting with terror; and so in the end she was dismissed, after which the phenomena ceased. The case, we are told, caused a sensation in London, but it was actually no more than one among many which made their way into print to titillate people's curiosity and exercise their ingenuities in finding some kind of explanation. Another case which had dominated the headlines more than half a century before was *A True Relation of the Apparition of one Mrs Veal*, published by Daniel Defoe in 1706. Defoe's version of the dead Mrs Veal's appearance to her friend Mrs Bargrave, and their subsequent discussion about death, is a piece of reportage whose veracity has since been questioned. Was Defoe consciously indulging in fiction, or had he been gulled by Mrs Bargrave? Typical, perhaps, of their different *mentalités*, the eighteenth century assumed the story was not true, whereas the twentieth was inclined to accept it. But whether true or false, the narrative struck the right note with its original public. As Parsons observes, 'What gave Defoe's relation greater currency than previous ones was not only its circumstantial wealth and the immediacy of the actual event, but the comforting assurance that "numbers of angels [hover] about us for our guard",

a message apparently delivered by "a good spirit, her discourse was so heavenly". In his optimism concerning the
supernatural activity that broke through to mortal sense,
Defoe was wisely keeping abreast of the times, like a good
journalist'. Defoe's reliance upon the apparent goodness of
Mrs Veal as a justification for treating both her and her
message seriously is of a part with his later remarks on how
one may judge the nature of an apparition. 'It is... difficult,
too, to determine whether the spirits that appear are good
or evil or both; the only conclusion upon that point is to
be made from the errand they come about; and it is a very
just conclusion, I think; for if a spirit or apparition comes to
or haunts us only to terrify or affright, to fill the mind with
horror, and the house with disorder, we cannot reasonably
suppose that to be a good spirit; and on the other hand, if
it comes to direct to any good, or to forewarn and preserve
from any approaching evil, it cannot then be reasonable to
suppose 'tis an evil spirit'.[11]

Ghosts of the dead not only continued to appear to the
living with messages from or revelations about the afterlife. They even invaded the courtroom from time to time
to bear witness against those who had harmed or killed
them, an accusatory role in the search for justice which
had long been one of the characteristics of the revenant.
On 10 June 1754, for example, Duncan Terig alias Clerk,
and Alexander Bain MacDonald were put on trial before
the High Court of Justiciary in Edinburgh on a charge
of murdering Sergeant Arthur Davies five and a half years
previously. The initial charge came from Sergeant Davies's
ghost which appeared to Alexander MacPherson, begging
him to see that his bones be buried. Guided by the ghost's
description, MacPherson and Donald Farquharson went
to a remote spot in the glens and found a body reduced
almost to a skeleton, but recognisable as Davies's from the

sergeant's mouse-coloured hair tied with a black silk ribbon, and fragments of clothing which were enough to identify the remains. Despite an agreement between the various parties to keep silent about the spectral visitation, news of it leaked out, with MacPherson swearing he had seen the ghost a second time, on which occasion he was told the names of the murderers.

During its first appearance, the ghost was clad in blue and MacPherson took it to be 'a real living man'; on the second occasion, however, it was naked. Both sets of conversation with the ghost – and one notices the interaction between it and MacPherson – were conducted in Gaelic, a language which Sergeant Davies had not known when he was alive but to which he resorted after death, presumably because it was the customary tongue used by Alexander MacPherson, although the defence advocate at the trial endeavoured to make a sarcastic point about it. But, as Sir Walter Scott observed, 'the inference was rather smart and plausible than sound, for, the apparition of the ghost being admitted, we know too little of the other world to judge whether all languages may not be alike familiar to those who belong to it'. The most interesting feature of the evidence, however, is that it was admitted in court in the first place and allowed to stand for consideration by the assize. So we may take, perhaps, either that the Lord Advocate presiding over the trial assumed the assize would dismiss this evidence out of hand – yet one is bound to ask why he did not instruct them to disregard it the moment it was presented – or that in his opinion the evidence was admissible, in which case we have an interesting light thrown on the psychology of this particular legal process and all those taking part in it.[12]

Needless to say, attempts at rationalisation were made subsequently, all dependent on the notion of fraud or deception in some form, and fraud, it must be said, was not only possible when it came to ghosts: it could be both sensational and popular. The Cock Lane ghost is perhaps the most obvious English example. A young woman called Fanny Lynes had died in February 1760 and her ghost returned to a room in Cock Lane in London, which she and her brother-in-law had rented for a while. Her former landlord, alarmed by the loud noises she made in response to people's questions, alerted a number of clergymen who then took up the case, and from then on the fame of the haunting rapidly grew. It was reported in the newspapers; sightseers came to the house in droves to hear the deceased Fanny give one knock to signify 'Yes' to a question and two knocks for 'No'. Samuel Johnson wrote a report on the spectral visitations, which was then published in London's daily newspaper, *The Public Ledger*. Books about ghosts, which had already been published, were reprinted; news pamphlets, ballads, and poems about Fanny were issued; Hogarth included a reference to Cock Lane in a fresh version of his engraving *Credulity, Superstition, and Fanaticism, a Medley* (1762); and both Drury Lane and Covent Garden theatres made haste to stage rival productions of Addison's comedy, *The Drummer, or, The Haunted House*, which had first been performed, to a lacklustre reception, in 1715. The smart set came to visit – Horace Walpole and the Duke of York, to name but two – but were disappointed to be told that there would be no phenomenon that night until seven o'clock the next morning. Even so, they stayed on in hope until half past one. The focus of everyone's attention (and Walpole records that there were fifty people beside him and his party crammed into a very small room), was the landlord's twelve-year old daughter, Elizabeth, since it was in her vicinity the ghost almost always seemed to operate. So it is not surprising that when 'Fanny' was exposed as a fraud in February 1762, it was because of the discovery of a block of wood in Elizabeth's

bed. This, apparently, had been used to make the characteristic scratching and knocking visitors heard when 'Fanny'
replied to their questions.[13]

Discovery of the deception, however, made no difference
to the public's interest in all manifestations of the preternatural. For typical of the period was the Gothic novel,
a medium which, by creating for its plot and characters
a circumambient atmosphere of tenebrous irrationality
affording the reader a pleasurable terror, in fact drew attention to the presumptions within 'enlightenment' and thus
presented him or her with a creative intellectual tension
out of which criticism (or at least a judicious re-assessment)
of the present could grow and fructify. Clery's comments
on Radcliffe's *Mysteries of Udolpho* (1794) illustrate the point
perfectly. 'The reader progressively moves from the sense of
mystery that encourages fearful, false ideas to full knowledge of the facts, intelligibility of causes, means and ends,
and confirmation of the truth of reason: in other words,
reliving the passage from gothic to modern times, a process
here invested with a pleasurable blend of relaxation and
control, licence and restraint'.[14] Side by side with this, the
rationalists sought to banish astonishment and its companion secret (i.e. occult) knowledge, both of which had
been identifying characteristics of the medieval and early
modern periods, and to replace them with mathematical
explanation of phenomena and a secular reinterpretation
of both religion and history. But we may note that this
latter shift occurred in intellectuals rather than in society
at large and that if the intellectuals' changed perception
of things gradually made an impression on others, it was
because, through the growth of popular education during
the nineteenth century in particular, those others came to
identify intellectuals as their superiors in understanding and
therefore hankered after joining their ranks for the sake of

increased personal and social esteem, rather than because they had cast off their instinctive traditionalism in some kind of enthusiastic embracing of 'enlightenment'. As the Roman poet Horace said, 'If you drive out Nature with a pitchfork, she will come running back, as full and complete as before' (*Epistles* 1.10.24).

What was the nature of these shifts in outlook during the eighteenth century? It was profound and affected not only the way subsequent generations have thought about their place in the world and the context in which they view it, but also their assumptions about religion, art, and desirable politics. In a word, it may be said that the 'enlightenment' set up an antithesis between Christianity and what were said to be preceding pagan religions, those of Greece and Rome in particular. Christianity (and, incidentally, the other major monotheistic religions such as Judaism and Islam) was viewed as patriarchal and authoritarian. Hence the 'enlightenment' emphasised the importance of the autonomy of the individual in the face of both historical and contemporary social, religious, and political structures. To justify this it turned (somewhat paradoxically) to the authority of Greek and Roman writers whom it misinterpreted in order to make Nature the great repository of the new ideals it was espousing. Exaltation of Nature – by happy chance a feminine noun in Latin – meant an exaltation of just those psychological traits which had hitherto been adversely criticised for being 'feminine': artlessness and irrationality. Thus a fundamental shift in perception of and response to the natural world had a deep impact on people's perception of and response to the supernatural and preternatural worlds, allowing on the one hand a certain scepticism towards the latter, based upon increasing acts of faith in humankind's ability to explain creation in purely material terms, and on the other a willingness to be swept away by the emotions of the moment as though these had an innate validity and purpose peculiar to themselves.[15]

Still, not all intellectuals were willing to adopt a sceptical tone if they had direct, personal experience of a haunting. At the Collegium Carolinum in Brunswick in 1747, for example, a recently deceased Hofmeister appeared to several of his former colleagues over a period of nine days, quite recognisable, although he sometimes failed to materialise completely. The apparition did not speak, but on one or two occasions manifested a melancholic disposition, while on others he behaved as a poltergeist by tickling and making noises and rapping at a door. Once the haunting ceased, the college authorities reverted to type by talking of silly deception and student pranks, and in 1748 one of their theologians published an essay in which he dismissed the whole episode as a fraud, libelled one of the professors involved as mentally unbalanced, and called for investigation and punishment of those responsible. There was, however, no evidence of any hoax, nor was any forthcoming, and the principals to whom the Hofmeister had appeared remained firm in their version of events; and it is worth bearing in mind that although sometimes there may appear to be a considerable gap between the relatively few learned and the much more frequent unlearned, that gap can easily be exaggerated. Consider the following. For thirty years at the start of the nineteenth century, Robert Hawker was vicar of Morwenstow in Cornwall, to which was added the nearby parish of Wellcombe in 1851. 'The people of Wellcombe', remarked Hawker's biographer in the typically lofty fashion of the Victorian *bien pensant*, 'are very ignorant. Indeed, a good deal of ignorance lingers still in the West of England. The schoolmaster has not yet thrown a great blaze of light on the Devonian mind, and the Cornish mind is not much better illuminated'. Mr Hawker, however, shared much of his parishioners' outlook. Whenever he came across anyone with an unusual eye, for example, he would make the sign of horns with his fingers in order to ward off the evil eye, and there was an old woman in Morwenstow he fully believed was a witch:

> If anyone combatted his statement, he would answer, 'I have seen the five black spots placed diagonally under her tongue, which are evidences of what she is. They are like those in the feet of swine, made by the entrance into them of the demons at Gadara'.
>
> This old woman came every day to the vicarage for skimmed milk. One day there was none, and she had to leave with an empty can. 'As she went away', said the Vicar, 'I saw her go mumbling something beside the pig-stye. She looked over at the pigs, and her eye and incantation worked. I ran out, ten minutes after, to look at my sow, which had farrowed lately. And there I saw the sow, which, like Medea had taken a hatred to her own offspring, spurning them away from her milk with their fore-paws in the air, begging in piteous fashion; but the evil eye of old Cherry had turned the mother's heart to stone, and she let them die one by one before her eyes'.
>
> Some years agone a violent thunderstorm passed over the parish, and wrought great damage in its course. Trees were rooted up, cattle killed, and a rick or two set on fire.
>
> 'It so befell', [said the Vicar], 'that I visited, the day after, one of the chief agricultural inhabitants of the village, and I found the farmer and his men standing by a ditch wherein lay, heels upward, a fine young horse, quite dead.
>
> 'Here, sir', he shouted, as I came on, 'only please to look; is not this a sight to see?'

I looked at the poor animal, and uttered my sympathy and regret at the loss. 'One of the fearful results', I said, 'of the storm yesterday.'

'There, Jem', said he to one of his men, triumphantly, 'didn't I say the parson would find it out?'

'Yes, sir,' he said, 'it is as you say; it is all that wretched old Cherry Parnell's doing, with her vengeance and her noise'.

I stared with astonishment at this unlooked-for interpretation which he had put into my mouth, and waited for him to explain.

'You see, sir', he went on to say, 'the case is this: old Cherry came up to my place, tottering along, and mumbling that she wanted a faggot of wood. I said to her, "Cherry, I gave you one only two days agone, and another two days before that, and I must say that I didn't make up my woodrick altogether for you". So she turned away, looking very grany, and muttering something. Well, sir, last night, as I was in bed, I and my wife, all to once there bursted a thunderbolt, and shaked the very room and house. Up we started, and my wife says, "Oh, father, old Cherry's up. I wish I had gone after her with that there faggot". I confess I thought in my mind I wish she had; but it was too late then, and I would try to hope for the best. But now, sir, you see with your own eyes what that revengeful old woman has been and done. And I do think, sir,' he went on to say, changing his tone to a kind of indignant growl, 'I do think that, when I call to mind how I've paid tithe and rates faithfully all these years, and kept my place in church before your reverence every Sunday, and always voted in the vestries that what hath and be ought to be − I do think that such ones as old Cherry Parnell never ought to be allowed to meddle with such things as thunder and lightning'.

A farmer came to Mr Hawker once with the complaint, "Parson! I've lost my brown speckled hen. I reckon
old Cherry have been and conjured her away. I wish
you'd be so good as to draw a circle and find out where
my brown speckled hen have been spirited away to".

The Vicar had his cross-handled walking-stick in his
hand, a sort of Oriental pastoral staff, and he forthwith
drew a circle in the dust and sketched a pentacle within
it – Solomon's seal, in fact – whilst he thought the matter
over.

'I believe, Thomas', said he, 'the brown speckled hen
has never got out of your lane, the hedges are walled
and high'.

In the afternoon back came the farmer. 'Parson, you've
done for old Cherry with your circle. I found the brown
speckled hen in our lane'.[16]

'Superstition', said Mrs Thrale in 1790, 'is said to be driven
out of the world; no such thing, it is only driven out of
books and talk'. One knows what she meant, but in fact
books (if by 'books' one means popular novels and plays),
continued to be positively eager to employ all manner of
preternatural machinery to keep their plots in motion and
enthral their public. One obvious example of this is the
vampire. The English word 'vampire' was first used in *The
London Journal* in March 1732 to report the hideous discovery that dead bodies in Hungary had been killing a
number of people by sucking them dry of their blood. At
once a controversy started in London's polite society, with
some supporting the credibility of the original sources and
others maintaining the impossibility of the phenomenon.
The argument spread to other parts of Europe, and suddenly
vampire scholarship became the rage, with some Catholic
writers' willingness not to dismiss the subject out of hand

serving to feed the presumptions of those already convinced that Catholicism = backwardness and superstition, with the French *philosophes* headed by Voltaire in the vanguard of indignation. Nevertheless, poets and novelists of whatever religious confession were happy to seize on the possibilities afforded by the subject, and the end of the eighteenth century and the beginning of the nineteenth saw such diverse figures as Coleridge, Southey, Goethe, Byron, and Polidori exploit the sexual potential inherent in the new Gothic version of the *vrykolax*.[17]

It was an exploitation one can see in one of the original illustrations to James Rymer's *Varney the Vampire* (1847). Here, a young girl is asleep in her bed, her neck and the top of her bosom and exposed to the mouth of a vampire in the form of a young man who is pressing his body spreadeagled against hers with his lips about to suck, not her neck but the top of her breast.[18] Crude though the engraving is, the bat-like posture of the youth contrasted with the composed sleeping pose of the woman is enough to engender a frisson of recognition. This is predatory male imposing himself on helpless female, and the voluptuous agitation of the bedclothes says all that needs to be said about the context. Once can see a similar, but very interestingly inverted message to the reader at the end of the same century in Bram Stoker's definitive novel about the vampire, *Dracula* (1897). Lucy Westenra has been turned into a vampire and recently buried, but she makes an expected appearance soon afterwards. Her features cause fear to the male party which is keeping watch, because of the contrast between the innocent Victorian maid she used to be and the sexually explicit woman who has taken her place. 'The sweetness was turned to adamantine, heartless cruelty, and the purity to voluptuous wantonness... By the concentrated light that fell on Lucy's face we could see that the lips were crimson with fresh blood, and that the stream had trickled over her chin and stained the purity of her lawn death-robe... She still advanced, however... with a languorous, voluptuous grace.' A picture by Dante Gabriel Rossetti has, apparently, turned into a drawing by Aubrey Beardsley. A similar emphasis on sexuality is made in relation to Dracula himself when he tries to seduce Mina Murray. The Count materialises from a mist beside her bed and then 'he pulled open his shirt, and with his long sharp nails opened a vein in his breast. When the blood began to spurt out, he... pressed my mouth to the wound, so that I must either suffocate or swallow'. What these examples do, of course, is to illustrate that fiction, whether poetry or prose, transmuted the original *vrykolax*, bloated with blood and bearing many of the signs of natural putrefaction, into a fully recognisable if somewhat disturbing figure which seems to be as alive as the genuine living. Dracula's first appearance in Stoker's novel, for example, gives no hint that he is dead, however striking he may have seemed to the young man who was visiting him: 'a tall old man, clean shaven save for a long white moustache, and clad in black from head to foot, without a single speck of colour about him anywhere'. The way is thus paved for the anodyne modern version of the vampire which, however theatrical its props, bears little resemblance to the more truly dreadful concept of the *vrykolax* of medieval and early modern times.[19]

But there are two particularly interesting points to note in connection with the eighteenth and nineteenth centuries' attitude not only to fictional vampires but also to other preternatural phenomena. The first is that in spite of the period's disdain in Protestant countries for what it saw as the superstitious backwardness of Catholicism and Catholic practices, it seemed willing to agree that only Catholic rites and sacramentals were effective in dealing with ghosts or

demons or vampires, and indeed there was a long Protestant
tradition that actually Catholic priests were more powerful than Protestant ministers when it came to the business
of exorcism of any kind. It is noticeable, for example, that
in *Dracula*, when Professor Van Helsing comes to confront
the vampiric Lucy, he brings with him a consecrated Host,
and a study of ghost stories in nineteenth-century Denmark
reveals that Lutheran ministers were not successful in getting
rid of ghosts, and that this inability affected their standing in the community. Secondly, there was an increasing
eagerness to explain preternatural phenomena by reference
to Nature rather than God or Satan. Thus, in 1823 a Dr
Alderson published an essay based on one or two cases
he had attended personally, intended to show that ghosts,
while real enough in a certain sense, could be accounted
for by various physical causes. His cure was to administer
purgatives. In one of these cases these were accompanied by
leeches, in another by foot-plasters. Dr Alderson thus had no
doubt that 'when there is no art, no attempt at imposition,
the whole is clearly made to appear a mere delusion, a *decep-
tio visus*, arising from a temporary disordered state of the
animal functions', and observed that the mind is capable of
producing remarkable effects on the body, adding, 'we may
fairly conclude that great mental anxiety, inordinate ambi-
tion, and guilt may produce similar effects'. He also noted
the possibility that ghosts could be produced artificially. 'A
celebrated conjuror or mystic mason with whom I had a
conversation some years ago told me he could give me a
receipt for a preparation of antimony, sulphur, etc. which,
when burnt in a confined room, would so affect the person
shut up in it that he would fancy that he saw spectres and
apparitions; and that by throwing his voice into a particular
part of the room, he could make the person believe he was
holding converse with spirits'. Likewise, the French physi-

cian, Alexandre Brierre de Boismont, who published an extensive study of hallucinations in 1845, observed, 'It must be borne in mind that an hallucination is composed of two distinct elements, the sensible sign and the mental conception...The hallucination which is the material embodiment, a daguerreotype of the idea, is only the bodily portion, while the mental conception is the psychical portion'.[20]

Now, this mention of daguerreotype reminds us that the eighteenth and nineteenth centuries had developed mechanical means either of creating illusions which could look to those who originally saw them remarkably real, or of recording physical presence by fixing it on a glass plate in the form of a picture. Optical illusions, for example, called 'phantasmagoria', were produced largely by means of the so-called magic lantern which for this purpose had the particular effect of making pictures projected on a screen appear to grow larger or smaller, or increase or diminish in brightness. The invention of the lantern is often attributed to the seventeenth-century Jesuit Athanasius Kircher who gives detailed instructions on how to make a device which will cause ghosts to appear and behave in just such a fashion, and the possibilities of his idea were then fully exploited to entertain the French Court at Versailles in the second half of the eighteenth century. The spectacle afforded by these phantasmagoria was described by William Nicolson in 1802:

All the lights of the small theatre of exhibition were removed, except one hanging lamp, which could be drawn up so that its flame should be perfectly enveloped in a cylindrical chimney, or opake shade. In this gloomy and wavering light the curtain was drawn up, and presented to the spectator a cave or place exhibiting skeletons and other figures of terror in relief, and painted

on the sides or walls. After a short interval the lamp was
drawn up, and the audience were in total darkness, succeeded by thunder and lightning; which last appearance
was formed by the magic lanthorn upon a thin cloth or
screen, let down after the disappearance of the light, and
consequently unknown to the spectators. These appearances were followed by figures of departed men, ghosts,
skeletons, transmutations, etc. produced on the screen by
the magic lanthorn on the other side, and moving their
eyes, mouth, etc. by the well known contrivance of two
or more sliders.[21]

The effect of all this on members of the audience was
profound. Accustomed to the obviously solid flesh of
actors mimicking the dead upon the stage, they were now
presented with figures which gave every appearance of
insubstantial reality – and indeed of recognisability – but
which behaved in ways no human actor could manage,
seeming to appear from the air and disappear silently into it
again. People forgot they were looking at artifice and tried
to embrace the ghosts, or struck out at them with a stick.
To eyes which had not had the opportunity to become
accustomed to the tricks of film or television, these spectres
which could appear from nowhere, alter their size, or vanish
by sinking into the ground seemed both astonishing and
disturbing. They were, after all, not projections from the
audience's imagination – an explanation for ghostly phenomena which was becoming popular among rationalists,
and physicians especially – but real images, even though
their reality was different from the reality they purported
to demonstrate.

But the psychological dislocation which these specta-
cles set in train was soon shifted back into the individual's
theatre of the mind by novelists and poets for whom the

very word 'phantasmagoric' became sufficient to trigger the desired heightened or even neurasthenic responses. Victor Hugo, Lord Byron, Sir Walter Scott, and Bulwer Lytton all made use of its possibilities, on the one hand employing the theatrical phantasmagoria as a device to further the plot of a novel (as in Bulwer Lytton's *Last Days of Pompeii*, 1834), or as a synonym for mental disturbance, hallucination, and other frightening evidences of extreme psychic alienation or delirium (as in Edgar Allen Poe's *Fall of the House of Usher*, 1839). But Castle makes a pertinent observation:

> The rationalists did not so much negate the traditional spirit world or displace it into the realm of psychology. Ghosts were not exorcised – only internalised and reinterpreted as hallucinatory thoughts. Yet this internalisation of apparitions introduced a latent irrationalism into the realm of mental experience... By relocating the world of ghosts in the enclosed space of the imagination, one ended up supernaturalising the mind itself.[22]

A good example of this point can be seen in a famous incident which took place in the gardens of Versailles in August 1901. Two English women, Charlotte Moberly, first Principal of St Hughes Hall in Oxford, and Eleanor Jourdain, a schoolmistress, were visiting the château for the first time. After touring the château itself, they went into the gardens with the intention of looking at the Petit Trianon, the house built for Marie Antoinette in 1774. The two women followed a somewhat circuitous route and thought they had lost their way; so they asked directions of two men in grey-green coats, whom they took to be gardeners. Not long after, they felt oppressed and wearied, but pressed on until they came in sight of the Petit Trianon. There they saw various people, including a middle-aged woman in a summer dress, and finally arrived at the house in time to join a wedding party which was having a guided tour. During the course of the next few months, Charlotte and Eleanor came to the tentative notion that what they had seen during the course of their detour was a vision of that part of the gardens, not as they were in 1901, but as they had been in the mid-eighteenth century, and that the people they had met were entities of that earlier period. Subsequent repeated visits to the Petit Trianon and its environs by Eleanor revealed that the geography of the present time was different from that which she and Charlotte had encountered, and after the two women had investigated further the history of the Petit Trianon and its inhabitants, they published, in January 1911, an account of their visionary experience under the title *An Adventure*.

The little book attracted supporters and sceptics from the start. Sceptics have tended to follow the suggestion that Charlotte and Eleanor had come across a rehearsal for a fancy-dress party staged by Comte Robert Montesquiou-Fezenzac, and make much of differences in the two women's original written account, the fact that they were feeling faint and tired in the heat of the day, and that the Petit Trianon is a romantic spot, so that a degree of unconscious wish-fulfilment to see the place as it used to be may have been involved. In other words, the women constructed a scene within the theatre of their minds, one which seemed real both at the time and in retrospect. Supporters, however, have challenged these versions of events (pointing out, for example, that actually Montesquiou was nowhere near Versailles in August 1901), and have advanced instead the thesis that modern physics allow us to envisage the possibility that past, present, and future can exist simultaneously from the point of view of an observer located in space-time, and that in consequence a metaphysical experience such as Charlotte and Eleanor claimed to have undergone might be possible and valid. One is reminded of William James's observation after his experiments with breathing nitrous oxide:

> One conclusion was forced upon my mind at the time, and my impression of its truth has ever since remained unshaken. It is that our normal waking consciousness, rational consciousness as we call it, is but one special type of consciousness, whilst all about it, parted from it by the filmiest of screens, there lie potential forms of consciousness entirely different.[23]

But if there has never been any serious suggestion that Charlotte and Eleanor were actually lying, the same cannot be said for spirit photography which, unfortunately, has been seen to lend itself to fraud both on the part of the sitter and of the photographer, although it should be added that fraud cannot always explain the presence of unexpected entities in the finished picture. The earliest spirit photograph was exhibited in 1860 at a meeting of the American Photographic Society. It showed a chair which had been empty at the time of the glass plate's exposure, but which was now seen to be occupied by a small boy who had not been in the studio at all. The most famous American spirit photographer of the period was William Mumler who claimed to be a medium through whom the spirits worked, if they chose, to make themselves visible on film. Spiritualists, it must be said, were not convinced and attacked him as a fraud. He was indicted and brought to trial in April–May 1869 and then acquitted, although the trial judge openly said after the verdict that he himself was morally convinced there actually had been deception. Spirit photography came to London in March 1872 in the studio of Frederick Hudson who photographed a couple, Samuel and Elizabeth Guppy, with Elizabeth intentionally trying to influence the camera to produce vital evidence of spirits. She seems to have been successful, since the three photographs which were taken showed an unfocussed figure standing behind Samuel. Again, as in Mumler's case, accusations of fraud followed an initial rush of interest, and people were split between those who thought they detected evidence of superimposition or double exposure and those who were convinced that some, at least, of Hudson's spirit photographs were genuine. Various theories were adduced to show that spirit photography worked according to rules from the regular version, and spirits themselves were consulted about the problem. Their explanation was straightforward enough. 'The success of our manifestations in these cases', they said, 'is to bring ourselves within the sphere of the sitter, and to amalgam that sphere with our own. When rays of light pass through the mixed aura, they are refracted and often cause things to be apparent on the plate which you cannot account for'. The spirits also played an active role in the photographic process, giving instructions, for example, via movements of the table on which the camera was placed, on how the photographer and his medium-assistant should proceed. In the end, however, despite every attempt to establish a dossier of photographs whose authenticity would prove beyond challenge, public confidence in spirit photography waned and has never since been re-established.[24]

Interest in this technique had been generated by the relatively recent phenomenon of table-rapping or table-turning or 'Spiritualism', as it was to be known later; and it can be said of Spiritualism, as it has been said of the occult sciences, that it was important to many because it directly challenged the scientific materialism of the nineteenth century:

The lure of the occult, from the 1870s to World War I, lay precisely in its antipathy to the strictly rational, empiricist outlook that was increasingly perceived as the hallmark of Victorian thought. Involvement in occult studies provided one means of challenging and of discarding a frame of mind that seemed to glory only in the concrete, the factual, and the substantive.[25]

Believers in Spiritualism consisted of the professional middle classes and the better educated working class. Indeed, working men in particular were supportive of Spiritualism, and it is thus no accident that the greatest concentration of Spiritualist societies in England was to be found in the industrialised north. Here especially could be found a rejection of Christianity as exemplified by the mainstream churches, either because its doctrines were perceived as inadequate or incredible, or because its demands upon the individual's behaviour were felt to be excessively narrow; and Darwin's theory of evolving species presented Spiritualists with the very attractive notion of continuous evolution beyond the death of the body. 'What Spiritualism does bring to light', wrote an Oxford essayist,

> is the prospect of a progressive future for human beings – no sudden break, no violent transformation – death but the birth into another sphere of existence, a sphere in which every human being is exactly that which himself and society have made him…There, as here, are all grades and varieties of being, and it is the work of the higher to lead up the lower.[26]

Table-rapping began at Hydesville in up-state New York in 1848. There, two teenage sisters, Kate and Margaret Fox, were found to have mediumistic powers. Ghosts manifested themselves audibly by a series of raps which were quickly regulated into a code whereby meaningful answers to questions posed by the living could be given by the dead. The girls' mother was not slow to permit them to demonstrate their skills in public séances all round the United States, where their growing fame generated an extraordinary interest in Spiritualism in many different forms. That Margaret confessed in 1888 that she and her sister had faked the ghostly noises by popping their toe or knee joints made no difference to this enthusiasm. Spirit writing on slates or paper, communications via the planchette, and materialisations of the dead through ectoplasm produced by both male and female mediums rapidly became commonplace in both the United States and Europe. For these séances answered a deep-felt need of the time.

> A shadow flits before me,
> Not thou, but like to thee:
> Ah Christ, that it were possible
> For one short hour to see
> The souls we loved that they might tell us
> What and where they be.

Thus Tennyson wrote in *Maud*, 1855. In consequence, the nineteenth century found a certain comfort in ghost stories which proliferated in its literature. These narratives which treated of the spirit world provided the living with a means of retaining contact with the dead and a way of exploring their mutual relationship. But Tennyson's melancholy is not surprising. Nineteenth-century intellectuals had inherited a combination of deism and doubt from their eighteenth-century predecessors, and after the publication of Lyell's *Elements of Geology* (1838), Chambers's *Vestiges of Creation* (1844), and Darwin's *Origin of Species* (1859), turned from one fundamentalism called 'Biblical Christianity' to another called 'Science' for answers to their longings for an explanation of the mysteries of the universe. It was a new faith inherited by the twentieth century. As Gordon points out, the rationality of modernism has a technological commitment to finding solutions for everything, and it believes, as fervently as any medieval mystic who turned his faith towards God, that one or other of the sciences will answer all questions of any kind which may occur to humanity. Nevertheless, the nineteenth century did not give way entirely to technological science. It is notable, for example, that several influential Socialists such as Fourier, Leroux, and Esquinos, inheritors, one might think, of anticlericalism and an atheistic determinism, developed ideologies in which speculation about the afterlife played an important role; while after 1850, Spiritualism became almost as much a pervasive activity in French intellectual circles as it was in those across the Channel, although French Spiritualism emphasised the importance of astronomy in its concept of how the soul evolved after death and where it did so, as opposed to England where psychology, biology, and physics were more prominent in debates between Spiritualism and the sciences.[27]

Attendance at and investigation of séances, then, should not be regarded as merely the diversion of the immovably credulous. To some extent they were the natural successors to phantasmagoric performances, and both had certain things in common. They took place in darkness; there was an expectation of seeing non-material phenomena; apparently unearthly sounds added to the heightened atmosphere and were meant to provide verification to any visual apparitions which might be manifested; such phenomena as did appear were often taken to be real; and both kinds of session were open to fraudulent manipulation of their audience. Doubts, of course, there were and they were frequently expressed from unexpected quarters. Daniel Dunglas Home, for example (about whom, it must be admitted, there has been controversy right from the start), was one of the most famous mediums of the nineteenth century. Yet it was he who, most successfully, exposed mediumistic fraud in a chapter of his book, *Lights and Shadows of Spiritualism*, published in 1877. It might be said, of course, that he was in a perfect position to do so: both poacher and gamekeeper. His own activities were remarkable, judge them how we may. Some were the same as those performed by other mediums; during sessions at which he was present, furniture rose from the floor, objects soared through the air, and spirit limbs manifested. But others were peculiar to himself. On one occasion, in the presence of three witnesses, he is reputed to have levitated and floated out of the window of one room of a private house, re-entering via the window of an adjacent room. On another, again in a private house, with several witnesses, it was recorded that 'Home flung himself back in his chair, looking wild and white; and then rising slowly and solemnly, went to the still bright fire, into which he thrust his unprotected hands, and taking out a double handful of live coals, placed them – as a fire offering – upon Mr Hall's snow-white head, combing the hair over them with his fingers, all which our host appeared to receive more than patiently'. Needless to say, Home, like many other mediums of his day, was investigated several times by sceptics intent on exposing him as a fraud; but, unlike many other mediums, he never suffered any such exposure, although there were those who could not bring themselves to accept that he was genuine. The most famous of those doubters was Robert Browning whose poem, *Mr Sludge, the Medium*, is a vitriolic attack on both Home in particular and Spiritualism in general.[28]

Séances differed, of course, from medium to medium and occasion to occasion. Flournoy has classified medi-

ums as 'real', 'pseudo', and 'false', the difference between
the last two being that pseudo-mediums do not possess
genuine psychic abilities but, by luck or coincidence, appear
to be able to summon or interpret real phenomena, and
false mediums are simply frauds. Spiritualist phenomena
may also be classified. There are, for example, those that
are significant because of their intellectual content, such
as messages or prophecies; those that are not significant in
themselves – noises, sudden movements, and so forth – but
that may become significant if allied with other meaningful
signs; those that produce a sudden access of emotion such
as sadness or deep pain; those that result from intuition; and
those that stem from a person's physical condition, such as
sleeping or reverie. In consequence, what happened during
a séance depended very much on an interplay between
these various possibilities as well, of course, as the psychic
complexity created by the various predispositions of the
various members of the audience. Generally speaking, however, séances tended to have certain features more or less
in common. They usually took place in near darkness, with
perhaps one light turned very low to give minimal illumination. The medium, most often a woman, would enter a
'cabinet', a small area screened by curtains, in which she
seated herself and went into a trance. Spirits might then
appear. These could take the form of full human shapes
coagulated from ectoplasm; or ghostly musical instruments
were made to sound by invisible spirits; or voices without form gave messages to or held conversations with the
living. Clearly, as I have said already, there are parallels here
between the theatricality of the phantasmagoria and that
of the ectoplasmic materialisations, some of which were
self-evidently a combination of muslin cloth and mask, but
some of which convinced individual members of the audience that a genuine manifestation had occurred. In either

case, the audience was likely to be split in its reactions, just as the audiences of the phantasmagoria had been, between those who retained awareness that they were witnessing a preconstructed dramatic performance and those whose disbelief was suspended entirely.[29]

But the very fact that the nineteenth century was the age of both technological advance and religious doubt meant that people were almost bound to take a special interest in communicating with the dead. After all, if it was possible to talk to someone who was not physically present by using the new device of the telephone, why should it not also be possible to communicate with the dead by using the age-old instrument of the medium? Moreover, if this last could be proved possible according to scientific criteria, would this not provide irrefutable proof of survival after death, and therefore proof also of the validity of religious doctrine concerning it? It was in Cambridge in 1874 that a group of scholars and political men began to investigate Spiritualist claims, thought transference, and similar occult phenomena in a series of experiments which led to the foundation of the Society for Psychical Research. One of the original members, later President, of the Society, Henry Sidgwick, explained their motives in his presidential address of 1888:

> We believed unreservedly in the methods of modern science, and were prepared to accept submissively her reasoned conclusions, when sustained by the agreement of experts; but we were not prepared to bow with equal docility to the mere prejudices of scientific men. And it appeared to us that there was an important body of evidence – tending prima facie to establish the independence of soul or spirit – which modern science had simply left on one side with ignorant contempt; and that in so leaving it she had been untrue to her professed

method, and had arrived prematurely at her negative conclusions.

Consequently, members of the SPR undertook an immense programme of investigation of ghostly phenomena, stimulated thereto by the thousands of letters they received from people all over Britain. The results were published in a number of surveys which noted how many cases had been examined and discussed many of them in some detail. Many of the reported apparitions were traditional, in the sense that the ghosts seemed to have returned in order to convey a message, fulfil a pact with the living, or reveal the existence of lost items or treasure-trove. Others gave, by their very appearing, an unexpected notice that they had died. Haunted houses figure frequently in the reports, and when these make their way into literature it is clear that the legacy of the Gothic novel had not been forgotten, since the locus of the action so often takes place in a ruined monastery or converted convent.[30] But some of the statistics revealed by the report are particularly interesting. More women than men reported apparitions (sixty-one per cent to thirty-nine per cent); a much larger percentage of these apparitions were of people known to be alive than of figures known to be dead (forty-four per cent to sixteen per cent), while forty per cent were of complete strangers, quite a contrast with earlier times when ghosts were almost always known to the viewer. Apparitions, it seems, may also be seen by anyone at all, regardless of the individual's education, social status, religious belief, or lack of it. They appear in daylight as often as during the hours of darkness; they can be seen both indoors and out; and their appearance may be entirely lifelike or filmy. The ghost may be seen or heard or both, although it is not at all common for the apparition to speak, another contrast between the modern ghost and its earlier counterpart which usually appeared precisely in order to convey a spoken message to the living. The ghost may interact with the onlookers or ignore them; but the drop in surrounding temperature, so well known as a distinctive accompaniment to a haunting, actually may not always occur. All this the SPR took in its stride, resolutely adhering in its interpretation of the data to the scientific method or frame of mind which Henry Sidgwick declared was the bedrock of its method.

Of course, Spiritualism in its various forms attracted not only scepticism but also opposition, not least from the Catholic Church which saw several dangers in it. First, it was becoming allied with undesirable forces in nineteenth-century intellectual life, which led (it was felt) to atheism and materialism. Secondly, in both France and Spain especially it appealed to anticlerical sentiment and thus to rebellion against the Church's teaching and discipline. It was claimed, for example, that in April 1864 the dead Bishop of Cadiz appeared to a group of citizens and declared he was no longer a Catholic and put his trust in science instead. Thirdly, by accepting the reality of preternatural phenomena it posed a difficulty for the Church, in as much as while the Church obviously agreed that such phenomena both might and did exist, she was aware, as she had always been, of the role played by Satan in manufacturing illusions for his own purposes, and therefore thought it best for the individual's spiritual safety that he or she avoid any occasion which might tempt Satan to practise his potentially damnable arts of deception. But Sharp reminds us of the important additional point that, far from being a rural phenomenon, Spiritualism was especially attractive to urban dwellers who were more easily exposed to the rationalism of contemporary science. These people therefore represent a major and swiftly expanding section of society which was both prepared and eager to re-interpret traditional notions according to the precepts of available scientific knowledge. Their eagerness to trust science, however, came at a price. For science helped to emphasise the deep feelings of separation and alienation which afflicted the age and therefore, in Gillis's striking observation, 'knowing the dead could not return to haunt the living, the Victorian middle classes began to haunt the dead, visiting them in cemeteries and communicating with them through spiritualist mediums'.[31]

VI

THE TWENTIETH CENTURY:
MANUFACTURING GHOSTS ON AN
INDUSTRIAL SCALE

In 1907, after falling to what appeared for a while to be her death, three-year-old Dorothy Eady began to have vivid dreams and to insist that she wanted to go home. 'Home' turned out to be ancient Egypt and during the next eleven years Dorothy did not deviate from this notion. Then one night, just before the First World War ended, she had an unusual experience. 'I was asleep', she recalled years later,

> and I half woke up, feeling a weight on my chest. Then I fully woke up, and I saw this face bending over me with both hands on the neck of my nightdress. I recognised the photo I had seen years before of the mummy of Sety [*Pharaoh Seti I*]. I was astonished and shocked and I cried out, and yet I was overjoyed. I can remember it as if it were yesterday, but still it's difficult to explain. It was the feeling of something you have waited for that has come at last, and yet it gives you a shock... And then he tore open my nightdress from neck to rim.

At first glance, this is reminiscent of a vampire story in which the heroine suffers her first assault from Dracula; or perhaps a somewhat racy boudoir novel whose principal character is rather more explicit than usual about her mixed feelings prior to being ravished by the villain of the piece. But for Dorothy it represented the start of a long period of waiting before she could go to Egypt and renew an ancient love-affair, tantalising glimpses of which she caught in her constant dreams.

These played in the background of her marriage to an Egyptian, and produced phenomena by no means peculiar to Dorothy's imagination. One day, for example, her father-in-law walked into her bedroom while she was recuperating from an illness, but rushed out again shouting that there was a Pharaoh sitting on her bed; and on another, her mother, who was stay-ing with her and sleeping in the same room, woke up to see a man standing by Dorothy's bed. She took this to be Dorothy's husband, even though she knew he was away overnight, and was frightened when Dorothy explained that the figure was, in fact, Seti I. The Pharaoh had apparently begun to visit her almost as soon as she had arrived in Egypt, not in his mummy-form, but as he had looked in life. 'Every time I tried to touch him or he tried to touch me, however, it was as if there were a thick pane of glass between us', Dorothy remembered.

> I had difficulty in understanding him, and I used to make funny mistakes when I talked... But one night he discovered that by placing his hand on me – and especially by holding my hand – I could understand and speak properly to him, as if some intimate power from His Majesty had entered into me.[1]

(This is reminiscent of something we have come across already, the temporary transmission of second sight to those normally without the ability, by standing on the feet of the seer.)

Dorothy's subsequent life found her working by day as an archaeologist in Giza, largely by transcribing and translating hieroglyphic manuscripts. Her nights, however, were filled with worship of the Sphinx to whom she offered incense and prayers in the ancient language. She also spent one or two nights alone in the King's or Queen's Chamber of the Great Pyramid, and frequently saw the ghosts of those who had died centuries ago. At last, after the revolution of July 1952, Dorothy made up her mind that she was going to go to Abydos and live permanently next to the temple there, an intention she finally fulfilled in 1956. It was there she acquired the name *Omm Sety* ('Mother of Seti'), and lived and worshipped in happy reunion with her lover-Pharaoh until her death in 1981.

How unusual was Dorothy? In her visions and her pursuit of them, most unusual, of course; but why did an Edwardian, heir to the sceptical, pro-scientific outlook of the nineteenth century on the one hand and on the other to a renewed, somewhat combative Christian faith, plunge headlong, without hesitation, into a world of spirits, ghostly visitants, and the mixed pleasure and fearfulness of reincarnation? The answer by now should be obvious. The nineteenth century had a split mind and the twentieth century inherited it. This split had been acknowledged decades before by Charles MacKay, the stout debunker of popular beliefs:

These tales of haunted houses, especially those of the last and present century, however they may make us blush for popular folly, are yet gratifying in their results; for they shew that society had made a vast improvement... Thus it is pleasant to reflect, that though there may be as much folly and credulity in the world as ever in one class of society, there is more wisdom and mercy in another than ever were known before. Lawgivers, by blotting from the statute-book the absurd or sanguinary enactments of their predecessors, have made one step towards teaching the people. It is to be hoped that the day is not far distant when lawgivers will teach the people by some more direct means, and prevent the recurrence of delusions like these, and many worse, which might be cited, by securing to every child born within their dominions an education in accordance with the advancing state of civilisation. If ghosts and witches are not yet altogether exploded, it is the fault, not so much of the ignorant people, as of the law and the government that have neglected to enlighten them.[2]

Science and rationalism had failed to penetrate the irresponsible foolishness of the lower classes, although certain progress had been made in the law. Much remained to be done, especially via education – one cannot help but think MacKay would have approved of Mr Gradgrind's 'Facts, facts, facts!' in Charles Dickens's *Hard Times* – and yet that very admission, expressed in class terms, but still the admission of something he could not deny, illustrates how pertinaciously attractive people found the seductions of what was preternatural and otherworldly. MacKay was quite wrong to confine such things to the lower classes, of course. Interest in spirits and ghosts, for example, was to be found throughout society. Spiritualist séances flourished, ghosts appeared in numbers which did not diminish, houses were still infested by spectral phenomena, and the cast of mind which dealt with these could be little different in the early 1900s from what it had been during the previous Victorian decades.

Let us take as an example the haunting of Beth-Oni, a comfortable dwelling in the village of Tackley in Oxfordshire, which was subject to a restless ghost for three years between 1905 and 1908. The attendant disturbances, however, were not consistently manifested. In April 1905 the household experienced a variety of unexplained noises at night, and in May one or two minor oddities during the day. Then the phenomena ceased until autumn 1906 when Ada Sharpe, who wrote several years later an account of the haunting, was woken by what felt like a violent blow to her head, but was rendered too afraid by the sense of someone's presence in the room to reach out for matches to light a candle. The noises continued throughout the first half of 1907. They were of various kinds: someone dragging a heavy weight across a wooden floor, footsteps, scratching, tapping, rustling, and ripping of wallpaper, and heavy blows as though a stone mason were at work. Every so often somebody in the house would see strange lights. 'Lois saw a starry light floating over Florrie's bed' (12 January); 'Willie was disturbed by starry lights on his ceiling' (20 January); '[I] saw two starry lights for a second in the corner of my room' (5 April); 'between 3 and 4 am, a long, dark shadow like a cloud seemed floating over my bed, occasionally relieved by dim sparks like rays of the sun' (13 April). People felt their bedclothes disturbed or a heavy weight pressing down on their feet or chest:

March 29, Good Friday. At 1.30 am Mrs Harris called out that she had felt the weight again, and someone seemed to push her from one side of the bed to the other. Afterwards, for two or three hours the room was full of starry lights and tiny sparks which eventually went out of the open door, and these were seen by Agnes, now sleeping in the Blue Room with the door open.
May 7, Tuesday. I felt something clawing outside my bedclothes between 11 and 12 pm before I went to sleep.
June 1, Saturday. Willie felt as though someone pressed the bedclothes between his knees, and then heard and felt something clawing off the bed.

Phenomena, however, were not confined to noises and sparkly lights and sensations of clawing. Occasionally there were apparent visual manifestations:

> *March 2, Saturday*. Lizzie saw a distinct form of a man in the pantry with his hand on the door, which clicked to in front of her.
>
> *30 March, Saturday, Easter Eve*. Lizzie was going up the second short staircase, and distinctly saw the form of a man (she describes him as 'a big burly farmer') standing in my bedroom doorway. It petrified her, but as she tried to move up another step he turned and went into my room.
>
> *April 1, Monday*. Lizzie and Agnes Floyd watching in the big attic from 7.30 to 8.30 pm saw the form of someone in a black cloak, afterwards also seen by Mrs Harris, which vanished as they approached it.
>
> *April 15, Monday*. Miss Bevan and Lizzie watching at dusk at top of the attic stairs between 7 and 8 pm felt an electric shock through them, and saw at entrance to the big attic a figure as of a man wrapped in a cloak, in kneeling posture, with clasped hands extended (hands not visible), then seeming to squat on its heels, then, extending itself again, seemed to turn a face towards them, which, although they defined no features, they felt wore an expression of derisive contempt.
>
> *July 5, Friday*. Alice had not been to sleep when she heard two taps at her open door, and while she was vainly trying to answer, a man came in, tapping the door as he came, walked to the bookshelves, snatched a book with both hands from the middle shelf, carried it to the dressing-table, laid it down while he looked at Alice's watch lying there, picked up the book, replaced it in the shelf, and seemed to go out at the door... The book was called *In*

Strange Company, and a distinct mark where it was drawn out was noticeable in the dust on the shelf next day, also two finger-marks on the top of the book. Alice looked at the time when he was gone, and found it 12.40.

On 12 July Ada collected from the station a clergyman with whom she had been corresponding for some months about all these phenomena, and he conducted a brief ceremony of exorcism which seemed to alter the whole atmosphere of the house. For three or four months, indeed, everything appeared to be quiet, although two women – maid servants – who came to the house in 1907 later confessed they had had unusual experiences, more or less of the kind Ada had been describing. But in January 1908 the noises began again and continued until 21 February when a second exorcism was carried out, this time successfully, because there was no repetition of any ghostly phenomena – 'absolute peace', as Ada thankfully expresses it.

There is little difficulty in offering all kinds of explanations for most of what Ada experienced, of course. An old village house lit only by candle-light provides an excellent setting for noises and shadows, and the expectation of all who stayed there that psychic phenomena could be and were being experienced may have encouraged interpretation of natural things as though they were preternatural. The vague and yet somewhat theatrical description of the figure by the attic on 15 April 1907 is a good example of this heightened expectancy. Seeing starry lights can easily be put down to atmospheric effects, and feeling an oppressive weight while one is in a state of half-sleep can be explained by reference to apnoea, a momentary stoppage of breathing during sleep, which results in feelings of suffocation and panic, and used to be called the 'night hag'.

What *is* interesting, and would have been worth closer

inquiry at the time, is the apparently solid and lifelike appearance of a man in Alice's room on 5 July. He was able to
handle a physical object, behaved in a quite random fashion,
ignored Alice completely, and then 'seemed' to go out of the
open door. 'Seemed' is annoying. Ada, who records the incident, presumably reproducing what Alice told her (though
with what exactitude we cannot tell), has used this verb
before. It occurs twice during the vague description of the
figure near the attic door: it seemed to squat, it seemed to
turn its face. We do not know how much light was available
during the April incident – Ada says Miss Bevan and Lizzie
were watching 'at dusk' between 7 and 8 pm – and we are
given no indication at all for the July apparition. But if Alice
could see the man perform the various actions she describes,
the room must have been lit by candle or by moonlight.
(Perhaps the former: on 15 and 16 April Ada notes that she
had a candle alight until 4am). It is also worth noting that
the man had been seen the previous night by Alice's three-
year old niece, and was seen by her again on his second
visit. '[Alice] had not known the child was awake till he had
vanished, when the child said, 'Didn't that man snatch the
books? and he tiggled me in the back. He hadn't half got
cheek!' *Seemed to go out* has now become the more specific
vanished, and the child adds two details which Alice/Ada
omitted before. The 'book' has become 'books', and the man
tickled the child's back while she was in the bed. How odd,
perhaps, that Alice did not remark on his doing so. Clearly
the man was a stranger, but we are given no information
about his appearance, and there the matter ends because we
are not told that anything more was done to find out who
he was. Ada had actually contacted the Society for Psychical
Research, but nothing seems to have come of it. (Did the
Society have its hands full at the time, or did it think the
case was not worth the trouble of further investigation?) She

also wrote to a bishop, whom she does not name, and he recommended a clergyman who came over from Oxford and said prayers in the hall – apparently to no effect. But it was suggested to her that 'the restless soul' was probably that of one Bart Chaudry who had lived in the house in 1875 and fell to his death over a landing banister, an attempt at explanation which rather suggests that people were looking for and happy to accept a conventional answer to the phenomena, rather than undertake a careful and detailed investigation to find out what was actually happening.

What resolved the haunting, if haunting it was, were the two exorcisms performed in July 1907 and February 1908. It is an interesting comment on the psychology of the principals. Ada had initially turned to science (which had apparently ignored her), and then to religion (which had not). It was a reaction entirely consistent with the priorities of educated individuals during the nineteenth century and a significant prologue to the twentieth century which inherited its predecessor's curious predilection for myth-making under the guise of anthropology and historicism – witness so many of the public 'traditions' of the British state, which were, in effect invented during Victoria's reign – and peopled its castles, stately homes, and ancient battlefields with ghost after ghost, to the thrill and pleasure of their increasing numbers of visitors. Ada's story got into print because there was a public appetite for such things. As an example of the genre, let us consider an anecdote taken from *The Haunted Homes and Family Traditions of Great Britain* by John Ingram, first published in 1884, which ran through nine more editions, some of them enlarged and illustrated, until 1929. It relates to a house in Plymouth.

Amongst the innumerable multitude of buildings whic'
have the reputation of being haunted it will be note'
by far the larger number are haunted by stran'

and mysterious sounds only, but few of them really attain to the dignity of being visited by visible beings. Some of the places, however, which have had the character of being disturbed by unusual and unaccountable noises are very interesting from the suggestiveness of these noises: in the following account, for instance, and indeed in many others, the ghostly but invisible visitants appear to be condemned to return to the occupations they followed before they shuffled off the mortal coil, and to resume, after their incorporeal fashion, the labours of their past life...

[Mrs Hunn, an actress, was looking for lodgings in Plymouth and was told of a place which would be very cheap, provided she was not afraid of the ghost]. Mrs Hunn, alluding to theatrical apparitions, said it would not be the first time she had had to do with a ghost, and that she was very willing to encounter this one; so she had her luggage taken into the house in question, and the bed prepared. At her usual hour, she sent her maid and her children to bed, and curious to see if there was any foundation for the rumour she had heard, she seated herself with a couple of candles and a book, to watch the event. Beneath the room she occupied was the carpenter's workshop, which had two doors; the one which opened into the street was barred and bolted from within; the other, a smaller one, opening into the passage, was only on the latch; and the house was, of course, closed for the night. She had read somewhat more than half an hour, when she perceived a noise issuing from this lower apartment, which sounded very much like the sawing of wood; presently, other such noises as usually proceed from a carpenter's workshop were added, till, by and by, there was a regular concert of knocking and hammering, and sawing and planning, etc; the whole sounding like half a dozen busy men in full employment. Being a woman of considerable courage, Mrs Hunn resolved, if possible, to penetrate the mystery; so, taking off her shoes, that her approach might not be heard, with her candle in her hand, she very softly opened her door and descended the stairs, the noise continuing as loud as ever, and evidently proceeding from the workshop, till she opened the door, when instantly all was silent – all was still – not a mouse was stirring; and the tools and the wood, and everything else, lay as they had been left by the workmen when they went away.

Having examined every part of the place, and satisfied herself that there was nobody there, and that nobody could get into it, Mrs Hunn ascended to her room again, beginning almost to doubt her own senses, and question with herself whether she had really heard the noise or not, when it recommenced, and continued, without intermission, for about half an hour. She however went to bed, and the next day told nobody what had occurred, having determined to watch another night before mentioning the affair to anyone. As, however, this strange scene was acted over again, without her being able to discover the cause of it, she now mentioned the circumstances to the owner of the house and to her friend Mr Bernard; and the former, who would not believe it, agreed to watch with her, which he did. The noise began as before, and he was so horror-struck that, instead of entering the workshop as she wished him to do, he rushed into the street. Mrs Hunn continued to inhabit the house the whole summer, and when referring afterwards to the adventure, she observed that use was second nature; and that she was sure, if any night these ghostly carpenters had not pursued their visionary labours, she should have been quite frightened lest they should pay her a visit upstairs.

This, and the hundreds of stories like it, can be said to represent the latest stage of the eighteenth century's Gothic novel, made genteel for the drawing room, all passion and horror removed, and drained of those elements which might prove over-disturbing to the notion that God is too much of a gentleman to do more than titillate the nerve-ends of His worshippers to a degree they can easily bear in polite company. A natural reaction to these tales is 'so what?' Ancient, medieval, and early modern ghosts largely appear for a specific purpose. Nineteenth-century ghosts, by contrast, generally do not. They appear or they make their presence felt, and that is that. Their one remaining purpose (or, if you like, their one remaining effect), was to bear largely silent witness to the reality of survival after death in the face of that doubting materialism which was constantly seeping into society's bones, and, this done, they were content to do no more.[3]

Then came the First World War and public psychology changed, if only for the time being. For the war stimulated a desire, almost a desperation, in the general public to know whether those who were absent, fighting, were alive or dead, and if dead, to establish contact with them again. This desire was not limited to those of religious belief, and it was one of the strengths of Spiritualism that it catered for those who simply wished to ascertain whether the spirit continues after death and whether communication between the living and the dead be possible, regardless of any attendant notion even of God, let alone the specific assertions about life after death explicitly or implicitly defined by the Christian faith, while it also claimed to answer the same questions raised by those who had a particular religious commitment. Nor should it be supposed that the queries were restricted to people who were personally and directly affected by bereavement in the war. Those, such as many members of the SPR, who had been motivated before the war by the odd mixture of scientific curiosity and religious aspiration continued to be so motivated both during and after it; and the soldiers at the front found both interest and immense comfort in Spiritualism and in other unorthodox expressions of religious sentiment. As one army chaplain put it, 'The British soldier has certainly got religion; I am not so sure, however, that he has got Christianity'.[4]

Still, there can be no argument that the emotional tensions generated by the Great War provided an extra stimulus to the public's interest in death and therefore to people's hopes of finding proof of post-mortem survival, and apparent success during séances generated immense and heartfelt gratitude. One woman wrote to the medium Helen Duncan, 'It was as though the gates of Heaven had opened and let me in for a short time. I cannot put into words the joy I felt'; and at another session in the 1930s, Helen materialised a woman's son who had died at an early age and 'as he sang a hymn and threw his arms round her neck, she was certain he had returned, and before leaving... [his mother] whispered to Helen, "I am a new woman. I have now something to live for. I know now that my boy is not dead. He lives"'. So it is not surprising to find that interest in Spiritualism continued to grow during the war years. In 1914 there were 145 societies affiliated to the Spiritualists' National Union; by 1919 there were 309. Part of the reason for this is that mediums were also ready to give advice along with comfort, not only on psychic matters but on physical health as well, some of them acting as spiritual therapists in the manner (although not, of course, employing the same methods), of faith and magical healers through the ages.[5]

Death on such a grand scale as this war was intent on furnishing naturally provided endless opportunities for the dead to return to the living. Harold Owen, brother of the poet Wilfred, recorded how he found out his brother had been killed:

We were lying off Victoria [Cameroons]. I had gone down to my cabin thinking to write some letters. I drew aside the door curtain and stepped inside and to my amazement I saw Wilfred sitting in my chair. I felt shock run through me with appalling force and with it I could feel the blood draining away from my face. I did not rush towards him but walked jerkily into the cabin – all my limbs stiff and slow to respond. I did not sit down but looking at him I spoke quietly: 'Wilfred, how did you get here?' He did not rise and I saw that he was involuntarily immobile, but his eyes which had never left mine were alive with the familiar look of trying to make me understand; when I spoke his whole face broke into his sweetest and most endearing dark smile. I felt no fear – I had not when I first drew my door curtain and saw him there; only exquisite mental pleasure at thus beholding him. All I was conscious of was a sensation of enormous shock and profound astonishment that he should be here in my cabin.

I spoke again. 'Wilfred, dear, how can you be here, it's just not possible'. But still he did not speak but only smiled his most gentle smile. This not speaking did not now as it had done at first seem strange or even unnatural; it was not only in some inexplicable way perfectly natural but radiated a quality which made his presence with me undeniably right and in no way out of the ordinary. I loved having him there: I could not, and did not want to try to understand how he had got there. I was content to accept him, that he was here with me was sufficient. I could not question anything, the meeting in itself was complete and strangely perfect. He was in uniform and

I remember thinking how out of place the khaki looked among the cabin furnishings. With this thought I must have turned my eyes away from him; when I looked back my cabin chair was empty.

I felt the blood run slowly back into my face and looseness into my limbs and with these an overpowering sense of emptiness and absolute loss... I wondered if I had been dreaming but looking down I saw that I was still standing. Suddenly I felt terribly tired and moving to my bunk I lay down; instantly I went into a deep oblivious sleep. When I woke up I knew with absolute certainty that Wilfred was dead.[6]

The Second World War saw the same interest and the same phenomenon. So much so that in 1941 the Royal Navy actually recognised Spiritualism as a religion and permitted sailors to hold services at sea. The role played by mediums was very much like that they had played twenty-five years earlier and by 1944, it was said, Spiritualists had a million members attending a thousand churches, with over fifty thousand home circles supplementing that public adherence. But this hunger for information during the restrictive conditions of war was not regarded with favour by many of those in authority, as the case of Helen Duncan shows. Helen Duncan was a Scottish medium who materialised spirits and produced a wide range of Spiritualist phenomena. By the late 1920s she had joined that relatively small group of mediums who were able to produce ectoplasm, a dingy white muslin-like substance issuing from the body of the medium and used by the summoned or waiting spirit to give physical substance to its appearance. She was able to extract information about people by feeling objects which had some connection with them, such as rings, watches, or brooches, to read sealed letters by running the envelope over her forehead and down her spine, and to interpret people's auras, areas of light round the body, supposedly caused by the body's magnetism. A clairvoyant healing medium, for example, would look at the colour of the patient's aura and so work out the individual's current emotional and physical health.[7] Helen travelled all over Britain, but in 1944 held a séance in Portsmouth during which, in advance of any official disclosure, she allegedly revealed that two British ships, HMS Hood and HMS Barham, had been sunk. In consequence she was arrested, and gained a certain notoriety from being the last person to be prosecuted under the Witchcraft Act of 1735 before it was repealed, largely as a result of her case, in favour of the Fraudulent Mediums Act of 1951.

Her story is remarkably complex, a complexity which is in part a reflection of the woman herself who has attracted over the years both adherents and detractors, and partly because of the curious legislative position in which she found herself. For the fact that she was prosecuted under the Witchcraft Act rather than the Vagrancy Act of 1824, which was perfectly adequate for dealing with what the authorities saw as fraud practised for money on gullible members of the public, has lent her case a certain glamour and given rise to the notion that there was some kind of official conspiracy against her. But to people eager for news of their dead, Helen's performances – regardless of the conscious fraud which undoubtedly accompanied them, at least during her later years – were extraordinary, and it is this widespread belief in her abilities, not the question of how far she was or was not deceptive, that makes her a significant figure in the history of Spiritualist contact with the dead. But the materialisations which formed a major part of her séances quickly fell out of favour. Twentieth-century mediums – Doris Stokes is an obvious example – tended to work as transmitters of messages by hearing the voices of the dead and relaying their words to the members of their audience. Other mediums allegedly operate with the assistance of a guide who may act as an unseen, unheard presence, so that the medium is, in effect, a reporter; or the spirit may actually possess the medium and speak through her (usually 'her'), so that her appearance and voice alter as long as the trance or possession lasts.[8]

This modern reluctance to materialise the dead may spring from several causes. First and foremost, perhaps, is the legacy of fraud. Far too many of the nineteenth- and early twentieth-century mediums were found to be engaged in fakery – indeed it is often surprising, at least to us, that their crude methods could have fooled even the most ardent hoper and believer – with the result that ectoplasmic materialisation suffered a blow from which its reputation has not recovered. Secondly, films, whether in the cinema or on television, still frequently show ghosts as immaterial in the tradition of eighteenth-century phantasmagoria and nineteenth-century spirit-photography – indeed, the early twentieth century chose to advertise this kind of film in the manner of old ghost shows[9] – and the widespread prevalence of their version both responds to and reinforces public expectation. Thirdly, there is now not such a pressing need to bring the dead physically before us, because photography and video technology enable the living to see and hear the dead as they were when they were alive, and so provide the living with perpetual icons which appear to be more authentic and more believable than any apparition conjured forth in a séance room. Fourthly, the personal experiences of many people who deliberately place themselves in a haunted environment tend to consist of physical harm such as cuts or bruising, or physical discomfort such as inability to breathe or feeling unnaturally cold – disembodied phenomena rather than solid-seeming, visual apparitions. This, of course, may be allied to the investigative methods of many modern ghost researchers who tend to employ infra-red cameras, digital sound recording equipment, electromagnetic field detectors, and thermal scanners which, not unsurprisingly, produce anomalous magnetic fields and low frequency standing air waves.

Fifthly, the nineteenth century produced a new science in its development of psychology which brought with it a new method of looking at occult phenomena. These enabled investigators to offer explanations other than those which were purely materialist or merely to withdraw the hems of their intellectual garments to cries of 'superstition'. Freudians, for example, were now able to explain ghosts as the return of repressed experiences stimulated, essentially, by unconscious emotional interaction between the living, or in answer to a particular environment which happens to elicit that repressed material. One consequence of this, of course, is that when people report they have had an experience of a ghost, they ought to be believed since although one may not be willing to take their description at face value, the return of a repressed personality or occurrence which it could be said they are describing is, according to this particular Freudian explanation, almost certainly genuine.[10]

But it was the suggestive link between ghostly communication and telepathy which particularly intrigued psychologists and members of the SPR alike, and Freud himself is said to have remarked, 'If I had my life to live over again I should devote myself to psychical research rather than psychoanalysis'. Experiments were carried out soon after the invention of the Morse code in 1837, since the connection between its tapping and that of the original Spiritualists was self-evidently waiting to be explored; and from the point of view of the century's longing for continued community with its dead, the possibility of thought-transference via means which might be explicable in scientific terms was irresistibly alluring, since it would combine scientific method with theological argument and so provide satisfactory solutions to problems hitherto confined to the realm of 'belief'.[11] Freud expressed the positive view of this research in a lecture on dreams and occultism, delivered in 1932.

When they first came into my range of vision more than ten years ago, I too felt a dread of a threat against our scientific *Weltanschauung*, which, I feared, was bound to give place to spiritualism or mysticism if portions of occultism were proved true. Today I think otherwise. In my opinion it shows no great confidence in science if one does not think it capable of assimilating and working over whatever may perhaps turn out to be true in the assertions of the occultists. And particularly so far as thought-transference is concerned, it seems actually to favour the extension of the scientific – or, as our opponents say, the mechanistic mode of thought to the mental phenomena which are so hard to lay hold of. The telepathic process is supposed to consist in a mental act in one person instigating the same mental act in another person. What lies between these two mental acts may easily be a physical process into which the mental one is transformed at one end and which is transformed back once more into the same mental one at the other end. The analogy with other transformations, such as occur in speaking and hearing by telephone, would then be unmistakeable... It would seem to me that psychoanalysis, by inserting the unconscious between what is physical and what was previously called 'psychical', has paved the way for the assumption of such processes as telepathy... If there is such a thing as telepathy as a real process, we may suspect that, in spite of its being so hard to demonstrate, it is quite a common phenomenon.[12]

The sixth and final reason for the near demise of spiritualist materialisations these days is likely to be that death does not play the part it once did in Western society. 'Dying', says Benjamin, 'was once a public process in the life of an individual and a most exemplary one; think of the medieval pictures in which the deathbed has turned into a throne towards which the people press through the wide-open doors of the death house. In the course of modern times dying has been pushed further and further out of the perceptual world of the living. There used to be no house, hardly a room, in which someone had not once died... Today people live in rooms that have never been touched by death, dry dwellers of eternity, and when their end approaches they are stowed away in sanatoria or hospitals by their heirs'. Consequently, death has been turned into a great mystery, at once alluring and repulsive, its reality obliterated partly by the kind of concealment to which Benjamin refers, and partly by the continuous suggestion of films and videos that dying is something which happens in fiction to actors, and that once the gaze of the spectator is turned away, the corpses get up and resume their normal life. Either that or, as in computer games in which dozens of figures are slaughtered by the living master of the machine, death is as unreal as the slaughtered figures themselves. Only the living exponent of the game is real, and he or she is, of course, alive. A ghost is thus different from those players of illusions, and its materialisation would be too disconcerting for the onlooker, for it would suggest either that somehow death had not really taken place, or that the onlooker was not really in charge of the action. It is also interesting to note the observation of three twenty-first-century investigators of ghosts that 'humans are intuitively biased towards holding mental representations of psychological continuity after death'. That *psychological* takes us far, far away not only from the materialisations of the séance room, but also from the belief in the physical resurrection of the dead which played so important a role in the Christian consciousness of earlier times. Perhaps this is at least partly because, in Callum Brown's incisive remark, 'we no longer articulate our lives as moral stories'. Reported voices, on the other hand, or film-like appearances, or a sudden unexpected manifestation and equally sudden disappearance, preserve that distance between the living and the dead which the twentieth and twenty-first century have come to expect. Nothing, it seems, could be more different from that sense of community which characterised their relationship during the Middle Ages and the early modern period.[13]

A sense of community seems, in fact, to be the greatest loss in religious consciousness during the twentieth century, especially from the 1960s onwards. Eighteenth-century intellectual inquiry may have appeared to produce a formidable opponent to religion, but did so effectively only among certain groups in society. By calling the established tenets of faith into question, it actually rallied support for them and stimulated evangelical counter-attacks, some of which we have seen in particular connection with ghosts. But the internalisation of religion, which had begun much earlier in the sixteenth and seventeenth centuries, joining hands with Freud's psychology, altered the way people were prepared to discuss what appeared to be external but non-material phenomena, and invited them to look inwards rather than outwards for a cause. If ghosts were not to be the result of electromagnetic fields, or draughts, or air waves, or any such physical causes, they were to arise from disturbances in the brain and prove no more independent of it than images projected from film on to a cinema screen.

It may also be worth bearing in mind Jeanne Favret-Saada's experiences when she went to investigate witchcraft in the French Bocage in 1969. People consistently poured scorn on the notion that any such thing could exist in their community (even though they knew perfectly well it did), and adopted ways of diverting Favret-Saada's attention. Their common tactic was to find an individual whom they could deride as 'superstitious' or 'backward' or 'foolish', and thus turn away her questions from themselves. 'To call oneself a French citizen today, descended from the tradition of the enlightenment', she observed, 'is to show that one is capable of repelling the irrational. When they are required to do so – as for example when the national newspapers make a fuss about the practices of an eccentric unwitcher – the inhabitants of the Bocage loudly sacrifice those who have provoked the scandal in the sacred cause of national unity'.[14] *Mutatis mutandis*, this is how many people are likely to react if asked whether they believe in ghosts or not. An immediate struggle often ensues, between the desire to seem rational and the impulsion to admit that they (or more likely 'a friend'), have had some kind of experience which might be interpreted as spectral.

This frame of mind, however, is one peculiar to, or perhaps more accurately, associated with Western Europe and North America. Elsewhere ghosts not only flourish but flourish 'officially', along with witches and sorcerers and diviners of every kind. What is more, the ghost as *vrykolax* enjoys continued life. Let us consider briefly the zombie. Originating in Central Africa and spreading thence to the West Indies and from there disseminated throughout much of what was the British Empire, the zombie – a word meaning 'spirit of a dead person' – underwent all kinds of conceptual changes, the most prevalent being that of a living body without a soul, a physical husk rendered so by the actions of a sorcerer to provide him with a slave-like automaton to work on his land. This, however, is a Haitian construct.

Elsewhere the zombie is not so much a body deprived of its soul, or a resurrected corpse unconsciously carrying out the will of a master it does not know it has; it is rather a live human being so dominated by a witch (male or female) that it has no will of its own. Diminutive, sexless, in some cases speechless because its tongue has been cut, the zombie in this instance actually has nothing to do with the dead and everything to do with a form of slavery. But traditions concerning the two types may become amalgamated; for because zombies are associated with witches and malevolent occult powers, it is not difficult for people to say that they cross the border between life and death, and so represent them as some kind of ghost returning to visit the living. Isak Niehaus tells the story of a schoolboy, Samuel Mohlala, from the South African lowveld, whose sister Rebecca died in 1993 after losing her unborn child as the result of a fall. A 'Zionist prophet' in his church kept telling Samuel that Rebecca was not really dead but would come back to the house at night to look for food. So it is not really surprising that Samuel was badly frightened, especially as other church members told him they had actually met Rebecca during the night. Here 'zombie' has clearly metamorphosed from a living person of a particular kind into something closer to an ordinary revenant, 'ordinary' in as much as Rebecca was conceived as the returning spirit of a dead person, although she was somewhat unusual in as far as the ostensible purpose of her return was to look for food. So she was not entirely spirit, and thus the connection with a functioning body lingered on in the community's view of her.

Elsewhere in Africa, stories about vampires and vampiric activities abound. In Kampala, it was said, when a man joined the police, he had to be trained how to suck blood from human beings, and victims were kept in pits for this very purpose. Something similar was done in the houses

of prostitutes in Nairobi, where male customers fell into a
pit whence they were later removed to be sources of blood
for 'firemen', a generic term for vampires; and during the
first half of the twentieth century in particular there were
rumours all over Northern Rhodesia that Africans working for Europeans captured other Africans for their blood.
As late as December 2002, the southern areas of Malawi,
too, found themselves awash with stories of people being
attacked for their blood, and (lest it be thought the phenomenon is confined to African states), in February 2004 in
Romania, it was reported that several relatives of one Toma
Petre thought he had become a vampire. So they dug up
his body, removed the heart, burned it, and drank its ashes
mixed with water.[15]

Perhaps the most striking feature of the twentieth century's attitude to ghosts and other occult phenomena, then,
was its continuing curiosity about them and its desire (often
expressed as one might expect through scientific operations
such as weighing, measuring, recoding, classifying, and all
the other enlightenment-inspired attempts to explain, to
solve, and to quantify everything), to establish once and for
all whether life in some form does continue after death and
if it does, whether it may be contacted or not. Yet while it is
true that part of the modern psyche wishes to conquer death
altogether and to prolong life here on earth by increasingly
sophisticated medical intervention and biological modification, nevertheless, it is also true, as Ballard has pointed out,
that sooner or later the living change sides and join the dead,
and therefore acquaintance or contact with even the most
terrifying ghost might actually offer the living some kind
of reassurance. Hence, perhaps, the continued attempts even
by unlikely individuals to seek out contact with the dead.
Lord Carnarvon tried to exorcise the ghost of Akhenaton
in Egypt; Himmler spoke to the ghost of King Henry the

Fowler at night; and even in Communist China during
the late 1950s and 1960s, there were constant stories about
ghosts, such as that of a mill girl who befriended a young
man she met in the street, only to be told by his mother
that he had been dead for two years.[16]

The methods of science, so dear to the modern period,
however, may not be considered appropriate to the inquiry
for life after death – as Jung tartly observed in 1957, 'Our
scientific age wants to know whether such things are "true",
without taking into account what the nature of any such
proof would have to be and how it could be furnished' – and
so, regardless of any of their overt obeisance to the spirit of
the enlightenment tradition, people tend to continue to seek
communion with the dead much as they have always done:
through prayer to the saints, through intercession for the souls
of dead relatives, through preservation of icons, both religious
and secular, such as relics or photographs, through leaving
flowers and toys and other physical expressions of loss at the
place where someone died unexpectedly – an apotropaic
gesture from somewhere deep in their unconscious against
the return of a restless, angry ghost? – and through visiting
, as tourists or curiosity-seekers, certain places known or
reputed to be haunted. People also continue to report personal experience of the dead through sight, through hearing, or simply through a sense of presence with which they
may conduct a one-sided conversation.[17] Why do they do
so? Lafcadio Hearn had an interesting observation to make.
'The impossible is much more closely related to reality than
the greater part of what we designate true and ordinary. The
impossible isn't perhaps the naked truth, but I believe that it is
often the truth, undoubtedly masked and veiled, but eternal.
He who claims he does not believe in ghosts lies in his own
heart.'[18] Perhaps, then, in spite of everything, the dead are
still conceived as integral to the complete sweep of human

existence, guarantors both of connection with the past and of continuance in the future, and hence mediators between realms which are otherwise considered distinct.

NOTES

1. THE ANCIENT WORLD: MAPPING THE AFTERLIFE, CALLING UP THE DEAD

1 Otloh of St Emmeram: *Liber visionum* in Migne: *Patrologia Latina* 146.360-61. Boccaccio: *Decameron*, fifth day, eighth story.
2 O. St. John Gogarty, quoted in Russell: 'The environment of ghosts', 109.
3 'Phantasmagoria', 29.
4 Merridale: *Night of Stone*, 433-4. Leaving messages for the dead is, of course, a very ancient tradition. See, for example, Ritner: *Mechanics of Ancient Egyptian Magical Practice*, 180-3. As always, of course, exceptions test the rule. There are cultures which are said not to believe in ghosts, an example being the Tiv in Nigeria. These, however, are few in comparison with the great majority of cultures which do subscribe to belief in communication between some form of afterlife and this present physical existence, and the exceptions need close investigation to ensure they have not been misunderstood. Rockwell: 'The ghosts of Evald Tang Kristensen', 43.
5 Porter: 'Ghosts in the Old Testament', 216.
6 I have borrowed the term 'otherworld' from Susan Greenwood. 'The cosmos is... alive with forces and energies, some of which exist in a time and space distinct from, but also very closely

connected to, everyday reality – the reality ordinarily perceived
by the five senses of the human body. This area is commonly
termed the 'otherworld'', *Magic, Witchcraft and the Otherworld*, 23.

7 See further Gordon: *Death is for the Living*, 9-14.

8 *The Crane Bag*, 26. Cf. (a) 'Knowledge commoditised… is
knowledge which is separable from context and situation,
and thus easily separated. Ignorance 'grows' only in someone
whose knowledge and context no longer fit each other'; and
(b) 'If local traditions are allowed to survive, they do so only
as "beliefs" and are encapsulated as "folk" or "little tradition"
and put into quotation marks'; and (c) 'Ignorance is knowledge
denied or denigrated', Vitebsky: 'Is death the same everywhere?'
107, 108, 114. Modern pagan movements in the West represent
at least one conscious attempt to resist *soi-disant* 'scientific'
thinking, and it may be no accident that these movements are
composed largely of the intellectual middle classes.

9 *Ghostly Matters*, 8, 19, 10.

10 *Ishtar's Descent into the Netherworld*, cited in Bottéro: *Religion in
Ancient Mesopotamia*, 108. Homer: *Odyssey* 24.6-14. Johnston:
Restless Dead, 14-16. Garland: *The Greek Way of Death*, 1-2, 49-
60. Johnson: 'Hesiod's descriptions of Tartarus', 12, 27. See also
Ballabriga: *Le soleil et le Tartare*, 258-9.

11 *Phaedo* 112a; 112e-113c; 113d-e. Aristotle, in a somewhat
po-faced manner, treated Plato's vision as though it were a
scientific treatise and explained in some detail that rivers could
not flow the way Plato described because water does not flow
upwards, Plato does not account for rain water, and in any
case, rivers flow into the sea, *Meteorologica* 2.2 (355b.33-356a.34).
Goldingay: 'Death and afterlife in the Psalms', in Avery-Peck &
Neusner: *Judaism in Late Antiquity*, 66-67.

12 See Edmonds: *Myths of the Underworld Journey*, 209-11.
The interiors of Etruscan tombs, too, were often designed
to represent patrician houses, as though their inhabitants
would continue to live a kind of shadow life reflecting,
with appropriate modifications, the one they had lived on
earth. F. Prayon: 'Tomb architecture', in M. Torrelli (ed.): *The
Etruscans* (London: Thames & Hudson 2001), 338. See further
I. Krauskopf: 'The grave and beyond in Etruscan religion',
in Thomson de Grummond & Simon: *The Religion of the
Etruscans*, chap. 5. One is reminded of the two halls of the dead

in Scandinavian mythology: the Hall of the Slain (Valhalla) for
those killed on the battlefield, where the dead pass their time
feasting and drinking, and Freya's Hall (Folkvang) for the others.

13 Fragment 113 in R. Kassel & C. Austin (edd.): *Poetae Comici
Graeci*, Vol. 7 (Berlin & New York: De Gruyter 1989), 156-7.

14 McKeever Furst: *The Natural History of the Soul in Ancient
Mexico*, 44, 178. León-Portilla: *Aztec Thought and Culture*, 124-5.
A separate place existed for the souls of those who died in
battle or as sacrifices, or of women who died in childbirth,
Ibid., 126. Knox: *The Development of Religion in Japan*, 17-20.
The Greeks seem to have had some notion of a post-mortem
judgement, and certainly an individual such as Tantalos is
portrayed as undergoing perpetual punishment, but belief in
a formal trial and subsequent admission to a happy state for
the innocent or a condition of retributive justice for the guilty
did not play a major part in either Greek or Roman official
religion. See further Brandon: *The Judgement of the Dead*, 76-97.

15 Faulkner: *The Ancient Egyptian Book of the Dead*, 31-2. Brandon:
The Judgement of the Dead, 31-5, 45-6. Hornung: *The Secret Lore
of Egypt*, 74. *The Tibetan Book of the Dead*, 166. Lipner: *Hindus*,
233. León-Portilla: *Aztec Thought and Culture*, 124. Cf. how the
dead Brynhild, on her way to be reunited with the dead Sigurd
in the kingdom of the dead, is challenged by a dead giantess
who seeks to stop her. C. Larrington (ed.): *The Poetic Edda*
(Oxford: Oxford University Press 1996), 192.

16 McKeever Furst: *The Natural History of the Soul in Ancient Mexico*,
148-50. This relationship between the corpse and the spirit could
be a phenomenon true of the animal as well as the human dead.
Thus Porphyry, 'So when animals meet a violent death, their
souls are forced to take pleasure in the body they are leaving,
and there the soul finds no impediment to its being in the place
to which it is drawn by that to which it is akin. This is why
people have seen many souls lamenting, and why the souls of the
unburied dead remain near their bodies', *De abstinentia* 2.47.

17 Wilson: *The Magical Universe*, 56. Riché: 'La magie à l'époque
carolingienne', in P. Riché: *Instruction et vie religieuse dans le Haut
Moyen Age* (London: Variorum 1981), 132. Thomsen: 'Witchcraft
and magic in ancient Mesopotamia', 79-81, 86-8.

18 Bhattacharya: *Indian Demonology*, 31. Parry: *Death in Banaras*,
231. Green: *Meeting the Invisible Man*, 208. The living could also

bully the dead. In seventeenth-century Scotland, for example, we find that Agnes Didup was hauled before the kirk session of Carrington for cursing a dead woman, Barbara Steill, and praying that the Devil would ryve her out of her grave and give her no rest until she returned to tell Agnes whether during life she had stolen some cloth from her, *CH2/62/1*: p.132.

19 Gager: *Curse Tablets*, 60-61. Versnel: 'Punish those who rejoice in our misery', 130. Cf. Johnston: *Restless Dead*, 71-80. R.K. Ritner: *The Mechanics of Ancient Egyptian Magical Practice*, 180-83. R. Merrifield: *The Archaeology of Ritual and Magic* (London: Guild Publishing 1987), 137-9.

20 Spencer: *Death in Ancient Egypt*, 54-60. David: *The Ancient Egyptians*, 78-80. Brandon: *The Judgement of the Dead*, 12-14. Morenz: *Egyptian Religion*, 157-8; 207-8. Burkes: *Death in Qoheleth*, 20-21. Cooper: *Body, Soul, and Life Everlasting*, 54-5. Egyptian religion, of course, did not have a unified theology, nor did it remain unchanged throughout the long history of its society. Variants upon belief and practice are therefore to be expected. Some elements ay have been borrowed. Cf., for example, the later Mesopotamian belief that the spirits of the dead went down to the otherworld in the west, and that the sun-god was as much concerned with the dead as with the living, Bottéro: *Mesopotamia*, 275. Parke: *Festivals of the Athenians*, 116-19. Dodds: *The Ancient Concept of Progress*, 147. Bremmer: *Ancient Greek Concept of the Soul*, 108-23. Ovid: *Fasti* 2.537-42. Wheeler: 'A Roman pipe-burial', 3-7. Lindsay: *Leisure and Pleasure in Roman Egypt*, 298-307, 56-8.

21 *De divinatione* 1.27.56. Cf. Suetonius: *Otho* 7.2. where Galba, Otho's dead predecessor, appears to him in a dream and violently throws him out of bed. *Letters* 5.5.7. For a commentary on this and similar passages, see further Felton: *Haunted Greece and Rome*, 74-5.

22 Toynbee: *Death and Burial*, 47-8. Novara: 'Les *imagines* de l'Elysée virgilien', 321-49. Ginzburg: *Night Battles*, 56-7. Cf. the reactions of Horatio and Marcellus to the ghost of Hamlet's father. *Horatio*: Is it not like the King? *Marcellus*: As thou art to thyself. / Such was the very armour he had on / When he th'ambitious Norway combated (Act 1, scene 1).

23 Seneca: *Hercules*, 48-9, 55-6, 60-1. Vergil: *Georgics* 4.467-77.

24 *Papyri Graeci Magici* 4.335-406. Lucan: *Pharsalia* 6.625-6, 667-9,

720-62, 824-6. Cf. the novelist Heliodoros who describes, with less horrific detail, the reanimation of a man's corpse by his mother. She too uses blood, this time her own, and incantations to compel the body to revivify and stand upright. At first it will not speak, but eventually her magic is powerful enough to induce it into speech; whereupon the corpse utters prophecies and then, having done so, suddenly collapses, *Aethiopika* 6.14-15.

25 Clement of Rome: *Homiliae*, no.2, chapters 26 & 30 = *Patrologia Graeca* 2.93, 97. Cf. *Homiliae* no.4, chapter 4 (*PG* 2.169) where it is said that Simon 'astonishes the whole city every day by making spectres and ghosts appear in the midst of the market-place; and when he goes out... many shadows go in front of him, which, he says, are souls of the dead'. Prodromos: *Rhodanthe and Dosikles* 4.217-42. See also Winkler: 'Lollianos and the desperadoes', *Journal of Hellenic Studies* 100)1980), 155-81.

26 I *Kings* (I *Samuel*) 28.3-25. Schmidt: *Israel's Beneficent Dead*, 201-8. For the oddity of the woman's referring to supernatural beings and Saul's question apparently involving only one, see *Ibid.*, 210-19. Cooper makes the useful observations that the ghost of Samuel is recognisably Samuel, not someone or something else; he is a typical resident of Sheol in that he does not seem to be in a peculiar state created by God for this necromantic occasion; it appears that the dead can be active even though they are described as 'sleeping'; and Samuel is a ghost, not a soul or an abstract 'mind', *Body, Soul, and Life Everlasting*, 58-9. For later interpretations of the incident, see Schmitt: 'Le spectre de Samuel', 43-50. Saul's request for necromantic divination was not particularly unusual. See Cogan: 'The road to En-Dor', 319-26.

27 Plutarch: *Moralia* (De defectu oraculorum 9) 414E. See further Connor: *Dumbstruck*, 76-95. Gaskill: *Hellish Nell*, 75, 82. Early Christian Fathers – Justin Martyr, Origen, Hippolytus Romanus, Eustathius of Antioch – disputed whether the women of Endor had really raised Samuel's ghost or not, but regularly used the Greek word for ventriloquist to describe her. See further Hopfner: *Griechisch-Ägyptischer Offenbarungszauber* 2.2.276. Connor: *Dumbstruck*, 75-101.

28 Felton: *Haunted Greece and Rome*, 14-18. Barber: *Vampires, Burial, and Death*, 187-8, 104-5. Lucretius: *De rerum natura* 4.30-8. It is actually quite difficult to cremate a body because of its high

water content. The temperature of the burning agent must be
kept at *c.*870° centigrade for about an hour. Hence the Indian
practice of pouring clarified butter on the pyre, and the ancient
Greek custom of wrapping the body in fat before setting light
to the wood. See further Barber: *Vampires*, 76-7. Noy: 'Half-
burnt on an emergency pyre', 186-96.

29 *John* 11.1-44; 20.27. Ghost or revenant stories are not always
solemn. See, for example, Apuleius, *Metamorphoses* 2.28-30
which tells the story of a man's corpse magically brought back
to life to explain how he was murdered by his new wife. See
also Fenton: *Haunted Greece and Rome*, 27-9 for further examples
of Classical revenants, all of whom resemble (or, if one prefers,
actually are), the originally living individual. Pierre de l'Ancre:
L'Incredulité, treatise 7 (pp.363-4). Johnston: *Restless Dead*, 9-11;
127-8. Apuleius: *De deo Socratis* 15.

30 Augustine: *De civitate Dei* 9.11. Verginia's story is told in Livy
3.48.5 and 3.58.11. The verb *quiescere* which he uses means 'to
find rest, to stop travelling, to fall asleep', and this latter sense
reminds us of the ancient connection made between sleep and
death. Cf. Apuleius's story in *Metamorphoses* 9.29-30 of a woman
who arranged for a ghost to kill her adulterous husband. The
ghost appeared in the guise of an old woman and led the man
into his bedroom, as though she had something to say to him
in private. But there he was later discovered hanging from a
beam and the woman was nowhere to be found.

31 Felton: *Haunted Greece and Rome*, xii. Dodds: *The Ancient Concept
of Progress*, 208-9. Cooper: *Body, Soul, and Life Everlasting*, 59-
62. Bremmer: *Early Greek Concept*, 80-2. Lavater: *Ghostes and
Spirits*, 92. Sands: 'De kommo tvänne dufvor', 366. Bockie:
Death and the Invisible Powers, 132. Andrew Lang, expressing
himself in the inimitable fashion of many nineteenth-century
scholars, observed anent the appearance of ghosts in the form
of animals, 'This is the kind of story one seldom or never
hears in drawing-rooms, but it is the prevalent and fashionable
kind among the peasantry, for example, in Shropshire', 'The
comparative study of ghost stories', *The Nineteenth Century* 98
(April 1885), 624.

2. THE MIDDLE AGES: PITEOUS REVENANTS, NECROMANTIC SPIRITS, AND VAMPIRES

1   Friedman & Overton: 'Death and afterlife', 39-40. Nathan: 'Le
     mort et son représentant', 106. DuBois: *Nordic Religions*, 75.
     Klapisch-Zuber: *Women, Family, and Ritual*, 305. Fine: 'Le parrain,
     le filleul, et l'au-delà', 129-33. Canziani: *Through the Apennines*,
     39. Almquist: *Viking Ale*, 162. (Translation given in Almquist).
     Evans-Pritchard: *Nuer Religion*, 163, 164. Cf. *Deuteronomy* 25.5-6:
     'If brethren dwell together, and one of them die, and have no
     child, the wife of the dead shall not marry without to a stranger:
     her husband's brother shall go in unto her, and take her to him to
     wife, and perform the duty of an husband's brother to her. And it
     shall be that the firstborn which she beareth shall succeed *in the
     name of the brother which is dead*, that his name be not put out of
     the world' (my italics). Bockie: *Death and the Invisible Powers*, 131.
2   See Copeland: 'The earthly monastery', 142-58.
3   Trans. R.H. Charles (London: SPCK 1917), 37-8.
4   Wright: *The Early History of Heaven*, 164-81. A.Y. Collins:
     Cosmology and Eschatology in Jewish and Christian Apocalypticism
     (Leiden: Brill 1996), 21-54.
5   Caesarius: *Dialogus miraculorum* Book 11, chapter 12. King
     Louis's vision, *Chronicon Centulense* Book 3, chapter 21 =
     Patrologia Latina 174.1288. Lady Gregory: *Visions and Beliefs*, 107.
     This physicality of popular conceptions of Purgatory continued
     in some places into the twentieth century. See, for example,
     Bloch-Raymond & Frayssenge: *Les êtres de la brume*, 70. Russell:
     A History of Heaven, 64-90. Camporesi: *The Fear of Hell*, 3-23. Le
     Goff: The Birth of Purgatory, 1-12, 96-127, 154-76. On Limbo,
     see the article s.v. in the *Catholic Encyclopaedia* 8.762-5 and the
     literature there cited. Heaven, Hell, and Purgatory could be,
     and were, visited in vision by living individuals. Dante's *Divina
     Commedia* is the most obvious example of such an account, but
     see also the twelfth-century *Vision of Tundal* in which a knight
     visits seven places of the otherworld under the guidance of an
     angel, Haas: 'Otherworldly journeys', 455-9.
6   Nardi: *Saggi di filosofia dantesca*, 311-40. Dante places Purgatory
     directly at the antipodes of Jerusalem, Cornish: *Reading Dante's
     Stars*, 65, fig.1. On Lough Derg, see Greenblatt: *Hamlet in*

Purgatory, 93-8. For this and other accounts, see Le Goff: *The Birth of Purgatory*, 177-208. Classical parallels for such a cave include the entrance to Hades, which was also the object of pilgrimage in ancient times. See Paget: *In the Footsteps of Orpheus*, 111-15, and Temple: *Netherworld*, 3-68, with his plates 4-19 which show the entrance to the complex of passages and rooms making up the underground sanctuary at Baiae, known as the 'Oracle of the Dead'.

7 Cf. Schmitt: 'The living and the dead are united... The individual contractual ties that people establish before death remain in effect after death and underlie apparitions of the dead', *Ghosts in the Middle Ages*, 66. See further Polo de Beaulieu: 'De Beaucaire (1211) à Alès (1323)', 319-41. The dead could also be used to satisfy people's legitimate curiosity about certain aspects of life after death. This is what a Dominican did in 1323. Called by a widow to exorcise the ghost of her late husband, he took the opportunity to quiz the spirit about several theological points, including Purgatory. See Girolamo Menghi: *Compendio dell'arte essorcistica* (Bologna 1584), 430-35.

8 Schmitt: *Op,cit.* supra, 59-60. Cf. the ghost of Jacob Walch who returned to his friend Chonrad Stoecklin in fulfilment of a pact the two had made in life, Ginzburg: *Shaman of Oberstdorf*, 9-16.

9 Schmitt: *Ghosts in the Middle Ages*, 35, 41-3, 136-40. Polo de Beaulieu: 'Le lundi des trépassés', 1191-2. McLoughlin: 'On communion with the dead', 23-34. Spinaeus: *Utrum sonus campanarum*, 8-9. Jones & Pennick: *History of Pagan Europe*, 132-7, 156-64.

10 DuBois: *Nordic Religions in the Viking Age*, 70, 75, 87, 89-90, 195-6. Davidson: 'The restless dead', 155-75. The dead could take a remarkably solid physical form, as in the long-lasting Icelandic belief that they could wrestle with the living. See Adalsteinsson: 'Wrestling with a ghost', 7-20. Involvement with the dead is also a feature of the Germanic sagas, 'in which the dead regularly return to inflict punishment, share meals, exact revenge, give advice, teach, or give gifts', Geary: *Living With the Dead*, 83. In Anglo-Saxon culture there may have been a close link between the benevolent ancestral dead and elves, 'aelf' being a general name for non-human spirits. See Griffiths: *Aspects of Anglo-Saxon Magic*, 32-3. Nedkvitne: 'Beyond historical anthropology', 41-2.

11 Vitalis: *Historia Ecclesiastica* Book 8, chapter 17 = *Patrologia Latina* 188.607-12. This is but one version of the ghostly procession of the dead, on which see further Ginzburg: *Night Battles*, 40-1, 47-50 and *Shaman of Oberstdorf*, 26-34.

12 *Ghosts in the Middle Ages*, 7. Cf. *Ibid*., 221.

13 Cameron: *The Reformation of the Heretics*, 73-4, 96-7. Gonet & Molnar: *Les Vaudois au Moyen Age*, 437-41. Le Roy Ladurie: *Montaillou*, 344-50. Even outwith the Cathar heresy there was a popular, though unorthodox, belief that the soul stayed near the body for the first month after death. See Roberts: 'Contesting sacred space', 133.

14 In Iceland, the returning dead are easily recognisable, but they are not wraiths or spirits. They are the revivified bodies of the dead. Davidson: 'The restless dead', 164-7, 169. Cf. Bowyer on visions of the otherworld by people who die and then return to life to give an account of what they have seen and experienced. 'All these visions encourage the reader to think of the dead as continuing their existence in apparently physical bodies in an apparently physical world; and while certain theologians doubted whether these visions could be taken literally, it is clear that for the majority of mediaeval men the next world was conceived as a mode of existence barely different from this life. All these visions place the Other World within the confines of the physical universe', 'The role of the ghost story', 182-3.

15 *De miraculis* 1.28 = *Patrologia Latina* 189.904-6. Cf. the incident from nineteenth-century Ireland, recorded by Lady Gregory, in which a female ghost appeared to a man and explained that she needed to have twenty Masses said for her to make up for twenty she missed in life, and that she still had small debts left unpaid, which were keeping her from rest, *Visions and Beliefs*, 95-6. One must always bear in mind of course, the possibility that the whole narrative may be a fiction devised by Peter the Venerable for the purpose of making certain theological and moral points to his readers. If we take this line, there is not much point in our proceeding further, since deliberate fiction is deliberate fiction. But if we allow the possibility that Peter is relating (at second hand) the elements of a real experience, however these may or may not have been embellished in the first or second tellings, there are components worth discussing, which is the course I have chosen to pursue here.

16 *Exodus* 12.29. *Job* 34.20, 'In a moment shall they die, and the people shall be troubled at midnight, and pass away'. *Psalm* 118.62 (Vulgate). On sleep patterns, see Ekirch: *At Day's Close*, 300-4.

17 Trachtenberg: *Jewish Magic and Superstition*, 66-7.

18 *Seeing Ghosts*, 25-6.

19 Watt: 'Some personal experiences of the second sight', 29-30.

20 *Seeing Ghosts*, 234.

21 See further Schmitt: *Ghosts in the Middle Ages*, 71-8. Cf. Bowyer: 'The mediaeval ghost or spirit appears as an integral part of an immense and ordered spiritual world which includes not merely tormented sinners and devils, but also guardian angels and benevolent saints', 'The role of the ghost story in Mediaeval Christianity', 177.

22 *Description of the Western Isles*, 322. Cf. Campbell: *Witchcraft and Second Sight*, 125-6, 137-41. A MacGregor: *Highland Superstitions* (Stirling: Eneas MacKay 1922), 34-40. F. MacDonald has recorded modern instances of the same ability to have premonitions of death, *Island Voices* (Irvine: Carrick Media 1992), 163-8.

23 Ralph Higden: *Polychronicon* Book 1, chapter 44. Sacheverell: *An Account of the Isle of Man* (1702), ed. J.G. Cumming (Douglas: Manx Society 1859), 20. Kvideland & Sehmsdorf: *Scandinavian Folk Belief and Legend*, 61, 63.

24 Trachtenberg: *Jewish Magic and Superstition*, 222-4. Schmidt: *Israel's Beneficent Dead*, 147-58. On texts from Mesopotamia, see *Ibid.*, 215-16. Nihan: 'I Samuel 28 and the condemnation of necromancy', 24-32, 43-6. Alexander: 'Sefer Ha Razim and the problem of black magic', 174-8. P.G. Maxwell-Stuart: 'Myrtle and the Eleusinian Mysteries', *Wiener Studien* 85 (1972), 145-61. Interestingly enough, apart from the use of *Deuteronomy* 18.14 in the Temple Scroll, there is no allusion to necromancy in the Qumran archive.

25 *Odyssey* 11.207-8. See also Ogden: *Greek and Roman Necromancy*, 163-90. Bremmer: *Rise and Fall of the Afterlife*, 71-6.

26 Bremmer: *Rise and Fall of the Afterlife*, 76-83. It is against such a background of magical practice that we should read the episodes of Jesus's raising Jairus's daughter and Lazarus from the dead: *Matthew* 9.18, 23-6, repeated in *Mark* 5.22-4, 35-42, and *Luke* 8.41-2, 49-55; *John* 11.3-4, 14, 17, 38-44. In 210/213

Tertullian spoke out against those who promised to call the
dead from the otherworld, *De Anima* 57.2; and St Isidore of
Seville (560-636) referred to *necromantici* who resuscitate and
interrogate the dead, *Etymologiae* 8.9. According to Talmudic
tradition, the time in which the dead could be raised was
limited. 'A certain Sadducee said to Rabbi Abbahu, "You
maintain that the souls of the righteous are hidden under
the Throne of Glory. Then how did the bone-[practising]
necromancer bring up Samuel by means of his necromancy?"
"There it was within twelve months [of death]", he replied. For
it was taught: "For full [twelve months] the body is in existence
and the soul ascends and descends; after twelve months
the body ceases to exist, and the soul ascends but descends
nevermore"' *Shabbath* 152b.

27 Poulin: *L'idéal de sainteté*, 148-9. Anent the witch of Endor, see
Rabanus Maurus: *De magicis artibus* = Migne, *Patrologia Latina*
11.1097-99. Nider: *Formicarius* 3.1. Nider summarises the change
in the use of the word *necromantici* in 5.4.

28 *The Awntyrs off Arthure at the Terne Wathelyn*, ed. R. Hanna
(Manchester: Manchester University Press 1974), verses 105-110.
The date of the poem is c.1400-1430. There is a Hungarian
tradition which says that a ghost may appear as a flame or a
fiery man. 'I saw them myself, I was still a child at the time.
These fiery men were coming nearer, and when they met up
they struck out at each other, the sparks just flew from them!
This one lashed out, then the other one, and we couldn't see
what with, you know, but they really went for each other, they
clashed head on so to speak! Well, I'm telling you, I saw this
myself. People were mighty scared of these men in flames, but
they didn't cause any harm anywhere at all. They didn't injure
or attack a living soul', T. Dömötör: *Hungarian Folk Beliefs*,
English trans. (Bloomington: Indiana University Press 1981), 104.

29 Avery-Peck: 'Death and afterlife in the early Rabbinic sources',
265. Acceptance of universal bodily resurrection is to be found
in Zoroastrianism where it is described as 'a miraculous work of
Ahura Mazda's, carried out as part of his plan for the perfecting
of all things', Cohn: *Cosmos, Chance, and the World to Come*, 97.
Cf. the Hindu notion that burial is disgusting, insanitary, and
theologically nonsensical, C.A. Bayly: 'From ritual to ceremony:
death ritual and society in Hindu North India since 1600', in

J. Whaley: *Mirrors of Mortality* q.v. 179. On the development of Christian belief, see Bremmer: *The Rise and Fall of the Afterlife*, 41-55. Odo of Ourschamp: *Quaestiones* 39, ed. Cardinal J.B. Pitra: *Analecta Novissima* Vol. 2 (1888), 40-1. Cf. St Thomas Aquinas: *Summa theologiae* Part 3 (supplement), question 80, articles 1-5. On the thirteenth century's concentration on the moment of death, see Gragnolati: *Experiencing the Afterlife*, 1-52.

30 Oldridge: *Strange Histories*, 66-7.

31 Campbell Thompson: *Semitic Magic*, 52. Lawson: *Modern Greek Folklore*, 454. I have suggested elsewhere that the Choephoroi may have been shown on the Greek stage as bats, which would make them akin to the later notion of vampires, 'The appearance of Aeschylus's Erinyes', *Greece & Rome*, 2nd series, 20 (1973), 81-4. Trachtenberg: *Jewish Magic and Superstition*, 38-9. Barber: *Vampires*, 39-45, 7-8. Lawson: *Modern Greek Folklore*, 381-2. Abbott: *Macedonian Folklore*, 217-22. Quotation from Allacci in Lawson: *op.cit.*, 366-7.

32 Wilson: *The Magical Universe*, 203, 212, 284, 302-3. William of Newburgh: *Historia* Book 5, chapters 22 & 23. Bogatyrëv: *Vampires in the Carpathians*, 133-4. Barber: *Vampires*, 66-81. Schmitt: *Ghosts in the Middle Ages*, 83.

33 Dabrowska: 'Passeport pour l'au-delà', 320. St Bernard of Clairvaux, we are told, even asked to have relics of St Judas Thaddaeus with him in his grave to help him on the Day of Judgement. Wilson: *The After Death Experience*, 18. While the Incas' customs are unusual, one must bear in mind Victoria's instructions anent the dead Prince Albert. Servants were to lay out fresh clothes for him every morning, and bring hot shaving water, just as they had done while the Prince was alive.

3. EARLY MODERN GHOSTS: PERSISTENT APPEARANCES, STAGE PHANTOMS, AND POLTERGEISTS

1 St Dunstan, Anon: *Vita Sancti Oswaldi*, in J. Rain (ed.): *The Historians of the Church of York and their Archbishops*, 3 vols. (London: Longman 1879-94), 1.458. P. Ariès: *L'homme devant la mort* (Paris: Éditions du Seuil 1977), 73-4, 75-6. R. Muchembled:

Popular Culture and Elite Culture in France, 1400-1750, English
trans. (Baton Rouge & London: Louisiana State University
1985), 63. Marshall: *Beliefs and the Dead*, 14-15, 20-1. Trithemius,
P. Ball: The Devil's Doctor (London: William Heinemann 2006),
45. Finucane: *Appearances of the Dead*, 60-75.

2   Koslofsky: *The Reformation of the Dead*, 35-6, where the
quotations from Luther are given. Greenblatt: *Hamlet in
Purgatory*, 33-5. Note that Hamlet describes the otherworld
in orthodox Protestant terms as 'the undiscovered country,
from whose bourn/No traveller returns', although his father's
ghost's explanation of where he usually resides suggests a
Catholic Purgatory. The most interesting modern study of post-
reformation relations between the living and the dead is the
final section of Wilhelm-Schaffer's *Gottes Beamter und Spielmann
des Teufels*, Gordon: 'Malevolent ghosts', 98. Cf. John Webster:
'What do the dead do, uncle? Do they eat,/Hear music, go
a-hunting, and be merry/ As we that live? No, coz, they sleep',
The White Devil Act 1, scene 2. Marshall: 'The map of God's
word', 120-3. Cf. the Jewish belief that the dead exist in a
conscious intermediate state during the period between their
personal death and their eventual personal resurrection, Cooper:
Body, Soul, and Life Everlasting, 81-5. Bath & Newton: 'Sensible
proof of spirits', 7. A Spicer: 'Defile not Christ's kirk with your
carrion: burial and the development of burial aisles in post-
reformation Scotland', in Gordon & Marshall : *The Place of the
Dead* q.v. 149-51. Cf. the attitude of the descendants of the Inca
who 'confided to local priests that they were tormented by
the voices of their dead parents and grandparents, who called
out to them piteously through the church floors. Unable to
rest comfortably in their new tombs, the dead told them they
felt like prisoners. They could no longer sit upright and move
around as they had in their old shrines: they were pinned
down in graves that felt like straitjackets', Pringle: *The Mummy
Congress*, 316.

3   Luther: *Sermons on John, Chapters 14-16*, at 14.11 and 1613; *Table
Talk*, 10 January 1538. Lavater: *Of Ghostes and Spirites*, 127-33.
Lavater also appeals to earlier authorities to show that belief
in ghosts (that is, dead people's souls parted from their bodies),
was ejected by many of the Church Fathers, *Ibid.* 116-23. But
Lavater cannot resist recording a supposed exchange between 'a

professor of the Gospel' and 'a Papist'. 'Here I cannot overpass
with silence a certain merry jest: when once there chanced
to be talk in a certain place of visions and spirits, a certain
professor of the Gospel said unto a Papist in this manner: "You
ought", quoth he, "even by this to gather that our religion is
true and yours false, for that since the Gospel was preached unto
us, very few spirits have been seen of any man". To whom the
other made answer by way of reasoning called *violentum*: "Nay",
saith he, "hereby ye may gather that your religion is naught and
ours good: for the Devil assaulteth those whom he feareth will
shortly revolt from him"', *Ibid.* 183-4. Bruce Gordon makes the
useful observation that much sixteenth-century material anent
ghosts is to be found either in chronicles, or in the works of
religious writers who want to make a point about the ubiquity
of Satan and the iniquity of Catholicism, 'Malevolent ghosts',
93. Thomas: *Religion and the Decline of Magic*, 602-5. West: *The
Invisible World*, 181. On Catholic defence of Purgatory, see St
Robert Bellarmine: *De purgatorio* Book 1, chaps. 3 & 4, 13 & 14
and Book 2, chap.3. From time to time there were reports even
of demons who testified to the reality of Purgatory, as in the
case of Verin, the evil spirit who spoke through Sister Louise
Capeau during incidents of possession affecting the convent of
Aix-en-Provence in 1610/11. But see further Walker: *Unclean
Spirits* 75-6. Rosina Blökhl-Huber, in Lederer: Living with the
dead', 40-7.

4 Newton: 'Reading ghosts', 57. W.E. Burns: *An Age of Wonders*
(Manchester: Manchester University Press 2002), 1-3. Marshall:
'Deceptive appearances', 199-200.

5 *Religion and Culture*, 294-7, 312-14. Quotation from p.296.

6 Erasmus: *Colloquies*, trans. C.R. Thompson in Collected
Works, Vol. 39 (Toronto: University of Toronto 1997), 531-44.
Bolognese chronicle quoted in Camporesi: *Bread of Dreams*, 100.
Thomas: *Religion and the Decline of Magic*, 592, 596. Marshall:
Beliefs and the Dead, 242-5. Taillepied: *A Treatise of Ghosts* 16.113.
Del Rio: *Disquisitiones Magicae* Book 2, question 26, section 1.

7 West: *The Invisible World*, 193. Malcolm Gaskill has pointed
out that in early modern literature a large number of ghosts is
reported to have returned in order to protest against injustice or
to confess to a crime, and that in court cases at least, 'ghosts and
dreams can be interpreted as fictions enabling witnesses not just

to testify with conviction, but to distance themselves from the origin of their evidence', 'Reporting murder', 14-16. Quotation from p.16.

8 Thomas: *Religion and the Decline of Magic*, 590-2. Sadducism was so called from *Luke* 23.8: 'For the Sadducees say there is no resurrection, neither angel nor spirit'. Howard: *Defensative*, 90r. More in Glanvill: *Essays on Several Important Subjects*, 16.

9 Cardano: *De rerum varietate* Book 16, chap.93. Cf. the ghost of Mrs Leakey who was able to kick a living man's backside, Brown: 'The ghost of old Mrs. Leakey', 142; and that of Thomas Goddard's father-in-law who had on 'the same clothes, hat, stockings, and shoes he did usually wear when he was living', and held a rational conversation with his son-in-law. Glanvill: *Saducismus Triumphatus* Part 2, p.172. Marshall: 'Deceptive appearances', 201-2. For modern examples, see Green & MacCreery: *Apparitions*, 102-13. The Breslau incident is recorded in J. Grasse: *Sagenbuch des preussischen Staats* (Glogau 1868), quoted by Barber: *Vampires*, 10-13. The sensation of being smothered was common to many ghostly assaults. It was known by several names – the old hag, ephialtes, incubus, nightmare – and the victim usually felt paralysed during the attack. See further Hufford: *The Terror that Comes in the Night*, 148-9, 171-244. Corrector of Burchard of Worms: *Decreta* Book 19, chap.5 = Migne, *Patrologia Latina* 140.974. Stewart: *Demons and the Devil*, 268, note 16. Bogatyrëv recounts an incident from 1916. A dead mother kept visiting her daughter and trying to choke her. No kind of remedy seemed to have any effect, and the conclusion was that the mother, realising she was dead, wanted her daughter dead, too: *Vampires in the Carpathians*, 129. This kind of behaviour is not restricted to ghosts of the western tradition. See, for example, Hardman: *Other Worlds*, 91-2 which describes a similar malevolence among the ghosts of Lohorung Rai. Klaniczay: *The Uses of Supernatural Power*, 178. Fermor: *Roumeli*, 41. The belief was still prevalent among Greek communities in the USA during the 1930s. See Lee: 'Folklore of the Greeks in America', 302-5.

10 'Protestantism, pragmatism, and popular religion', 85-6.

11 Marshall: 'Old Mother Leakey', 92. Taillepied: *A Treatise of Ghosts* (1588), English trans. (London: Fortune Press 1933), 80. Eleanor Prosser has noted the argument that the ghost of Hamlet's

father is actually malevolent and gives the initial impression of being a demon. It is hardly conceivable, it runs, that God would have permitted the release of a soul from Purgatory (which is where Hamlet's father says he has been in torment because he died unshriven), to corrupt Hamlet into sin by getting him to commit a murder, Prosser: *Hamlet and Revenge*, 138-42.

12 For a detailed discussion of western European theatrical conventions, see P. Butterworth: *Magic on the Early English Stage* (Cambridge: Cambridge University Press 2005), 74-86.

13 Sohmer: *Shakespeare's Mystery Play*, 219-23. The modern theatrical convention – not always adopted – of having no ghost appear and leaving its presence to the imagination of the audience, is thus nonsensical since it deprives the onlookers of that very sense of the physical dead which is important to the play.

14 Plautus: *Mostellaria* 470-528. Otloh: *Liber visionum* chap. 16 = Migne, *Patrologia Latina* 146.571-2. Geraldus: *Itinerarium Cambriae* Book 1, chap. 12. See also Finucane: *Appearances of the Dead*, 101-6. Owen: *Can We Explain the Poltergeist* ? 92-6. Del Rio: *Disquisitiones Magicae* Book 2, question 27, section 2. Physical phenomena were not always malign. The Blessed Beatrice d'Este II used to warn the people of Ferrara of impending calamities by making loud noises within her tomb, sometimes underlining the monition by changing its colour and causing it to ooze a great deal of liquid. See Camporesi: *Bread of Dreams*, 92. Puhle: 'Ghosts, apparitions, and poltergeist incidents', 292-305.

15 The following account is based on Perreaud's own account , but see also Labrousse: 'Le démon de Mâcon' in *Conscience et Conviction*, 16-41. Gauld & Cornell: *Poltergeists*, 226-8, 366-98.

16 *Disquisitiones Magicae* Book 2, question 27, section 2.

17 Gauld & Cornell: *Poltergeists*, 226-28, 366-98.

18 Lamb, Gauld, Cornell: 'A East Midlands poltergeist', 1-20, 139-55. Owen: *Can We Explain the Poltergeist*? 368-87. Fontana: 'A responsive poltergeist', 385-402; and 'The responsive South Wales poltergeist', 225-31. In the case of poltergeist activity, it seems that it is not actually an absolute requirement that one be dead to act as a stimulus for what appear to be preternatural phenomena. Note, for example, the case of William Drury of Tedworth, who was imprisoned for vagrancy and yet managed

to set off a series of poltergeist disturbances in the house of the magistrate who had sentenced him. See Holroyd: 'The mark of fear', 435-6.

19 Fontana: 'A responsive poltergeist', 402.

20 Lazare Meyssonier, a doctor in Mâcon, included an account of Perreaud's experience in the introduction to his 1650 translation of Giambattista della Porta's *Magia Naturalis*. This was very much more theatrical than Perreaud's own version. See further Labrousse: *Conscience et Conviction*, 36.

21 *Arminian Magazine* 7 (1784), 548-50, 606-8, 654-6.

4. THE SEVENTEENTH CENTURY: BOLSTERING RELIGION, PARTNERING WITCHCRAFT

1 Bath & Newton: 'Sensible proof of spirits', 1-14. Handley: 'Reclaiming ghosts in 1690s England', 345-55. Clark: *Thinking With Demons*, 294-311. Thomas: *Religion and the Decline of Magic*, 655-6. The seventeenth-century historian, Thomas Sprat, referring to the recent civil wars, maintained that the study of nature provided an attractive refuge for those who were tired of 'the passions and madness of that dismal age', *The History of the Royal Society of London* (London 1667), 53.

2 Glanvill: *Saducismus Triumphatus* Part 2, pp.181-4.

3 On Stoeckhlin, see Behringer: *Shaman of Oberstdorf*, 10-16. On the Bellamy incident, see E. Gurney, F.W.H. Myers, F. Podmore: *Phantasms of the Living* 2 vols. (London: Trübner & Co 1886), 2.216.

4 *Sermons Preached Upon Several Occasions* 2 vols. (Oxford 1842), 1.287-8.

5 See further S. Schaffer: 'Halley's atheism and the end of the world', *Notes and Records of the Royal Society of London* 32 (1977-78), 17-40.

6 Thomas: *Religion and the Decline of Magic*, 227, 270-1, 275, 375, 590-1. C.W. Marsh: *The Family of Love in English Society, 1550-1630* (Cambridge: Cambridge University Press 1994), 70-4. Jakob Boehme: *Aurora*, English trans. (London: J.M. Watkins 1914), 658-66. An excellent example of the permeative part played by astrology in some people's lives can be seen in the

diary of the lawyer and nonconformist preacher, Samuel Jeake, who carefully noted the position of the planets at significant moments in his life. See M. Hunter & A. Gregory (edd.): *An Astrological Diary of the Seventeenth Century: Samuel Jeake of Rye, 1652-1699* (Oxford: Oxford University Press 1988).

7   H. Berry: *Gender, Society, and Print Culture in Late Stuart England: The Cultural World of the Athenian Mercury* (Aldershot: Ashgate 2003), 18-25.G.D. McEwen, true to the spirit of the 1970s, noted the Mercury's interest in wonders of all kinds, but immediately played these down in favour of its 'scientific' questions, *The Oracle of the Coffee House: John Dunton's Athenian Mercury* (San Marino, California: Huntingdon Library 1972), 125. S. Handley: 'Reclaiming ghosts in 1690s England', 346-7.

8   'Reclaiming ghosts in 1690s England', 355. See also Finucane: *Appearances of the Dead*, 119-25.

9   Sinclair: *Satan's Invisible World Discovered*, supplement xxi-xxxix. R. Law: *Memorialls*, 269-77.

10 *The Statistical Account of Scotland*, ed. Sir John Sinclair (reissued Wakefield: EP Publishing 1983), Vol. 5, p.314.

11 On Masonry, see D. Stevenson: *The First Freemasons: Scotland's Early Lodges and their Members* (Aberdeen: Aberdeen University Press 1988), 4, 82-3.

12 Danish troops were called on to reinforce William of Orange's army in subduing Ireland during the Jacobite War, 1689-91. They sailed from the west of Scotland in spring 1690. By 1691, however, many were deserting and trying to make their way back to Europe, initially to France. Rerrick is a coastal parish on the Solway Firth, so it is possible that the foreign soldiers this lad met were deserters. From the text, it seems as though they were making their way eastwards, since we are told they and the lad went to Flanders. On these Danish troops, see K. Danaher & J.G. Simmons (edd.): *The Danish Force in Ireland, 1690-1691* (Dublin: Irish Manuscripts Commission 1962), 5-24. It is worth noting that there were also Dutch troops in the west of Scotland at this time.

13 Glanvill: *Saducismus Triumphatus* Part 2, pp.143-4. Cf. *Ibid.* 211-13, and Richard Chamberlain's *Lithobolia, or. The Stone-Throwing Devil* (London 1698) where he says that the incident he describes 'has confirmed myself and others in the opinion that there are such things as witches and the effects of witchcraft,

or at least the mischievous actions of evil spirits'. See further
Owen: *Can We Explain the Poltergeist?* 94-100, 181-7. Ramón
de Aguilar has recorded several modern instances of poltergeist
fire-raising in Panama, which are interesting for their detail,
but none is connected with witches or witchcraft, *Las casas
que se incendian solas: psicopirosis en Panamá* (Panama: Editorial
Universitoria 1995).

14 Puhle: 'Ghosts, apparitions, and poltergeist incidents', 300.

15 Further incidents of violence against the house itself include
staves being thrust through the wall and the roof. A barn door
and a mid-wall were also broken down.

16 Gauld and Cornell record the observation of Fr. Herbert
Thurston, who wrote on ghosts and poltergeists in the mid-
twentieth century, that poltergeists tend to show themselves to
children rather than adults, *Poltergeist* 111-12. The Rerrick case
clearly proves an exception to this rule, if rule there be.

17 On percentages, see Gauld & Cornell: *Poltergeist*, 226-7. It is also
worth noting that they found the phenomenon of a hand seen
or felt in only seven per cent of these cases. So that, too, is a
somewhat unusual feature of the MacKie incident, whether we
regard is as susceptible to non-preternatural explanation or not.
Evans: *Seeing Ghosts*, 134-42.

18 *Poltergeist*, 168-70.

19 'The charge of atheism and the language of radical speculation,
1640-1660' in M. Hunter & D. Wootton (edd.): *Atheism from the
Reformation to the Enlightenment* (Oxford: Clarendon Press 1992),
134, 158.

20 *A Whip for the Droll*, 18.

5. THE EIGHTEENTH AND NINETEENTH CENTURIES: UNNERVING THE PUBLIC, INTRIGUING SCIENCE, PHOTOGRAPHING SPIRITS.

1 *The Rise of Supernatural Fiction*, 37. This continues with many of
the ghosts of Gothic fiction. In Walpole's *Castle of Otranto*, for
example, the ghost of the murdered Prince of Otranto is so vast
that it causes a castle to fall down – pure theatre, designed almost
to be represented by the elaborate stage machinery of the period.

2 G.C. Lichtenberg: *Visits to England, as described in his Letters and Diaries,* ed. & trans. M.L. Mare & W.H. Quarrell (Oxford: Clarendon Press 1938), 9-11. The actual mechanics of having a ghost appear and disappear are described by John Ripley: *Julius Caesar on Stage in England and America, 1599-1973* (Cambridge: Cambridge University Press 1980), 38.

3 See further F. Lentzsch: 'London's theatre – Drury Lane and Somerset House: all the city's a stage' in F. Lentzsch (ed.): *Fuseli, the Wild Swiss,* English trans. (Zurich: Scheidegger & Speiss 2005), 210-11. Quotation from Lewis = Act 2, scene 1. Jonathan Swift in his own sardonic fashion took a swipe at the ghost phenomenon. When Gulliver visits the land of Glubbdubdrib he is entertained by the Governor, a skilled necromancer, who summons for Gulliver's diversion and instruction all manner of ghosts including many of the famous dead. Unfortunately, as Gulliver soon realises, these heroes of history turn out to be, as he puts it, 'the vilest rogues and traitors, and thus a grave disappointment to his high hopes for edification, *Gulliver's Travels* Book 3, chapters 7 and 8.

4 Farge: *Fragile Lives,* 199. Sawday: *The Body Emblazoned,* 110. See also *Ibid.* 64, 72-5, 87, 98. It is interesting that the reformer Philipp Melanchthon begins his treatise on the soul (*De anima,* Paris 1540), with pagan definitions which tied it into physical substance (*materia*), proceeds to define its meaning in Christian theology as 'a spirit endowed with understanding, which is the second part of a human's material constitution', and then devotes most of the rest of his book to a description of the constituent parts of the human body, natural enough in view of his intention to demonstrate that the body is the temple of the soul, and that by anatomising the body we have demonstrated for us the wisdom and foresight of God. See further French: *Dissection and Vivisection,* 216-21 and Cunningham: *The Anatomical Renaissance,* 231-4.

5 *Disquisitiones Magicae* Book 2, question 26, section 2. It is also relevant to note that during the seventeenth century, Protestant funerals had become less and less elaborate, to the point that contemporaries were complaining about the disrespect shown to the dead. See Thomas: *Religion and the Decline of Magic,* 722-3. Hence the dead body tended to be seen as something quite distinct from the spirit with neither requiring much, if any

ritual from the living, the corpse because it was mere flesh, the
spirit because its abode was now fixed and it neither could nor
would return. Porter: *Flesh in the Age of Reason*, 218-23.

6   *An Essay on the Nature of the Human Body*, 46.

7   *Essays, Moral and Political*, 105-6. See also Porter: 'Witchcraft and
    magic in enlightenment, Romantic, and liberal thought', 197-9.

8   Gargett: *Voltaire and Protestantism*, 471-2. Cf. 'There was to be no
    half-hearted compromise with the enemy Voltaire had fought
    all his life [*i.e. Catholicism*]. The Enlightenment would supersede,
    not complete, the Reformation', *Ibid.* 479. See also Finucane:
    Appearances of the Dead, 161-9. Ellis: *The History of Gothic
    Fiction*, 83-96, 105-6. Ellis underlines the connection between
    Lewis's novel and the recent French revolution. Cf. Watt:
    Contesting the Gothic, 92. It is interesting that Lewis should have
    mentioned a thirst for information in connection with hearing
    Mass. The Mass is a religious ritual, not a seminar; but his
    phrase is redolent of the outlook of his time and class. Porter:
    Enlightenment, 96-129. Roche: *France in the Enlightenment*, 578-
    607. On German attitudes, see Hadley: *The Undiscovered Genre*,
    84-109, especially 96-7. See also Watt: *Contesting the Gothic*, 70-
    84. Huet: 'Deadly fear', 222-31.

9   *Hamburgische Dramaturgie* (Leipzig: Philipp Reclam c.1910), 51.
    Translation of Idris Parry. Cf. Martin Martin who raised, for
    the purposes of argument, three objections to accepting the
    reality of second sight but found himself obliged, by the sheer
    improbability of the sceptical points of dissent and his own
    direct experiences of the phenomenon, to acknowledge that *soi-
    disant* rational answers were inadequate, *Description of the Western
    Isles*, 326-8. On 18 August 1773, Boswell recorded that he saw
    the face of his dead daughter while he was in a chaise travelling
    to St Andrews, a confession which, along with other references
    to ghostly visions, he subsequently eliminated or neutralised
    so that he might not seem to be superstitious. See Jemielity: 'A
    keener eye on vacancy', 24-40.

10 Rack: *Reasonable Enthusiast*, 59, 431-6. Quotation from *Letters*,
    ed. J. Telford, 8 vols. (London: Epworth Press 1960), 1.48.

11 Ashton: *Chapbooks of the Eighteenth Century*, 68-73. Pictures
    could also be used with humorous intent. Samuel Johnson,
    for example, was satirised as a ghost in a series of engravings,
    Brownell: 'Dr Johnson's ghost', 339-57. A final note on the

title page of *An Authentic narrative* records, 'Published with the content and approbation of the family and other parties concerned, to authenticate which, the original copy is signed by them'. Parsons: 'Ghost stories before Defoe', 293-8. See also Secord: 'A September day', 639-50; Earle: *The World of Defoe*, 43; Damrosch: 'Defoe as ambiguous impersonator', 153-5. Defoe: *Essay on the History and Reality of Apparitions*, 7.

12 Roughead: *Twelve Scots Trials*, 85-105. Scott: *Letters on Demonology and Witchcraft*, 217.

13 See further Clery: *The Rise of Supernatural Fiction*, 13-32.

14 Clery: *op.cit.* supra, 107-8. See also *Ibid.* 53-67. Ellis: *The History of Gothic Fiction*, 1-14. Watt sees the Gothic novel as a genre rooted in the frivolity of Walpole's *Castle of Otranto* and thence deviating into a wide range of perceptions and agenda according to the individual preoccupations of its various writers, *Contesting the Gothic*, 3-11.

15 See further R. Hutton: *The Triumph of the Moon: A History of Modern Pagan Witchcraft* (Oxford: Oxford University Press 1999), 21-2. P.G. Maxwell-Stuart: *Wizards, A History* (Stroud: Tempus Publishing 2004), 150-3.

16 The Hofmeister's ghost, Cassirer: 'An 18th century haunt', 114-19. Mr Hawker, S. Baring-Gould: *The Vicar of Morwenstow: A Life of Robert Stephen Hawker, MA* (London: Henry S. King & Co. 1876), 152, 153, 156-9. The situation in the towns was not necessarily different, as Owen Davies has pointed out in his studies of eighteenth- and nineteenth-century witchcraft; nor has the twentieth century been immune, as the work of Jeanne Favret-Saada and Perle Møhl attests.

17 Mrs Thrale quoted in Porter: *Enlightenment*, 229. Ellis: *The History of Gothic Fiction*, 161-204. The principal Catholic source which excited them most, as Ellis points out (pp.172-4), was Augustin Calmet whose *Dissertations upon the Apparitions of Angels, Demons, and Ghosts, and concerning the Vampires of Hungary, Bohemia, Moravia, and Silesia*, published in 1746, became available in English translation in 1759. On the early history of vampirism, see McNally & Florescu: *In Search of Dracula*, 117-32.

18 Reprinted in McNally & Florescu: *op. cit.* supra, 144.

19 Quotations from *Dracula*, 272-4, 369-71, 25. Porter: Witchcraft and magic', 214-18. On the background to Stoker's novel, see Murray: *From the Shadow of Dracula*, 172-97. Vampirism was

common in New England during the nineteenth century.
People were afraid that those who had died of tuberculosis
could return as vampires, so they dug up the bodies and
mutilated them in order to prevent this eventuality. See Sledzik
& Bellatoni: 'Bioarchaeological and biocultural evidence for the
New England vampire belief', 269-74.

20 See further Ballard: 'Before death and beyond', 41. Rockwell: 'The
ghosts of Evald Tang Kristensen', 51. Tangherlini: 'Who ya gonna
call?' 153-78. Alderson: *Essay on Apparitions*, 42-3, 51-2, 46. De
Boismont: *On Hallucinations*, 270. See *Ibid*. 312 where De Boismont
arranges the physical causes of hallucination under five heads:
special physical conditions, alcohol and neurotics, insanity, nervous
diseases, and inflammatory, acute, chronic, or other diseases.

21 Kircher: *Ars magna lucis et umbrae*, 773, 804. There is an excellent
illustration of his contraption in Georgius de Sepibus: *Romani
Collegii Societatis Jesu Musaeum Celeberrimum* (Rome 1678).
Nicolson, quoted in Castle: 'Phantasmagoria', 38. See also the
illustrations there on pp.33 and 41. The following paragraph
is based on Castle's article, but see also Castle: *The Female
Thermometer*, 140-67.

22 *Op.cit*. supra, 52. Schiller's influential but unfinished novel, *Der
Geisterseher* (The Ghost-Seeker), translated into English in 1795,
uses the device of phantasmagoria as well as the fashionable
subject of conjurations and secret societies as vehicles for the
eventual moral regeneration of his principal character.

23 See Coleman: *The Ghosts of the Trianon*, 15-17, 114-25. Senelier:
Le Mystère du Petit Trianon, 163-72. James: *The Varieties of
Religious Experience*, 388.

24 Cloutier: 'Mumler's ghosts', 20-8. Fischer: 'A photographer of
marvels', 29-43. Chéroux: 'Ghost dialectics', 45-71. Permutt:
Photographing the Spirit World, 11-36, 140-82. Photographs are not
the only way to record the presence of a dead person, of course.
Attempts, allegedly successful, have been made during the last
few years to record the voices of the dead; and sporadic efforts
have been made ever since the nineteenth century to receive
the imprints of spirit hands in wax. See further Coleman: 'Wax-
moulds of spirit limbs', 340-6, with a reply to his scepticism by
Barrington: 'The Kluski hands', 347-51.

25 Oppenheim: *The Other World*, 161-2. Cf. Bernard Shaw in his
preface to *Heartbreak House*, '[Society was] addicted to table-

rapping, materialisation séances, clairvoyance, palmistry, crystal-gazing, and the like to such an extent that it may be doubted whether before in the history of the world did sooth-sayers, astrologers, and unregistered therapeutic specialists of all sorts flourish as they did during this half century of the drift to the abyss'.

26 Quoted in Oppenheim: *op.cit.* supra, 94. Gillis has argued that some middle class Victorians re-imagined Heaven as an idealised extension of middle class Britain. 'In earlier periods, Christians had imagined Heaven to be one endless Sabbath, an eternity beyond the spectrum of ordinary time. Now, however, Heaven was endowed with temporality, a place where change, growth, and progress were all equally present... By the mid-nineteenth century, Heaven had ceased to be seen as a place of repose, worship, and contemplation of the divine and taken on all the attributes of the bourgeois ethic of hard work and ceaseless striving', *A World of Their Own Making*, 218. Cf. Jalland: *Death in the Victorian Family*, 266-70. On working class involvement in Spiritualism, see further Barrow: *Independent Spirits*, 96-145. The evolutionary theme was also taken up by literature which now frequently portrayed the ghost as an ape-like creature. See Ledwon: 'Darwin's ghosts', 10-16.

27 Finucane: *Appearances of the Dead*, 181-8. The short stories of the Scottish novelist Margaret Oliphant (1828-97) illustrate her belief and that of so many others of the time that science, for all its pretensions, could not explain everything. See J. Calder's introduction to Oliphant's collected stories, *A Beleaguered City* (Edinburgh: Canongate 2000). For a discussion of nineteenth-century female novelists' treatment of ghosts and the supernatural in general, see V.D. Dickerson: *Victorian Ghosts in the Noon tide: Women Writers and the Supernatural* (Columbia: University of Columbia Press 1998). Wilson: *God's Funeral*, 223-60. Gordon: *Ghostly Matters*, 10. Kselman: 'Alternative afterlives', 111-23.

28 The account of Home and the coals is given by Martin Tupper (1883), quoted in Oppenheim: *The Other World*, 34-5. See also *Ibid.* 13-15. Gaskill: *Hellish Nell*, 85-6. Lamont: *The First Psychic*, 158-62. Lamont makes the important point that the phenomena of the séance room represented not so much a religious crisis in mid-nineteenth-century society as a problem in how to

interpret evidence which ran counter to the accepted scientific theories of the period. See his 'Spiritualism and a mid-Victorian crisis of evidence', 897-920.

29 Flournoy: *Esprits et Médiums*, 186-92. Adolescent girls and young females formed an important segment of the mediumistic profession. Oppenheim points to a degree of sensuality inherent in their performances, which was noted by contemporaries, *The Other World*, 21. Cf.. Barrow: *Independent Spirits*, 261-3. On ectoplasm and the convincing nature of some of the materialisations, see further Gaskill: *Hellish Nell*, 89-90. Cf. Oppenheim, 'Not only did these materialised forms separate themselves entirely from the medium; they walked around the room, wrote messages, lifted [the author of this extract] off the ground, and ate baked apples', *The Other World*, 70. See also Finucane: *Appearances of the Dead*, 187-90. Accounts of a clergyman's visits to séances in London during the early 1870s may be read in Davies: *Unorthodox London*, 305-43.

30 Sidgwick: *Proceedings of the Society for Psychical Research* 5 (1888-89), 272. But notice Wilson's perceptive comment that 'among Victorian men of science, Christian commitment was not the exception but the rule', *God's Funeral*, 241-2. We sometimes allow the agnostic and atheist to loom too large in our view of the period. On the early years of the SPR, see further Thurschwell: *Literature, Technology, and Magical Thinking*, 12-36. Oppenheim: *The Other World*, 111-58. Wicke has argued that Bram Stoker's *Dracula* is a novel which owes more to the development of the technology of communication in the late 1890s than to the Gothic tradition of novel-writing, 'Vampiric writing', 467-93. Finucane: *Appearances of the Dead*, 190-210. Marquis: *Loups, sorciers, criminals*, 93-9.

31 Finucane: *Appearances of the Dead*, 192. Nisbet: 'Apparitions', 91-2. Green & McCreery: *Apparitions*, 95. Abend: 'Spectres of the secular', 507. Sharp: 'Fighting for the afterlife', 282-95. The Catholic Church was not alone in objecting to Spiritualism, of course. There were denunciations from the Anglican and nonconformist churches, too. See Oppenheim: *The Other World*, 64-5. Winter: 'Spiritualism and the First World War', 186, 190. It is important not to assume, along with many ecclesiastical and scientific voices of the period, that belief in ghosts and other occult phenomena was now more or less limited to the

uneducated peasantry. The history of Spiritualism alone shows this was not so. Gillis: *A World of Their Own Making*, 210.

6. THE TWENTIETH CENTURY: MANUFACTURING GHOSTS ON AN INDUSTRIAL SCALE

1   Note, too, that in Madagascar dead bodies are touched by their closest living kinspeople as a means of preserving the strength of kinship ties through this gesture of strong emotional attachment. Women are especially important here, because they are thought to be the vessels of such emotions, Bloch: *Placing the Dead*, 156. Some such belief may also underlie the role of the women who came with spices to anoint the body of Jesus in its tomb, *Luke* 23.56; 24.1. Dorothy's quotations come from Cott: *Omm Sety*, 23, 41.

2   *Memoirs of Extraordinary Popular Delusions*, 3 vols. (London: Richard Bentley 1841), 2.405-6.

3   The tendency to read a preternatural source into what may have been a natural event was not restricted to Britain, of course. Harry Middleton Hyatt, for example, recorded an incident from *c.*1895 in which a cabin on board a ship was in good order for a while and then later found to be in complete disorder. The sailors were of the opinion that those responsible were the ghosts of two people, occupants of that same cabin, who had died during a previous trip, *Hoodoo, Conjuration, Witchcraft, Rootwork* 1.37 (no.93).

4   The dead also appeared to soldiers fighting in the trenches. Robert Graves, for example, recorded that in June he saw a ghost at Béthune, whom he recognised as a Private Challoner who had been killed at Festubert in May. He passed by C Company billet at dinner time, saluted, and passed on. 'There was no mistaking him', says Graves, 'or the cap-badge he was wearing', to which he added the remark, 'Ghosts were numerous in France at the time', *Goodbye to All That*, 161. Army chaplain quoted in Winter: 'Spiritualism and the First World War', 190. D. Clarke: 'Mud, blood, and spirits', *Fortean Times* (June 2006), 32-40.

5   Cassirer: 'Helen Victoria Duncan', 143. Gaskill: *Hellish Nell*, 102-3.

6   *Journey From Obscurity: Wilfred Owen, 1893-1918: Memoirs of the*

Owen Family, 3 vols. (London: Oxford University Press 1963–65), 3.198–9.

7 Hazelgrove: *Spiritualism and British Society*, 14, 36–7. Gaskill: *Hellish Nell*, 174–5, 71–106. Andreas Fischer traces various attempts to photograph materialisations and circumvent fraud in the process, and the rapid decrease of such phenomena in the twentieth century, 'The reciprocal adaptation of optics and phenomena', 171–215.

8 Barrington: 'Mediumship', 59–77.

9 See Castle: *The Female Thermometer*, 154 and the material cited in his notes, to which add J. Mathête & L. Mannoni: *Méliès, magie et cinéma* (Paris: Musées 2002), 51–8. The ghost film was a popular genre. The American film industry alone produced sixty-two such films in the thirty years between 1912 and 1942, and the representation of ghosts remained substantially (perhaps insubstantially), the same throughout that period.

10 On television etc., see Berthod: 'La vie des morts', 533–4. On cuts, bruising, and feeling cold, see the accounts of people's experiences during the 1990s in Greyfriars cemetery in Edinburgh and the immediate environs of the graveyard, both notoriously haunted places, J-A Henderson: *The Ghost that Haunted Itself* (Edinburgh: Mainstream 2001). Krivyanski: 'Probing the phenomena called ghosts', 140–44. Tandy: 'Something in the cellar', 129–40. Russell: 'The environment of ghosts', 110–13, 124–6. Freud himself remarked somewhat impatiently on the prevalence of belief in ghosts among the educated people of his day, *Jensen's Gradiva* in *Collected Works*, English trans. Vol. 9 (London: Hogarth Press 1959), 71.

11 See further: Thurschwell: *Literature, Technology, and Magical Thinking*, 20–36. The quotation attributed to Freud comes from p.1.

12 *Collected Works*, Vol.22 (London: Hogarth Press 1964), 54–5.

13 Benjamin quoted in Dollimore: *Death, Desire, and Loss*, 119. Geoffrey Gorer coined the phrase 'pornography of death' in 1955 in an article suggesting that death had replaced sex as the great unmentionable in modern society, *Encounter* 5 (October 1955), 49–52. Bering, MacCleod, Shackelford: 'Reasoning about dead agents', 363. C.B. Brown: *The Death of Christian Britain*, 194. Gordon observes, 'In a culture seemingly ruled by technologies of hypervisibility, we are led to believe that neither

repression nor the return of the repressed, in the form of either improperly buried bodies or countervailing systems of value or difference, occurs with any meaningful result', *Ghostly Matters*, 16. The word 'ghost', as will have been made clear by now, covers, at least in popular usage, a wide range of manifestations whose functions differ from one another. See further, Evans: *Seeing Ghosts*, 13-57.

14 *Deadly Words: Witchcraft in the Bocage*, English trans. (Cambridge: Cambridge University Press 1980), 37.

15 M. Warner: *Fantastic Metamorphoses*, 122-32. Niehaus: 'Witches and zombies of the South African lowveld', 191-210. The Samuel and Rebecca anecdote appears on pp.204-5. Vampires in Africa, White: *Speaking with Vampires*, 36-7, 72, 181. Malawi, BBC News Report, 23 December 2002. Toma Petre, Knight Ridder Newspapers Report, 24 March 2004.

16 Classification of the dead is not peculiar to the scientific method, of course. Russians, for example, commonly divided the dead into two major categories: those who die at the time appointed by God, and those who die prematurely whether through murder, suicide, unforeseen natural causes such as drowning, or drink. It is this latter group which comes back as ghosts. See Warner: 'Russian peasant beliefs', 74-5. Hungarian belief is very similar. See Dömötör: *Hungarian Folk Beliefs*, 101-2. Zaleski: 'Death and near-death today', 387-90. Ballard: 'Before death and beyond', 30. Levenda: *Unholy Alliance*, 176. Smith: 'Talking toads and chinless ghosts', 417.

17 Jung: *Collected Works*, English trans. Vol. 18 (London: Routledge & Kegan Paul 1977), 328. Cf. Samuel Johnson's reply to Boswell who observed that although people did not believe Bishop Berkeley's contention that matter did not exist, they were satisfied it was not true. Johnson then kicked a stone hard and said, 'I refute it thus', a crass resort to theatricality which does not begin to take Berkeley's argument seriously, *Life*, 6 August, 1763.

18 Quoted in Warner: *Fantastic Metamorphoses*, 127.

ILLUSTRATION LIST

All illustrations are from author's collection unless otherwise stated.

BIBLIOGRAPHY

Abbott J: *Macedonian Folklore* (Cambridge:Cambridge University Press 1903).

Abend L: 'Spectres of the secular: spiritism in nineteenth-century Spain', *European History* 34 (2004), 507-33.

Adalsteinsson: 'Wrestling with a ghost in Icelandic popular belief', *Arv* (Sweden) 43 (1987), 7-20.

Alderson J: *An Essay on Apparitions in which their Appearance is accounted for by Causes wholly independent of Preternatural Agency* (London: Longman etc. 1823).

Alexander P.S: 'Sefer Ha-Razim and the problem of black magic in early Judaism', in Klutz: *Magic in the Biblical World* q.v. 170-90.

Almquist B: *Viking Ale: Studies on Folklore Contacts between the Northern and the Western Worlds* (Aberystwyth: Boethius Press 1991).

Argenti P.P & Rose H.J: *The Folklore of Chios*, 2 vols. (Cambridge: Cambridge University Press 1949).

Ashton J: *Chapbooks of the Eighteenth Century* (London: Chatto & Windus 1882).

Avery-Peck A.J: 'Death and afterlife in the early Rabbinic sources', in Avery-Peck & Neusner: *Judaism in Late Antiquity* q.v.

Avery-Peck A.J. & Neusner J (edd.): *Judaism in Late Antiquity*: Part 4, *Death, Life-After-Death, Resurrection and the World-To-Come in the Judaisms of Antiquity* (Leiden: Brill 2000).

Ballabriga A: *Le soleil et le Tartare: l'image mythique du monde en*

Grèce archaïque (Paris: Editions de l'Ecole des Hautes Etudes en Sciences Sociales 1986).

Ballard L-M: 'Before death and beyond: a preliminary survey of death and ghost traditions with particular reference to Ulster', in Davidson & Russell: *The Folklore of Ghosts* q.v. 13-42.

Barber P: *Vampires, Burial, and Death: Folklore and Reality* (New Haven & London: Yale University Press 1988).

Barrington M.R: 'The Kluski hands', *Journal of the Society for Psychical Research* 59 (1994), 347-51.

Barrow L : *Independent Spirits: Spiritualism and the English Plebeians, 1850-1910* (London: Routledge & Kegan Paul 1986).

Bath J: 'In the Divell's likenesse: interpretation and confusion in popular ghost belief', in J. Newton: *Early Modern Ghosts* q.v. 70-8.

Bath J & Newton J: 'Sensible proof of ghosts: ghost belief during the later seventeenth century', *Folklore* 117 (April 2006), 1-14.

Behringer W: *Shaman of Oberstdorf: Chonrad Stoeckhlin and the Phantoms of the Night*, English trans. (Virginia: University Press of Virginia 1998).

Bennett G: 'Ghost and witch in the sixteenth and seventeenth centuries', *Folklore* 97 (1986), 3-14.

—: *Traditions of Belief: Women, Folklore and the Supernatural Today* (London: Penguin Books 1987).

Bering J.M, McLeod K, Shackelford T.K: 'Reasoning about dead agents reveals possible adaptive trends', *Human Nature* 16 (2005), 360-81.

Bernand A: *Sorciers grecs* (Paris: Fayard 1991).

Berthod M.A: 'La vie des mort sans le regard des anthropologues', *Anthropos* 100 (2005), 521-36.

Bhattacharya: *Indian Demonology: The Inverted Pantheon* (Delhi: Manohar 2000).

Blacker C: 'Angry ghosts in Japan', in Davidson & Russell: *The Folklore of Ghosts* q.v. 95-105.

Bloch M: *Placing the Dead: Tombs, Ancestral Villages, and Kinship Organisation in Madagascar* (London & New York: Seminar Press 1971).

Bloch-Raymond A & Frayssenge J: *Les êtres de la brume: peurs, revenants, et sorcières des Grands Causses hier et aujourd'hui* (Montpellier: Les Presses de Languedoc 1987).

Bockie S: *Death and the Invisible Powers: The World of Kongo Belief*

(Bloomington: Indiana University Press *c.*1993).

Bogatyrëv P: *Vampires in the Carpathians: Magical Acts, Rites, and Beliefs in Subcarpathian Rus'*, English trans. (New York: Columbia University Press 1998).

Bottéro J: *Religion in Ancient Mesopotamia*, English trans. (Chicago & London: University of Chicago Press 2001).

Boustan R.S. & A.Y. Reed (edd.): *Heavenly Realms and Earthly Realities in Late Antique Religions* (Cambridge: Cambridge University Press 2004).

Bowyer R: 'The role of the ghost story in Mediaeval Christianity', in Davidson & Russell: *The Folklore of Ghosts* q.v. 177-92.

Brandon S.G.F: *The Judgement of the Dead* (London: Weidenfeld & Nicolson 1967).

Bremmer J.N: *The Early Greek Concept of the Soul* (Princeton: Princeton University Press 1987).

—: *The Rise and Fall of the Afterlife* (London & New York: Routledge 2002).

Brown C.B: *The Death of Christian Britain* (London & New York: Routledge 2001).

Brown T: *The Fate of the Dead: A Study in Folk-Eschatology in the West Country after the Reformation* (Cambridge: Cambridge University Press 1979).

Brown T.M: 'The ghost of old Mrs Leakey', in Davidson & Russell: *The Folklore of Ghosts* q.v. 141-54.

Brownell M.R: 'Dr Johnson's ghost: genesis of a satirical engraving', *Huntingdon Library Quarterly* 50 (1987), 339-57.

Burkes S: *Death in Qoheleth and Egyptian Biographies of the Late Period* (Atlanta, Georgia: Society of Biblical Literature 1999).

Cameron E: *The Reformation of the Heretics: The Waldenses of the Alps, 1480-1580* (Oxford: Clarendon Press 1984).

Campbell J.L & Hall T.H: *Strange Things* (London: Routledge & Kegan Paul 1968).

Campbell Thompson A: *Semitic Magic: Its Origins and Development* (London: Luzac & Co 1908).

Camporesi P: *Bread of Dreams*, English trans (Cambridge: Polity Press 1989).

—: *The Fear of Hell: Images of Damnation and Salvation in Early Modern Europe*, English trans. (Cambridge: Polity Press 1990).

Canziani E: *Through the Apennines and the Lands of the Abruzzi:*

Landscape and Peasant Life (Cambridge: Heffer 1928).

Cassirer M: 'Helen Victoria Duncan: a reassessment', *Journal of the Society for Psychical Research* 53 (1985), 138-44.

—: 'An 18th century haunt and the precursors of CSICOP', *Journal of the Society for Psychical Research* 59 (1993), 114-19.

Castle T: 'Phantasmagoria: spectral technology and the metaphorics of modern reverie', *Critical Inquiry* 15 (1988), 26-61.

—: *The Female Thermometer: Eighteenth-Century Culture and the Invention of the Uncanny* (New York: Oxford University Press 1995).

Chéroux C, Fischer A, Apraxine P, Canguihem D, Schmidt S: *The Perfect Medium: Photography and the Occult* (New Haven & London: Yale University Press 2005).

Clark S: *Thinking With Demons* (Oxford: Clarendon Press 1997).

Clery E.J: *The Rise of Supernatural Fiction, 1762-1800* (Cambridge: Cambridge University Press 1995).

Cloutier C: 'Mumler's Ghosts', in Chéroux, Fischer, and others: *The Perfect Medium* q.v., 20-8.

Cogan M: 'The road to En-Dor', in D.P. Wright, D.N. Freedman, A. Hurvitz (edd.): *Pomegranates and Golden Bells* (Winona Lake, Indiana: J.E. Eisenbrauns 1995).

Cohn N: *Cosmos, Chaos, and the World To Come: The Ancient Roots of Apocalyptic Faith*, 2nd ed. (New Haven & London: Yale University Press 2001).

Cohn S.A: 'A questionnaire study on second sight experiences', *Journal of the Society for Psychical Research* 63 (1999), 129-49.

Coleman M.H (ed.): *The Ghosts of the Trianon* (Wellingborough: Aquarian Press 1988).

—: 'Wax moulds of spirit limbs', *Journal of the Society for Psychical Research* 59 (1994), 340-6.

Connor S: *Dumbstruck: A Cultural History of Ventriloquism* (Oxford: Oxford University Press 2000).

Cooper J.W: *Body, Soul, and Life Everlasting*, 2nd ed. (Michigan: University of Michigan Press 2000).

Copeland K.B: 'The earthly monastery and the transformation of the heavenly city in late antique Egypt', in Boustan & Reed: *Heavenly Realms* q.v. 142-58.

Cornish A: *Reading Dante's Stars* (Yale: Yale University Press 2000).

Cott J: *Omm Sety* (London: Rider 1987).

Coventry M: *Haunted Places of Scotland* (Musselburgh: Goblinshead 1999).

Cunningham A: *The Anatomical Renaissance: The Resurrection of the Anatomical Projects of the Ancients* (Aldershot: Scolar Press 1997).

Dabrowska E: 'Passeport pour l'au-delà: essai sur la mentalité médiévale', *Le Moyen Age* III (2005), 313-37.

Damrosch L: 'Defoe as ambiguous impersonator', *Modern Philology* 71 (November 1973), 153-9.

Davenport-Hines R: *Gothic* (New York: North Point Press 1998).

David R: *The Ancient Egyptians: Religious Beliefs and Practices* (London: Routledge & Kegan Paul 1982).

Davidson H.R.E: 'The restless dead': an Icelandic ghost story' in Davidson & Russell: *The Folklore of Ghosts* q.v. 155-75.

Davidson H.R.E & Russell W.M.S (edd.): *The Folklore of Ghosts* (Cambridge: D.S. Brewer 1981).

Davies D: *Death, Ritual, and Belief: the Rhetoric of Funerary Rites* (London: Continuum 2002).

Defoe D: *Essay on the History and Reality of Apparitions* (London 1727).

Delumeau J: *La Peur en Occident (XVIe–XVIIIe siècles): Une Cité Assiégée* (Paris: Fayard 1978).

Dodds E.R: *The Ancient Concept of Progress, and other essays on Greek Literature and Belief* (Oxford: Clarendon Press 1973).

Dollimore J: *Death, Desire, and Loss in Western Culture* (London: Penguin Books 1998).

DuBois T.A: *Nordic Religions: The Viking Age* (Philadelphia: University of Pennsylvania Press 1999).

Earle P: *The World of Defoe* (London: Weidenfeld & Nicolson 1976).

Edgeworth R.J: 'The eloquent ghost: Absyrtus in Seneca's Medea', *Classica et Mediaevalia* 41 (1990), 151-61.

Edmonds R.G: *Myths of the Underworld Journey: Plato, Aristophanes, and the 'Orphic' Gold Tablets* (Cambridge: Cambridge University Press 2004).

Ekirch A.R: *At Day's Close: A History of Nighttime* (London: Weidenfeld & Nicolson 2005).

Ellis M: *The History of Gothic Fiction* (Edinburgh: Edinburgh University Press 2000).

Evans H: *Seeing Ghosts: Experiences of the Paranormal* (London: John Murray 2002).

Evans-Pritchard E.E: *Nuer Religion* (Oxford: Clarendon Press 1956).

Farge A: *Fragile Lives: Violence, Power, and Solidarity in Eighteenth-Century Paris* (Oxford: Oxford University Press 1993).

Faulkner R.O: *The Ancient Egyptian Book of the Dead* (London: British Museum Publications 1985).

Favret-Saada J: *Deadly Words: Witchcraft in the Bocage*, English trans. (Cambridge: Cambridge University Press 1980).

Felton D: *Haunted Greece and Rome: Ghost Stories from Classical Antiquity* (Austin: University of Texas Press 1999).

Fenn R.K: *The Persistence of Purgatory* (Cambridge: Cambridge University Press 1995).

Fermor P.L: *Roumeli: Travels in Northern Greece* (London: John Murray 1966).

Fine A: 'Le parrain, le filleul, et l'au-delà', *Etudes rurales* 105-6 (1987), 123-46.

Finucane R.C: *Appearances of the Dead: A Cultural History of Ghosts* (London: Junction Books 1982).

Fischer A: 'The reciprocal adaptation of optics and phenomena: the photographic recording of materialisations' in Chéroux, Fischer, and others: *The Perfect Medium* q.v. 171-215.

Flournoy T: *Esprits et Médiums: Mélanges de Métapsychique et de Psychologie* (Geneva & Paris, 1911).

Fontana D: 'A responsive poltergeist, a case from South Wales', *Journal of the Society for Psychical Research* 57 (1991), 385-402.

—: 'The responsive South Wales poltergeist, a follow-up report', *Journal of the Society for Psychical Research* 58 (1992), 225-31.

—: 'Spirit moulds: observations on Kluski and his critics', *Journal of the Society for Psychical Research* 63 (1998), 43-5.

French R: *Dissection and Vivisection in the European Renaissance* (Aldershot: Ashgate 1999).

Friedman R.E. & Overton S.D: 'Death and afterlife: the Biblical silence', in Avery-Peck & Neusner: *Judaism in Late Antiquity* q.v. 35-59.

Gager J.G (ed.): *Curse Tablets and Binding Spells from the Ancient World* (New York: Oxford University Press 1992).

Gargett G: *Voltaire and Protestantism* (Oxford: The Voltaire Foundation 1980).

Garland R: *The Greek Way of Death* (London: Duckworth 1985).

Gaskill M: 'Reporting murder: fiction in the archives in early modern England', *Social History* 23 (1998), 1-30.

—: *Hellish Nell: Last of Britain's Witches* (London: Fourth Estate 2001).

Gauld A & Cornell A.D: *Poltergeist* (London: Routledge &

Kegan Paul 1979).

Geary P.J: *Living with the Dead in the Middle Ages* (Cornell: Cornell University Press 1994).

Gillis J.R: *A World of Their Own: A History of Myth and Ritual in Family Life* (Oxford: Oxford University Press 1997).

Ginzburg C: *The Night Battles: Witchcraft and Agrarian Cults in the Sixteenth and Seventeenth Centuries*, English trans. (London: Routledge & Kegan Paul 1983).

Glanvill J: *Essays on Several Important Subjects in Philosophy and Religion* (London 1676).

—: *Saducismus Triumphatus* 2nd ed. (London 1681-2).

Goldingay J: 'Death and afterlife in the Psalms', in Avery-Peck & Neusner: *Judaism in Late Antiquity* q.v. 61-85.

Gonnet J & Molnar A: *Les vaudois au moyen âge* (Turin: Claudian 1967).

Gordon A: *Death is for the Living* (Edinburgh: Paul Harris Publishing 1984).

Gordon AF: *Ghostly Matters: Haunting and the Sociological Imagination* (Minneapolis: University of Minnesota Press 1997).

Gordon B: 'Malevolent ghosts and ministering angels: apparitions and pastoral care in the Swiss reformation' in Gordon & Marshall: *The Place of the Dead* q.v. 87-109.

Gordon B & Marshall P (edd.): *The Place of the Dead: Death and Remembrance in Late Mediaeval and Early Modern Europe* (Cambridge: Cambridge University Press 2000).

Gottlieb R: 'The legend of the European vampire: object loss and corporeal preservation', *Psychoanalytic Study of the Child* 49 (1991), 465-80.

Graf F: *Eleusis und die orphische Dichtung Athens in hellenistischer Zeit* (Berlin: De Gruyter 1974).

—: *Magic in the Ancient World*, English trans. (Cambridge Mass & London: Harvard University Press 1997).

Gragnolati M: *Experiencing the Afterlife: Soul and Body in Dante and Mediaeval Culture* (Notre Dame, Indiana: University of Notre Dame Press 2005).

Graves R: *Goodbye to All That* (London: Jonathan Cape 1929).

—: *The Crane Bag* (London: Cassell 1969).

Green C & McCreery C: *Apparitions* (Oxford: Hamish Hamilton 1975).

Green T: *Meeting the Invisible Man: Secrets and Magic in West Africa*

(London: Weidenfeld & Nicolson 2001).

Greenblatt S: *Hamlet in Purgatory* (Princeton: Princeton University Press 2001).

Greenwood S: *Magic, Witchcraft, and the Otherworld* (Oxford & New York: Berg 2000).

Gregory, Lady: *Visions and Beliefs in the West of Ireland*, 2 vols. (New York & London: G.P. Putnam's Sons 1920).

Griffiths B: *Aspects of Anglo-Saxon Magic* (Norfolk: Anglo-Saxon Books 1996).

Guibert de Nogent: *Monodiae*, English trans. (Pennsylvania: University of Pennsylvania Press 1996).

Haas A.M: 'Otherworldly journeys in the Middle Ages', in B. McGinn (ed.): *The Encyclopaedia of Apocalypticism*: Vol. 2: *Apocalypticism in Western History and Culture* (London: Continuum 2000).

Handley S: 'Reclaiming ghosts in 1690s England' in K. Cooper & J. Gregory (edd.): *Signs, Wonders, Miracles: Representations of Divine Power in the Life of the Church* (Woodbridge: Boydell Press 2005), 345-55.

Harding V: 'Whose body? A study of attitudes towards the dead body in early modern England' in Gordon & Marshall: *The Place of the Dead* q.v. 170-87.

Hardman C.E: *Other Worlds: Notions of Self and Emotion among the Lohorung Rai* (Oxford: Berg 2000).

Hartley M.P (ed.): *A Revelation of Purgatory by an Unknown Fifteenth-Century Woman Visionary* (Lewiston: Edwin Mellen Press 1985).

Hazelgrove J: *Spiritualism and British Society between the Wars* (Manchester & New York: Manchester University Press 2000).

Holroyd J.E: 'The mark of fear', *Blackwood's Magazine* 328 (1980), 434-46.

Hopfner T: *Griechisch-ägyptischer Offenbarungszauber: seine Methoden*, Vols I & II (reprint, Amsterdam: Hakkert 1974-1990).

Huet M-H: 'Deadly fears: Dom Augustin Calmet's vampires and the rule over death', *Eighteenth-Century Life* 21 (1997), 222-32.

Hufford R: *The Terror that Comes in the Night* (Philadelphia: University of Pennsylvania Press 1982).

Huntingdon R & Metcalf P: *Celebrations of Death: the Anthropology of Mortuary Ritual* (Cambridge: Cambridge University Press 1979).

Hyatt H. Middleton: *Hoodoo, Conjuration, Witchcraft, Rootwork*

(Hannibal USA: Western Publishing Inc. 1970)

Jalland P: *Death in the Victorian Family* (Oxford: Oxford University Press 1996).

Jemielity T: 'A keener eye on vacancy: Boswell's second thoughts about second sight', *Prose Studies* 11 (1988), 24-40.

Johnson D.M: 'Hesiod's description of Tartaros (Theogony 721-819)', *Phoenix* 53 (1999), 8.28.

Johnston S.I: 'Songs for the ghosts: magical solutions to deadly problems', in Jordan, Montgomery, Thomassen: *The World of Ancient Magic*, q.v. 83-102.

—: *Restless Dead: Encounters between the Living and the Dead in Ancient Greece* (Berkeley: University of California Press 1999).

Jones P & Pennick N: *A History of Pagan Europe* (London: Routledge 1995).

Joyner A: *Mediaeval Ghost Stories* (Woodbridge: Boydell Press 2001).

Klaniczay G: *The Uses of Supernatural Power: The Transformation of Popular Religion in Mediaeval and Early Modern Europe*, English trans. (Cambridge: Polity Press 1990).

Klapisch-Zuber C: *Women, Family, and Ritual in Renaissance Italy* (Chicago & London: University of Chicago Press 1985).

Klutz T (ed.): *Magic in the Biblical World: From the Rod of Aaron to the Ring of Solomon* (London: T&T Clark International 2003).

Knox G.W: *The Development of Religion in Japan* (New York & London: G.P. Putnam's Sons 1907).

Koslofsky C.M: *The Reformation of the Dead: Death and Ritual in Early Modern Germany, 1450-1700* (London: Macmillan 2000).

Krivyanski J.M: 'Probing the phenomena called ghosts', *World and I* 16 (August 2001), 140-9.

Kselman T: 'Alternative afterlives in nineteenth-century France', in T. Kselman (ed.): *Belief in History: Innovative Approaches to European and American Religion* (Notre Dame: University of Notre Dame Press 1991), 107-36.

Kvideland R & Sehmsdorf H.K (edd.): *Scandinavian Folk Belief and Legend* (Oslo: Norwegian University Press 1991).

Labrousse E: *Conscience et Conviction: Études sur le xviie siècle* (Oxford: Voltaire Foundation 1996).

Lamb C, Gauld A, Cornell A.D: 'An East Midlands poltergeist', *Journal of the Society for Psychical Research* 47 (1973), 1-20, 139-55.

Lamont P: 'Spiritualism and a mid-Victorian crisis of evidence', *Historical Journal* 47 (2004), 897-920.

—: *The First Psychic: The Peculiar Mystery of a Notorious Victorian Wizard* (London: Little, Brown 2005).

Lavater L: *Of Ghosts and Spirits Walking by Night*, English translation 1572 (Oxford: Oxford University Press 1967).

Law R: *Memorialls, or, The Memorable Things that fell out within this Island of Brittain from 1638 to 1684*, ed. C.K. Sharpe (Edinburgh: Constable & Co. 1818).

Lawson J.C: *Modern Greek Folklore and Ancient Greek Religion* (Cambridge: Cambridge University Press 1910).

Lederer D: 'Living with the dead: ghosts in early modern Bavaria', in K.A. Edwards (ed.): *Werewolves, Witches, and Wandering Spirits: Traditional Belief and Folklore in Early Modern Europe* (Kirksville: Truman State University Press 2002), 25-53.

Ledwon L: 'Darwin's ghosts: the influence of Darwinism on the nineteenth-century ghost story', *Proteus* 6 (1989), 10-16.

Lee D.D: 'Folklore of the Greeks in America', *Folklore* 47 (1936), 294-310.

Le Goff J: *The Birth of Purgatory*, English trans. (London: Scolar Press 1984).

León-Portilla M: *Aztec Thought and Culture: A Study of the Ancient Nahuatl Mind*, English trans. (Norman: Oklahoma University Press 1963).

Le Roy Ladurie E: *Montaillou: Cathars and Catholics in a French Village, 1294-1324,* English trans. (London: Penguin Books 1980).

Levenda P: *Unholy Alliance*, 2nd ed. (New York & London: Continuum 2002).

Lewis B: 'Protestantism, pragmatism, and popular religion: a case study of early modern ghosts', in J. Newton: *Early Modern Ghosts* q.v. 79-91.

Lindsay J: *Leisure and Pleasure in Roman Egypt* (London: Muller 1965).

Lipner J: *Hindus: Their Religious Beliefs and Practices* (London & New York: Routledge 1994).

Marshall P: 'Old Mother Leakey and the Golden Chain: context and meaning in an early Stuart haunting', in J. Newton: *Early Modern Ghosts* q.v. 92-105.

—; 'The map of God's word: geographies of the afterlife in Tudor and early Stuart England' in Gordon & Marshall: *The Place of the Dead* q.v. 110-30.

—: 'Deceptive appearances: ghosts and reformers in Elizabethan and Jacobean England' in H. Parish & W. Naphy (edd.): *Religion and Superstition in Reformation Europe* (Manchester: Manchester University Press 2002), 188-203.

McKeever Furst J.L: *The Natural History of the Soul in Ancient Mexico* (New Haven & London: Yale University Press 1995).

McLoughlin M: 'On communion with the dead', *Journal of Mediaeval History* 17 (1991), 121-77.

McNally R.T & Florescu R: *In Search of Dracula* (Bury St Edmunds: Robson Books 1995).

Marquis J-C: *Loups, sorciers, criminels: faits divers en Seine-Inférieure au xixe siècle* (Luneray: Editions Bertout 1993).

Martin M: *A Description of the Western Isles of Scotland circa 1695*, [originally London 1702], ed. D.J. MacDonald (Edinburgh: Birlinn 1994).

Merridale C: *Night of Stone: Death and Memory in Russia* (London: Granta Books 2000).

Morenz S: *Egyptian Religion*, English trans. (London: Methuen 1960).

Morrissey S.K: 'Drinking to death: suicide, vodka, and religious burial in Russia', *Past and Present* 186 (2005), 117-46.

Murray P: *From the Shadow of Dracula* (London: Jonathan Cape 2004).

Nardi B: *Saggi di filosofia dantesca* (Florence 1967).

Nathan T: 'Le mort et son représentant', in F. Dagognet & T. Nathan: *La mort vue autrement* (Le Plessis-Robinson: Institut Synthélabo 1999).

Nedkvitne A: 'Beyond anthropology in the study of Mediaeval mentalities', *Scandinavian Journal of History* 25 (2000), 27-51.

Newton J: 'Reading ghosts: early modern interpretations of apparitions', in J. Newton (ed.): *Early Modern Ghosts* q.v. 57-69.

—: *Early Modern Ghosts* (Durham: Centre for Seventeenth-Century Studies 2002).

Niehaus I: 'Witches and zombies of the South African Lowveld: discourse, accusations, and subjective reality', *Journal of the Royal Anthropological Institute* n.s. 11 (2005), 191-210.

Nihan C.L: 'I Samuel 28 and the condemnation of necromancy in Persian Yehud', in Klutz: *Magic in the Biblical World* q.v. 23-54.

Nisbet B.C: 'Apparitions', in I. Grattan-Guinness (ed.): *Psychical Research: A Guide to its History, Principles, and Practices* (Wellingborough: Aquarian Press 1982), 50-100.

Novara A: 'Les imagines de l'Elysée virgilien', in F. Hinard (ed.):

La mort, les morts et l'au-delà (Caen: L'Université de Caen 1987), 321-49.

Noy D: 'Half-burnt on an emergency pyre: Roman cremations which went wrong', *Greece & Rome* 2nd series 47 (October 2000), 186-96.

Ogden D: *Greek and Roman Necromancy* (Princeton & Oxford: Princeton University Press 2001).

Oldridge D: *Strange Histories* (London & New York: Routledge 2005).

O'Neil M.R: 'Sacerdote ovvero strione: ecclesiastical and superstitious remedies in sixteenth-century Italy', in S.L. Kaplan (ed.): *Understanding Popular Culture: Europe from the Middle Ages to the Nineteenth Century* (Berlin: Monton 1984), 53-83.

Oppenheim J: *The Other World: Spiritualism and Psychical Research in England, 1850-1914* (Cambridge: Cambridge University Press 1985).

Owen A: *The Place of Enchantments: British Occultism and the Culture of the Modern* (Chicago & London: University of Chicago Press 2004).

Owen A.R.G: *Can We Explain the Poltergeist?* (New York: Garrett Publications 1964).

Paget L: *In the Footsteps of Orpheus* (London: Hale 1967).

Parke H.W: *Festivals of the Athenians* (London: Thames & Hudson 1977).

Parry J. P: *Death in Banaras* (Cambridge: Cambridge University Press 1994).

Parsons C.O: 'Ghost stories before Defoe', *Notes & Queries* 201 (July 1956), 293-8.

Perera S: 'Spirit possession and avenging ghosts: stories of supernatural activity as narratives of terror and mechanisms of coping and remembering', in V. Das, A. Kleinman, M. Lock, M. Ramphele, P. Reynolds (edd.): *Remaking a World: Violence, Social Suffering, and Recovery* (Berkeley: University of California Press 2001), 157-200.

Permutt C: *Photographing the Spirit World: Images from beyond the Spectrum* (Wellingborough: Aquarian Press 1988).

Perreaud F: *Demonologie* (Paris 1653).

—: *L'Antidemon de Mâcon* (Paris 1653).

Polo de Beaulieu M-A: 'De Beaucaire (1211) à Alès (1323), les revenants et leurs révélations sur l'au-delà', in J-L Biget (ed.):

La mort et l'au-delà en France méridionale, xiie-xve siècle (Toulouse: Editions Privat 1998), 319-41.

—: 'Le lundi des trépassés: création, diffusion, et réception d'un rituel', *Annales HSS* 6 (November-December 1998), 1191-1217.

Porter J.R: 'Ghosts in the Old Testament and the Ancient Near East', in Davidson & Russell: *The Folklore of Ghosts* q.v. 215-38.

Porter R: 'Witchcraft and magic in enlightenment, Romantic, and liberal thought' in B. Ankerloo & S. Clark (edd.): *The Athlone History of Witchcraft and Magic in Europe*: Vol. 5, *The Eighteenth and Nineteenth Centuries* (London: Athlone Press 1999), 193-274.

—: *Enlightenment: Britain and the Creation of the Modern World* (London: Penguin Press 2000).

—: *Flesh in the Age of Reason* (London: Penguin Books 2004).

Pringle H: *The Mummy Congress: Science, Obsession, and the Everlasting Dead* (London: Fourth Estate 2001).

Prosser E: *Hamlet and Revenge*, 2nd ed. (Stanford: Stanford University Press 1971).

Puhle A: 'Ghosts, apparitions, and poltergeist incidents in Germany between 1700 and 1900', *Journal of the Society for Psychical Research* 63 (1999), 292-305.

Rack H.D: *Reasonable Enthusiast: John Wesley and the Rise of Methodism*, 2nd ed. (London: Epworth 1992).

'Raphael': *The Familiar Astrologer* (London: John Bennett 1832).

Riché P: *L'instruction et vie religieuse dans le Haut Moyen Age* (London: Variorum 1981).

Ritner R.K: *The Mechanics of Ancient Egyptian Magical Practice* (Chicago: University of Chicago Press 1993).

Roberts P: 'Contesting sacred space: burial disputes in sixteenth-century France', in Gordon & Marshall: *The Place of the Dead* q.v. 131-48.

Roche D: *France in the Enlightenment*, English trans. (Harvard: Harvard University Press 1998).

Rockwell J: 'The ghosts of Evart Tang Kristensen', in Davidson & Russell: *The Folklore of Ghosts* q.v. 43-72.

Roughead W: 'The ghost of Sergeant Davies' in *Twelve Scots Trials* (Edinburgh: W. Green & Sons 1913), 85-105.

Russell C: 'The environment of ghosts', in Davidson & Russell: *The Folklore of Ghosts* q.v. 109-37.

Russell J.B: *A History of Heaven: The Singing Silence* (Princeton: Princeton University Press 1997).

Russell W.M.S: 'Greek and Roman ghosts', in Davidson & Russell: *The Folklore of Ghosts* q.v. 193-213.

Sands T.R: 'Det kommo tvänne dufvor... doves, ravens, and the dead in Scandinavian folk tradition', *Scandinavian Studies* 73 (2001), 349-74.

Sawday J: *The Body Emblazoned: Dissection and the Human Body in Renaissance Culture* (London: Routledge 1995).

Schmidt B: *Israel's Beneficent Dead* (Tübingen: Mohr 1994).

Schmitt J-C: 'Le spectre de Samuel et la sorcière d'En Dor', *Etudes rurales* 105-6 (1987), 37-64.

—: *Les revenants: les vivants et les morts dans la société médiévale* (Paris: Editions Gallimard 1994).

Scott, Sir Walter: *Letters on Demonology and Witchcraft* (London: The Folklore Society 2001).

Scribner R.W: *Religion and Culture in Germany, 1400-1800*, ed. L. Roper (Leiden: Brill 2001).

Sébillot P-Y: *Folklore et Curiosités du vieux Paris* (Paris: Maisonneuve et Laros 2002).

Secord A.W: 'A September day in Canterbury: the Veal-Bargrave story', *Journal of English and Germanic Philology* 54 (1955), 639-51.

Senelier J: *Le mystère du Petit Trianon: une vision dans l'espace-temps* (Nice: Collection Belisane 1982).

Sharp L.L: 'Fighting for the afterlife: Spiritists, Catholics, and popular religion in nineteenth-century France', *Journal of Religious History* 23 (1999), 282-95.

Sharpe A.M: *A Disturbed House and its Relief* (London: Oarker & Co. 1914).

Simon E: 'Sentiment religieux et vision de la mort chez les Étrusques dans les derniers siècles de leur histoire', in F. Gaultier & D. Briquel (edd.): *Les plus religieux des hommes: état de la recherche sur la religion étrusque* (Paris: La documentation française 1997), 449-57.

Sinclair G: *Satan's Invisible World Discovered* (Edinburgh: Thomas Stevenson 1871).

Sledzik P.S. & Bellatoni N: 'Bioarchaeological and biocultural evidence for the New England vampire belief', *American Journal of Physical Anthropology* 94 (1994), 269-74.

Smith S.A: 'Talking toads and chinless ghosts: the politics of superstitious rumours in the People's Republic of China, 1961-1965', *American Historical Review* 111 (April 2006), 405-26.

Sohmer S: *Shakespeare's Mystery Play* (Manchester: Manchester

University Press 1999).

Sourvinou-Inwood C: 'To die and enter the House of Hades: Homer before and after', in J. Whaley: *Mirrors of Mortality* q.v. 15-39.

Spence L: *Second Sight: Its History and Origins* (London: Rider & Co 1951).

Spencer A.J: *Death in Ancient Egypt* (London: Penguin Books 1982).

Stewart C: *Demons and the Devil: Moral Imagination in Modern Greek Culture* (Princeton: Princeton University Press 1991).

Strubbe J.H.M: 'Cursed be he that moves my bones', in C.A. Faraone & D. Obbink (edd.): *Magika Hiera: Ancient Greek Magic and Religion* (New York & Oxford: Oxford University Press 1991), 33-59.

Summers M: *The Vampire in Europe* (New York: University Books Inc. 1963).

Taillepied N: *A Treatise of Ghosts*, English trans. (London & Ann Arbor: Gryphon Books 1971).

Tandy V: 'Something in the cellar', *Journal of the Society for Psychical Research* 64 (2000), 129-40.

Tangherlini T.R: 'Who ya gonna call? Ministers and mediation of the ghostly threat in Danish legend and tradition', *Western Folklore* 57 (1998), 153-78.

Temple R: *Netherworld: Discovering the Oracle of the Dead and Ancient Techniques of Foretelling the Future* (London: Century 2002).

Thomas K: *Religion and the Decline of Magic* (London: Weidenfeld & Nicolson 1971).

Thomsen M-L: 'Witchcraft and magic in ancient Mesopotamia', in B. Ankarloo & S. Clark (edd.): *The Athlone History of Witchcraft and Magic in Europe*: Vol. 1: *Biblical and Pagan Societies* (London: Athlone Press 2001), 3-95.

Thomson de Grummond N & Simon E (edd.): *The Religion of the Etruscans* (Austin: University of Texas Press 2006).

Thurschwell P: *Literature, Technology, and Magical Thinking, 1880-1920* (Cambridge: Cambridge University Press 2001).

The Tibetan Book of the Dead, ed. W.Y. Evans-Wentz (New York: Oxford University Press 1960).

Toynbee J.M.C: *Death and Burial in the Roman World* (London: Thames & Hudson 1971).

Trachtenberg J: *Jewish Magic and Superstition* (New York: Behrman's Jewish Bookhouse 1938).

Valletta F: *Witchcraft, Magic and Superstition in England, 1640-70*

(Aldershot: Ashgate 2000).

Versnel H.S: '"Punish those who rejoice in our misery": on curse texts and Schadenfreude', in Jordan, Montgomery, Thomassen: *The World of Ancient Magic* q.v. 125-62.

Vitebsky P: 'Is death the same everywhere? Contents of knowing and doubting', in M. Hobart (ed.): *An Anthropological Critique of Development: The Growth of Ignorance* (London: Routledge 1993).

Vovelle M: *Les âmes du purgatoire, ou le travail du deuil* (Paris: Editions Gallimard 1996).

Walker D.P: *Unclean Spirits: Possession and Exorcism in France and England in the late Sixteenth and Early Seventeenth Centuries* (London: Scolar Press 1981).

Warner E.A: 'Russian peasant beliefs and practices concerning death and the supernatural, collected in Novosokol'niki region, Pskov Province, Russia, 1995: Part I, The restless dead, wizards, and spirit beings', *Folklore* 111 (2000), 67-90.

Warner M: *Fantastic Metamorphoses, Other Worlds* (Oxford: Oxford University Press 2002).

Watt E: 'Some personal experiences of the second sight', in H.E. Davidson (ed.): *The Seer in Celtic and Other Traditions* (Edinburgh: John Donald 1989).

Watt J: *Contesting the Gothic: Fiction, Genre, and Cultural Conflict, 1764-1832* (Cambridge: Cambridge University Press 1999).

West R.H: *The Invisible World: A Study of Pneumatology in Elizabethan Drama* (reprint New York: Octagon Books 1969).

Whaley J (ed.): *Mirrors of Mortality* (London: Europa 1981).

Wheeler R.E.M: 'A Roman pipe-burial from Caerleon, Monmouthshire', *Antiquaries Journal* 9 (1929), 1-7.

White L: *Speaking with Vampires: Rumour and History in Colonial Africa* (Berkeley: University of California Press 2000).

Wicke J: 'Vampiric typewriting: Dracula and its media', *English Literary History* 59 (1992), 467-93.

Wilhelm-Schaffer: *Gottes Beamter und Spielmann des Teufels: Der Tod in Spätmittelalter und Frühe Neuzeit* (Weimar: Bohlau 1999).

William of Newburgh: *History*, English trans. (London: Seeleys 1856).

Wilson A.N: *God's Funeral* (London: Abacus Publications 2000).

Wilson E (ed.): *The Living and the Dead: Social Dimensions of Death in South Asian Religions* (Albany: State University of New York Press 2003).

Wilson I: *The After Death Experience* (London: Sidgwick & Jackson 1987).

Wilson S: *The Magical Universe: Everyday Ritual and Magic in Pre-Modern Europe* (London & New York: Hambledon 2000).

Winter J.M: 'Spiritualism and the First World War', in R.W. Davis & R.J. Helmstadter (edd.): *Religion and Irreligion in Victorian Society* (London: Routledge 1992).

Wright J.E: *The Early History of Heaven* (New York & Oxford: Oxford University Press 2000).

Zaleski C: 'Death and near-death today', in J.J Collins & M. Fishbane (edd.): *Death, Ecstasy, and Other Worldly Journeys* (State University of New York 1995), 383-407.

Zemon Davis N: 'Ghosts, kin, and progeny: some features of family life in early modern France', *Daedalus* 106 (1977), 87-114.

Zonabend F: 'Les morts et les vivants: le cimetière de Minoten Chatillonnais', *Études Rurales* 52 (1973), 7-23.

INDEX

TEMPUS – REVEALING HISTORY

Britannia's Empire
A Short History of the British Empire
BILL NASSON

'Crisp, economical and witty' *TLS*
'An excellent introduction the subject' *THES*

£12.99   0 7524 3808 5

Madmen
A Social History of Madhouses,
Mad-Doctors & Lunatics
ROY PORTER

'Fascinating'
The Observer

£12.99   0 7524 3730 5

Born to be Gay
A History of Homosexuality
WILLIAM NAPHY

'Fascinating' *The Financial Times*
'Excellent' *Gay Times*

£9.99   0 7524 3694 5

William II
Rufus, the Red King
EMMA MASON

'A thoroughly new reappraisal of a much
maligned king. The dramatic story of his life is
told with great pace and insight'
John Gillingham

£25   0 7524 3528 0

To Kill Rasputin
The Life and Death of Grigori Rasputin
ANDREW COOK

'Andrew Cook is a brilliant investigative historian'
Andrew Roberts
'Astonishing' *The Daily Mail*

£9.99   0 7524 3906 5

The Unwritten Order
Hitler's Role in the Final Solution
PETER LONGERICH

'Compelling' *Richard Evans*
'The finest account to date of the many twists
and turns in Adolf Hitler's anti-semitic obsession'
Richard Overy

£12.99   0 7524 3328 8

Private 12768
Memoir of a Tommy
JOHN JACKSON
FOREWORD BY HEW STRACHAN

'A refreshing new perspective' *The Sunday Times*
'At last we have John Jackson's intensely
personal and heartfelt little book to remind us
there was a view of the Great War other than
Wilfred Owen's' *The Daily Mail*

£9.99   0 7524 3531 0

The Vikings
MAGNUS MAGNUSSON

'Serious, engaging history'
BBC History Magazine

£9.99   0 7524 2699 0

If you are interested in purchasing other books published by Tempus, or in case you have difficulty finding any
Tempus books in your local bookshop, you can also place orders directly through our website

www.tempus-publishing.com

TEMPUS – REVEALING HISTORY

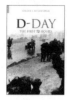 

D-Day The First 72 Hours
WILLIAM F. BUCKINGHAM

'A compelling narrative' **The Observer**
A **BBC History Magazine** Book of the Year 2004

£9.99   0 7524 2842 X

The London Monster
Terror on the Streets in 1790
JAN BONDESON

'Gripping' **The Guardian**
'Excellent... monster-mania brought a reign of
terror to the ill-lit streets of the capital'
The Independent

£9.99   0 7524 3327 X

London
A Historical Companion
KENNETH PANTON

'A readable and reliable work of reference that
deserves a place on every Londoner's bookshelf'
Stephen Inwood

£20   0 7524 3434 9

M: MI5's First Spymaster
ANDREW COOK

'Serious spook history' **Andrew Roberts**
'Groundbreaking' **The Sunday Telegraph**
'Brilliantly researched' **Dame Stella Rimington**

£20   0 7524 2896 9

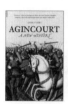   

Agincourt A New History
ANNE CURRY

'A highly distinguished and convincing account'
Christopher Hibbert
'A *tour de force*' **Alison Weir**
'*The* book on the battle' **Richard Holmes**
A **BBC History Magazine** Book of the Year 2005

£25   0 7524 2828 4

Battle of the Atlantic
MARC MILNER

'The most comprehensive short survey of the
U-boat battles' **Sir John Keegan**
'Some events are fortunate in their historian, none
more so than the Battle of the Atlantic. Marc
Milner is *the* historian of the Atlantic campaign... a
compelling narrative' **Andrew Lambert**

£12.99   0 7524 3332 6

The English Resistance
The Underground War Against the Normans
PETER REX

'An invaluable rehabilitation of an ignored
resistance movement' **The Sunday Times**
'Peter Rex's scholarship is remarkable'
The Sunday Express

£12.99   0 7524 3733 X

Elizabeth Wydeville: The Slandered Queen
ARLENE OKERLUND

'A penetrating, thorough and wholly convincing
vindication of this unlucky queen'
Sarah Gristwood
'A gripping tale of lust, loss and tragedy'
Alison Weir
A **BBC History Magazine** Book of the Year 2005

£18.99   0 7524 3384 9

If you are interested in purchasing other books published by Tempus, or in case you have difficulty finding any
Tempus books in your local bookshop, you can also place orders directly through our website
www.tempus-publishing.com

TEMPUS – REVEALING HISTORY

Quacks Fakers and Charlatans in Medicine
ROY PORTER

'A delightful book' *The Daily Telegraph*
'Hugely entertaining' *BBC History Magazine*

£12.99   0 7524 2590 0

The Tudors
RICHARD REX

'Up-to-date, readable and reliable. The best
introduction to England's most important
dynasty' *David Starkey*
'Vivid, entertaining... quite simply the best short
introduction' *Eamon Duffy*
'Told with enviable narrative skill... a delight for
any reader' *THES*

£9.99   0 7524 3333 4

The Kings & Queens of England
MARK ORMROD

'Of the numerous books on the kings and
queens of England, this is the best'
Alison Weir

£9.99   0 7524 2598 6

The Covent Garden Ladies
Pimp General Jack & the Extraordinary Story of Harris's List
HALLIE RUBENHOLD

'Sex toys, porn... forget Ann Summers, Miss
Love was at it 250 years ago' *The Times*
'Compelling' *The Independent on Sunday*
'Marvellous' *Leonie Frieda*
'Filthy' *The Guardian*

£9.99   0 7524 3739 9

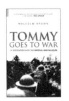

Okinawa 1945
GEORGE FEIFER

'A great book... Feifer's account of the three
sides and their experiences far surpasses most
books about war'
Stephen Ambrose

£17.99   0 7524 3324 5

Tommy Goes To War
MALCOLM BROWN

'A remarkably vivid and frank account of the
British soldier in the trenches'
Max Arthur
'The fury, fear, mud, blood, boredom and
bravery that made up life on the Western Front
are vividly presented and illustrated'
The Sunday Telegraph

£12.99   0 7524 2980 4

Ace of Spies The True Story of Sidney Reilly
ANDREW COOK

'The most definitive biography of the spying
ace yet written... both a compelling narrative
and a myth-shattering *tour de force*'
Simon Sebag Montefiore
'The absolute last word on the subject' *Nigel West*
'Makes poor 007 look like a bit of a wuss'
The Mail on Sunday

£12.99   0 7524 2959 0

Sex Crimes
From Renaissance to Enlightenment
W.M. NAPHY

'Wonderfully scandalous'
Diarmaid MacCulloch

£10.99   0 7524 2977 9

If you are interested in purchasing other books published by Tempus, or in case you have difficulty finding any
Tempus books in your local bookshop, you can also place orders directly through our website

www.tempus-publishing.com